HANNIBAL and ME

HANNIBAL AND ME

What History's Greatest Military Strategist
Can Teach Us About Success and Failure

ANDREAS KLUTH

RIVERHEAD BOOKS

a member of Penguin Group (USA) Inc.

New York

2011

RIVERHEAD BOOKS
Published by the Penguin Group
Penguin Group (USA) Inc., 375 Hudson Street, New York, New York 10014,
USA • Penguin Group (Canada), 90 Eglinton Avenue East, Suite 700, Toronto,
Ontario M4P 2Y3, Canada (a division of Pearson Penguin Canada Inc.) • Penguin Books Ltd,
80 Strand, London WC2R 0RL, England • Penguin Ireland, 25 St Stephen's Green,
Dublin 2, Ireland (a division of Penguin Books Ltd) • Penguin Group (Australia),
250 Camberwell Road, Camberwell, Victoria 3124, Australia (a division of Pearson
Australia Group Pty Ltd) • Penguin Books India Pvt Ltd, 11 Community Centre,
Panchsheel Park, New Delhi–110 017, India • Penguin Group (NZ), 67 Apollo Drive,
Rosedale, North Shore 0632, New Zealand (a division of Pearson New Zealand Ltd) •
Penguin Books (South Africa) (Pty) Ltd, 24 Sturdee Avenue,
Rosebank, Johannesburg 2196, South Africa

Penguin Books Ltd, Registered Offices: 80 Strand, London WC2R 0RL, England

Copyright © 2011 by Andreas Kluth
Map copyright © 2011 by David Lindroth

The epigraph on p. 92 is taken from *A Life in Aikido* by
Kisshomaru Ueshiba. Published by Kodansha International Ltd.
Copyright © 2008 by Moriteru Ueshiba. English translation copyright © 2008
by Kei Izawa and Mary Fuller. Reprinted by permission. All rights reserved.

Library of Congress Cataloging-in-Publication Data

Kluth, Andreas.
Hannibal and me : what history's greatest military strategist can teach as about success and
failure / Andreas Kluth.
p.   cm.
ISBN 978-1-59448-812-2
1. Hannibal 247–182 B.C. 2. Punic War, 2nd, 218–201 B.C. 3. Generals—Tunisia—
Carthage (Extinct city)—Biography. 4. Rome—History—Republic, 265–30 B.C.
5. Success. 6. Self-realization. I. Title.
DG249.K58   2011   2011027818
937'.03072—dc23

Printed in the United States of America
1   3   5   7   9   10   8   6   4   2

BOOK DESIGN BY NICOLE LAROCHE

While the author has made every effort to provide accurate telephone numbers and Internet
addresses at the time of publication, neither the publisher nor the author assumes any
responsibility for errors, or for changes that occur after publication. Further, the publisher
does not have any control over and does not assume any responsibility for author or third-
party websites or their content.

To SAS and S

CONTENTS

ONE. HANNIBAL AND ME   *1*

TWO. THE INFLUENCE OF PARENTS   *19*

THREE. DO YOU NEED A GOAL?   *44*

FOUR. TOWERING PEAKS   *67*

FIVE. THE ART OF WINNING   *92*

SIX. TACTICS AND STRATEGY IN LIFE   *119*

SEVEN. DEALING WITH DISASTER   *144*

EIGHT. THE PRISON OF SUCCESS   *169*

NINE. THE LIBERATION OF FAILURE   *192*

TEN. THE THRESHOLD OF MIDDLE AGE   *217*

ELEVEN. POLITICAL DEATH   *243*

TWELVE. AGING AND TRANSCENDING *265*

THIRTEEN. THE LESSONS OF HANNIBAL *284*

Acknowledgments 299
Notes 301
Bibliography 315
Index 319

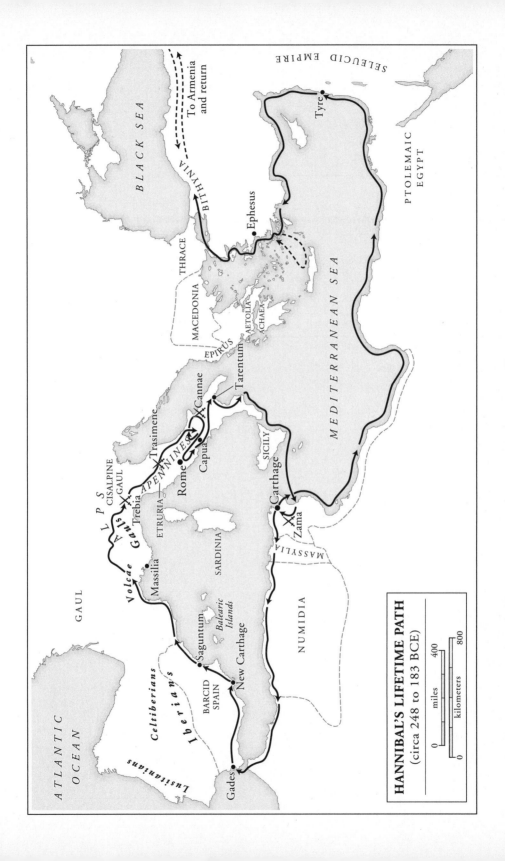

HANNIBAL'S LIFETIME PATH
(circa 248 to 183 BCE)

ONE

HANNIBAL
AND ME

If you can meet with Triumph and Disaster
And treat those two impostors just the same . . .
— Rudyard Kipling, "If"

Shivering but rapturous, the warrior stood in the snow on a wind-beaten pass in the Alps. His olive skin was chapped and his eyes were watery from the icy wind. But he felt no discomfort. As he looked across the white peaks, he saw faint green plains in the distance. Those plains were Italy, and the twenty-nine-year-old warrior, named Hannibal, had been dreaming about this moment since he was nine years old.

That was when, in his home city of Carthage in northern Africa, today's Tunisia, Hannibal had gone with his father to a temple and sworn an oath to conquer Carthage's enemy, Rome. Now, twenty years later, in the early winter of 218 BCE, Hannibal was commander in chief of the armies of Carthage, one of the great powers of the ancient world. As he stood on the Alpine pass, the young man felt that he was physically and symbolically at the threshold of his life dream, of an adventure that would change world history. For he knew that down there, on those green plains, he would find and fight the legions of Rome.

Behind Hannibal, on the long and winding slopes ascending to the pass, was an army of tens of thousands of soldiers, mules, horses, and even twenty-seven elephants. These men and beasts looked otherworldly in the snow and hoof-trodden, excrement-brown slush.

Their faces, weapons, and armor, their animals and language—everything about them looked alien in this place. The officers were Carthaginian, like Hannibal. Carthage had once been a colony of the Phoenicians, a people from what is today Lebanon. The rest of the army was a motley and Babel-tongued amalgam of tribes. Many of the horsemen, riding without stirrups, saddles, or even reins, as though they were fused with their mounts, were Numidians from northwestern Africa, the ancestors of the Berbers, with leathery skin, aquiline noses, and bright green eyes. On foot were masses of Iberians and Celtiberians from the land now called Spain, each band speaking its own tribal tongue. There were Gauls, somewhat paler and with brown or reddish hair, wrapped in thick, checkered wool scarves. There were Greeks, Libyans, and others from the Mediterranean world. All were now mercenaries of the richest city in the western Mediterranean, Carthage. But none had ever expected to stand on the white roof of the world.

As these soldiers paused in their climb to look up to their young general on the ridge, the collective raising of heads traveling back down the long line like a wave, they presented a surreal spectacle, one that would have been pitiable but for the pride on their faces. This army had been twice as large only a fortnight earlier: about half of the men had already died during just the previous two weeks of climbing to this lonely pass. Even the survivors looked frail. They had slipped and fallen, fought and bled, starved and frozen. They were haggard, emaciated, and frostbitten. Many had festering wounds, fevers, or dysentery. Men and elephants that were fearsome war wagers on hot, dry African or Spanish battlefields now appeared lost on this treeless, frozen mountaintop.

But the soldiers adored their general, and as they had followed Hannibal up to this pass, they would now follow him down the other side and into Italy. In that descent, many more would skid off the ice sheets and plunge to their deaths. But the toughest warriors and their mangy war elephants made it to the bottom.

That they did so—that they survived at all and appeared out of the mountains—came as a shock to the Romans. They had last sighted Hannibal's army several months earlier on the French side of the Alps, where it had suddenly *dis*appeared. Hannibal had, in that year of 218 BCE, surprised the Romans by marching his huge land army from Iberia, where his military base was, across the Pyrenees and into Gaul, today's France, apparently in order to attack Italy by land. A Roman army had tried to intercept the Carthaginians near the Rhône, but then Hannibal unexpectedly turned and marched straight toward the highest part of the Alps, just as fall was turning into the Alpine winter.

The Romans were sure that Hannibal's army would perish in these mountains. They themselves were afraid of the Alps and, for that very reason, regarded the mountains as an insurmountable barrier to other armies and thus as Italy's ultimate fortification against any land invasion. As far as the Romans knew, only the mythic hero Hercules and perhaps some barbarian Gallic tribesmen had ever crossed the Alps. And yet, suddenly, Hannibal, this young and mysterious Carthaginian, this new enemy about whom the Romans knew nothing except that he was the son of their greatest enemy in the previous war against Carthage, was now aiming the army of Carthage at Rome itself.

FOR THE NEXT YEAR and a half, Hannibal, even though he was always outnumbered, met one Roman army after another and routed them all in a crescendo of victories, each more crushing than the last. The names of these battles—Trebia, after a river; Trasimene, after a lake—would strike terror into Roman hearts for centuries to come. Hannibal's tactics in these battles are studied in military schools to this day.

In his greatest battle, named Cannae after the location of a nearby Roman grain depot, Hannibal killed some seventy thousand Romans in a single day, roughly as many as the atomic bomb dropped on Hiroshima killed on the day of its explosion more than two thousand years later.[1] But this was not high-tech warfare, in which a pilot opened a bomb bay above anonymous victims. This was slow and manual killing, with sword cuts and thrusts, spear gashes, broken necks, and crushed skulls. Hannibal, with his most genius maneuver, surrounded the Romans and turned that plain of Cannae into a shallow lake of blood clotted with heaps of limbs and corpses.

In those days of the Roman republic, all Roman citizens, from aristocrats to plebeians, served in the army. And on that evening at Cannae, almost the entire Roman nobility, including many of its senators, lay dead. The victorious Carthaginians were stepping over mounds of corpses, going from one dead nobleman to the next and cutting off fingers to collect the signet rings. They sent the rings in a big casket home to Carthage, where Hannibal's youngest brother poured them on the floor in front of the assembled senators of Carthage. It was a triumphant and dramatic gesture by Hannibal that signaled his imminent, complete, and glorious conquest of Rome.

For this much was clear to the Carthaginians, and even to most Romans: this war was over. Hannibal had won, Rome had lost. Roman surrender was inevitable; the rest was procedural detail. In the twenty-one months since Hannibal had crossed the Alps, he had slaughtered one out of every four men in Italy.[2] The Italian cities that had been allies of Rome were now coming over to Hannibal's side, just as he had expected. The Romans had practically nobody left to fight or resist. And Hannibal had demonstrated beyond any doubt that he was supreme in battle, indeed invincible.

Hannibal *was* triumph. He embodied it as Hercules personified strength and Odysseus cunning. Hannibal's striking face, with one eye gnarled shut and blind from conjunctivitis caught in an Italian swamp the previous year, was the face of victory and success.

AND THEN SOMETHING ODD began to unfold. Somehow the war was *not* over. Despite their litany of defeats, the Romans did *not* surrender. Hannibal, despite his string of astonishing, even legendary, victories, could *not* impose his will. He remained in Italy for another fourteen years and although he stayed unbeaten during this entire time, he never conquered Rome. In the many smaller Italian battles to come, Hannibal's genius never failed him, and the Romans acknowledged as much. And yet, all of Hannibal's successes on the battlefield seemed, mysteriously, to *amount* to a huge failure. His triumphs turned out to be, in a word, *impostors.*

The easiest way to know that they were impostors is to look at our American government buildings today: they are built to resemble Roman edifices. Or to listen to the Romance languages spoken to our south and in much of Europe, descended from the Latin of the Romans. Or to use a simple calendar, which dates, with only minor refinements, to the one the Romans used. Our Western civilization is a Roman world, not a Carthaginian one. We don't even know exactly how Carthaginian temples looked, how the Carthaginian language, Punic, sounded, or what exactly Hannibal might have worn.

That is because, a few decades after Hannibal died, the Romans erased Carthage—the city, the people, and the civilization—in an act of genocide. The Carthaginians were either killed or sold into slavery or chased into the interior of Africa. The last three Carthaginians taking refuge at the eternal fire inside the Temple of Baal, Carthage's greatest god, were a mother and her two children. The name Hannibal meant "favorite of Baal," and it was by this fire where Hannibal had sworn, when he was nine years old, to be Rome's enemy. Now, a generation after his death, this last Carthaginian mother hurled her children into the flames, then leaped in after them.

The Romans worked for a long time. Whatever was wood or flesh in Carthage they burned. The rest they pulled down stone by stone, tile by tile. Legend has it that they sowed the earth with salt so that nothing would ever grow there again. It was their posthumous revenge on Hannibal. It was a gesture that said: Hannibal has failed, Rome has triumphed.

I first read the story of Hannibal when I was a teenager. I loved it primarily for a teenager's reasons—the action and suspense and romance of it all. I was fascinated by the spectacle and grandeur of Hannibal's life, by his conquest of the Alps—with elephants, no less—and his victories.

These are the moments in his story that have been etched into Western culture and legend. One thousand years after Hannibal, Charlemagne, the great king of the Franks, tried to follow Hannibal's path across the Alps as a way of staking his claim to the same greatness. Another thousand years after that, Napoleon did the same thing and had the greatest French artist of the time, Jacques-Louis David, paint him in a flowing cape on a rearing horse while crossing an Alpine pass, with the names of both Hannibal and Charlemagne carved into a rock in the painting's corner. Boys like Harry Truman, the future U.S. president, read and reread the story of one-eyed Hannibal because "there is not in all history," as Truman said, "so wonderful an example of what a single man of genius may achieve against tremendous odds."[3]

If I noticed the existential riddle hidden in Hannibal's life story, in the sweeping arc between triumph and disaster, I did not dwell on it. I was too young to contemplate success and failure in life. For a teenager, successes are simply victories and failures are defeats. Hannibal, along with Alexander the Great and Julius Caesar, is thus antiquity's perfect boyhood hero: a winner, not a loser.

But it is a mark of the best and most timeless stories, as of the best poems and works of art, that they stay relevant throughout a lifetime, taking on different meanings and offering different messages at each stage of life. So, for example, at about the time I first learned about Hannibal I also first read Rudyard Kipling's beautiful poem "If," which included these lines: "Meet with triumph and disaster and treat those two impostors just the same." At the time I found it a good poem, but no more than that. My own life had not yet caught up with the message of the story or the poem.

THIS BEGAN TO CHANGE later, in my twenties. I remember one particular moment. I was alone at the time and sitting on a cheap IKEA chair that came with the London digs I was renting just behind Victoria Station. It was a typical London apartment: the sink had separate taps for hot and cold water, and you either froze or scalded yourself. There was a constant draft.

I was wearing a well-tailored Italian pinstripe suit that looked completely out of place in the flat. I had loosened my Hermès tie and was settling down to vegetate in front of mindless British television after a long and unhappy day working in mergers and acquisitions for a famous American investment bank in the City of London, Europe's equivalent of Wall Street. The work was considered glamorous but was intellectually and emotionally unsatisfying, physically exhausting, and spiritually draining.

That was my life. The long hours in my cubicle under fluorescent light left no time, and no emotional energy, for deep relationships. I was lonely and tired, and my plan that night was to cross over the brink of exhaustion and collapse into bed for a few hours, then to get up and do it all again.

But when I turned on the TV, a documentary about Hannibal was playing. There it was again: that familiar story of the man, the elephants, the Alps and the battles, the maps of his march from Spain through France and into Italy, the vector charts of his maneuvers, the reenacted scenes with Roman legionaries. But this time, I found the story unexpectedly perplexing. I suddenly had lots of questions, and they were personal. How come I, and most people, knew so much about the two years of Hannibal's life that made him famous—the span between his Alpine crossing and his great victory at Cannae—and so little about the next thirty-three years of his life? What exactly happened to Hannibal during that time?

Why had his triumphs turned to disaster? And could the same thing happen to me?

The fundamental tragedy of Hannibal's story usually forms only a dramatic—in the theatrical sense of Greek tragedy—backdrop to heighten the romance. The tragedy of Carthage, its demise as a civilization, is well known. When Truman, the boy who loved Hannibal, became president and visited bombed-out Berlin after World War II, he said, "I never saw such destruction" and "I thought of Carthage."[4] But the bitter irony, the fundamental enigma, of *how* Hannibal's triumphs had led to that tragedy did not occupy Truman at that moment. It was suddenly occupying me, however, as I sat on my cheap IKEA chair, trying to make sense of my life.

ALL PEOPLE, beginning in their twenties and continuing until the end of their lives, tell themselves stories about their own journeys to make sense of life. This is one of the biggest ideas in psychology: that identity *is* story.[5] The psychologists call these stories personal myths, life scripts, or self-narratives. The stories are not logical and linear strings of autobiographical facts. Rather, they're selective memories with magnified turning points—a trauma, for example—that give shape to a life so that the young adult can view himself as part of the complex, confusing, and demanding adult society around him. An adolescent does not yet know who he is. But a young adult—having to choose a career, sexual partners, political affiliations, and so much more—needs to believe that he knows who he is. So he begins making up a story line, with himself as the hero. And that's what I was doing, too.

That Hannibal should come to serve as one archetype for the hero in my own personal myth might seem ridiculous, but I didn't see it that way. Hannibal lived an epic life, full of soaring success and crushing failure, whereas I was living a small and ordinary life, full of little successes and trifling failures, none of them of any consequence to anybody but me. But it was the *trajectory* of Hannibal's story that fascinated me and that I chose to see as a warning that deliberately presented itself in this early "chapter" of my own life story. Hannibal was warning me to examine the successes that I had achieved up until then and might achieve next, and to ask whether they were leading me, as his had led him, down a treacherous path toward failure.

WHEN HANNIBAL was a boy, he went with his father, Hamilcar, from Carthage in northern Africa to Iberia, where Hamilcar, a general, was trying to build a new empire to replace the one that Carthage had just lost in a humiliating war against Rome. When I was a teenager, I moved with my father and mother from our comfortable and safe suburb of Munich to New York, where my father was planning a new chapter in his career. The years in Iberia forged Hannibal into a warrior, as he trained by the side of his father to lead men into battle and to victory. For me, the years in America were also a crucible, as I tried to get by at a respected but cruel and Dickensian boarding school in New England. My equivalent of Rome in those days was to get rid of my German accent and then to learn flawless English as my weapon for the future. I set out to memorize the English dictionary—getting as far as L, I believe—and declared success when my verbal SAT scores were higher than those of many Americans in my class.

As Hannibal succeeded in his twenties, I had my own little achievements as a young man. High test scores, college admissions, academic honors, a coveted job at an elite(ish) bank. There were failures, too, primarily on the ledger of friendships gone awry or missing. But in the story that I was telling myself at the time, I did not dwell on them. At most, they seemed inevitable costs of success—after all, Hannibal lost half of his army during that two-week Alpine crossing.

A psychologist analyzing my emerging story would have said that the theme of "agency"—self-mastery, achievement, status—dominated over the theme of "communion"—intimacy, friendship, love. But just as Hannibal won at the Trebia, at Lake Trasimene, and at Cannae, I could tell myself that I was doing quite well. I seemed to be winning my little battles.

What made me receptive to Hannibal's story just then was that I suspected, or feared, that the story I was telling myself was a lie. My victories and successes were too banal to take seriously. I was wearing Hermès ties even though I thought they looked tacky. I was working on deals that bored me. I wore myself out so that I had no time or energy left to do the things that I loved doing.

I began to suspect that my success, and my entire existence, might be a joke. Officially, I was achieving things, relatively speaking. When the bank hired me, it flew me and the other London recruits to the headquarters in

New York for our training program, and we were not allowed to travel on the same plane lest it crash and take all of us down at once. This suggested that we were important. Now, however, I was spending my days and my nights in the same cubicle under never-changing fluorescent light. Around me stretched an ocean of other cubicles, all of them filled with people like me. We had stiff necks and red eyes from staring at spreadsheets full of earnings ratios and other boring numbers day after day. We conversed in a strange language in which people were constantly "leveraging" something, usually "proactively." Our business cards called us "analysts," which meant that our job was to fiddle with these numbers until midnight or later every night. At that point a boss would call in from an expensive hotel room in some faraway time zone and tell us to fax documents to a client immediately. We faxed them. Then we waited in the cubicle for the fax confirmation, and kept waiting just in case the boss called again. Then we called a car service—the bank picked up the tab, because we were important—that took us home and the driver waited outside while we took a shower inside, so that we could take the same car back to the bank and start this process all over again.

This was my success. It was a success where booking a holiday was an act of masochism, because as soon as it was booked, I counted down to the moment—perhaps hours before departing for the airport—when a boss peered over my cubicle wall to announce that an "opportunity" had just presented itself for me to show my "commitment" to the "team" by canceling my holiday and staying in the cubicle to keep sending midnight faxes to executives in far-flung places. Then I got to tear up my plane tickets and settle back into my cubicle for more success.

I was alive—in a seething and angry way—to the irony of the situation, and so were a few of my friends at the bank. I took philosophical cigarette breaks with one of them, during which we walked along the Thames in front of the office. We were trying to figure out the personality types at the bank. Few of our colleagues appeared to see banking as a calling and nobody seemed to think that it was even remotely fun. So why were we all there? It must have been because we wanted to get somewhere else and saw the bank as a mountain range to cross. Perhaps we wanted training or experience of some sort for something bigger. But what? Neither my friend nor I wanted to be entrepreneurs or businessmen. We weren't sure what we wanted. Once, when I was in the men's room at work, an Italian colleague at the urinal next to me told me, sotto voce, that he couldn't wait to get out of the bank so that he could go back to Italy to breed horses, but I had to promise not to tell anybody. Most of us, it seemed, were investment bankers because that's what ambitious young people in the 1990s did, just as young aristocratic men in Hannibal's time became warriors.

My friend and I also noticed that there were patterns to success and failure at the bank. Success was defined as a huge bonus and a promotion from "analyst" to "associate" to "vice president" to "managing director." Bonus time came just before Christmas, and for weeks before, the atmosphere was tense and people behaved differently toward one another. On the bonus day, bankers filed out of the cubicle barracks, one by one, and entered the glass-walled offices along the perimeter to have their talk with the boss. Those still in the cubicles would peer through the glass walls to read the body language as the ones in the fish bowls received their envelopes.

The people I saw succeeding—with good envelopes and big titles—tended to stay at the bank, even though I could never get a straight answer from them whether they actually wanted to be bankers. Whatever life goal they couldn't quite name yet but were ultimately aiming for was delayed. The more they got promoted, the longer they delayed it. Perhaps they forgot about it altogether. As they rose from one victorious deal to another, from one promotion to the next, they changed. With power and importance came impatience. Nothing that others did was done fast enough or well enough. They were anxious. One of them, a bit older than I was and very successful, gradually but completely rubbed his eyebrows out as he worked through the nights in his cubicle. A friend and I kept track of the divorces and breakups around us, as bankers worked so hard and focused so exclusively on their financial battles and power struggles that they ignored their partners. During one of those philosophy-and-cigarette walks, my friend, paraphrasing Winston Churchill, said that the bank was a riddle wrapped in a mystery inside an enigma: "In went nice, promising, interesting young people; out came sad, pathetic assholes."

ALL THIS was gnawing at me as I sat watching the Hannibal documentary. Was I in my life at the same point where Hannibal was in his life after he crossed the Alps and as he was winning his victories? I decided that I needed to find out what came next in Hannibal's story, during the decade that he stayed in Italy, undefeated the entire time. What was he doing there? Did he have a plan? Did he realize he was trapped? The documentary gave no answers.

I wondered whether Hannibal at the end of his sixteen years in Italy could still remember the face of Imilce, his lovely Iberian wife, and his newborn son, whom he had last seen when he left Iberia for Italy and who disappeared without a trace from history.[6] Did success require sacrificing loved ones (as many of the top bankers around me did), or was sacrificing loved ones *already* the ultimate failure?

I wondered whether, in his dreams, Hannibal could *stop* seeing the face of Hasdrubal, his beloved younger brother. Hasdrubal had tried to lead another army from Iberia over the Alps to support Hannibal in Italy. But the Romans had intercepted his army and killed him. They cut off Hasdrubal's head and marched it to the other end of Italy, where they catapulted it into Hannibal's camp. Hannibal, who did not even know yet that Hasdrubal had arrived in Italy, last saw his little brother's face as it rolled toward his feet.

How much can success cost before it becomes disaster?

Hannibal, I later decided as I investigated his mystery, is only one half of the Hannibal story, a bit as yang is one half of a whole that also has yin. The other half that completes the story and makes it comprehensible is much less known.

It comes in the form of two Romans. One was named Fabius. He was a slow-walking and slow-talking Roman senator. He was old by the time Hannibal arrived in Italy, and his nickname was Warty for the big wart he had on his lip. This same Warty watched as Hannibal swept into Italy like an angry god and killed a quarter of the men in the Roman parts of the Italian peninsula. (The north of what is today Italy was then still part of Gaul.) To Fabius, as to all Romans, Hannibal's triumphs were utter disasters. Nothing in Rome's entire history even came close to the existential crisis that Hannibal represented to Rome.

Rome's fate, it appeared to almost all Romans at their nadir, was either extinction or slavery. The Romans had lost hope. In their despair, they were ready to give up. But just then, old Warty changed their minds. Like an inner voice of the Roman psyche, he told his countrymen that something about these disasters was phony, transient, incomplete. The devastating force of Hannibal's thrust could never be blocked, Fabius conceded, but perhaps it might be absorbed—or diverted, like a stream after a downpour, so that it might run its course in a different direction.

The other Roman, who would play a very different role in the story, was named Scipio. A decade younger than Hannibal and in many ways similar, he was a dashing, cosmopolitan, sophisticated Roman aristocrat. In his youth, Scipio was an eyewitness to the disasters Hannibal inflicted on the Romans. He served in the armies that Hannibal butchered and was one of the few survivors at Cannae. Like all Romans, he lost loved ones, but the blows were especially hard for him. His father and his uncle were Roman generals and went to Iberia to fight Hannibal's brothers. Both died in battle. Into his mid-twenties, Scipio saw only disaster in his life.

And yet Scipio did not succumb. He was so much younger than Fabius that he hardly needed to convince himself to absorb the disaster; it was simply life as he knew it. Scipio saw Hannibal as a force of nature, like volcanic eruptions or floods. He understood that Hannibal was a military genius, but instead of hating or fearing him, Scipio studied him from afar with the open and appreciative mind of a disciple. Like Fabius, he believed that the disaster of Hannibal might turn out to be an impostor.

Unlike Fabius, he wanted to do more than absorb, divert, or simply out-
last the disaster. Scipio wanted to be the one to turn it upside down, into
triumph.

THESE THREE MEN—Hannibal, Fabius, and Scipio—presented themselves to me together. The hero in my own emerging story was a potential blend of all three. If Hannibal was the impostor triumph, then Fabius
and Scipio were aspects of the impostor disaster. Fabius was the part of
me and of all other people who meet their worst fears and endure, overcome, and above all *accept*. Scipio was the part of me and of others that
stands in the rubble after disaster strikes and feels strangely, surprisingly
liberated by it. If Fabius is acceptance, Scipio is the freedom to start anew,
to aim higher, or at least elsewhere, to reinvent oneself.

Everyone has a story, and each story is simultaneously unique and
universal. The psychologist Carl Jung believed that what makes us
human is that we tell one another our stories, and that these stories are,
at some deep level, the same ones over and over again. The characters and
plots are different and yet the same. Jung called them *archetypes*. After
Jung, other scholars[7] found those archetypes—such as the *hero* on
a *quest*—in virtually all the great stories ever told, from antiquity to modern times, from the *Odyssey* to *Star Wars*, from the ancient Greeks to the
Navajo and to us.

We seem to need archetypes because we recognize ourselves in them.
"Ultimately, every individual life is at the same time the eternal life of the
species," wrote Jung. It does not matter how long ago or far away a hero
lived, or indeed whether he lived at all. It does not matter whether the
quest and the feats were epic as in myth or life-sized as in folktales. What
matters, as Jung put it, is that "in the archetype itself, there is no time; it

is a timeless condition where beginning, middle, and end are just the same. They are all given in one."[8]

THIS IS A BOOK of stories, some ancient, some modern, some personal, some mythical, some famous, some obscure, and all of them true in their own way. What the stories have in common is that they are about the archetypes of triumph and disaster, or success and failure, in life. Each chapter shines a light on one theme of this mysterious and universal journey with the two impostors, as Kipling called them. There are the themes of youth, when parents influence how we view success and failure; the themes of young adulthood, when we pursue our dreams, when we dare, win, or lose; the themes of middle age, when we need to reexamine our dreams and identities and our successes and failures up to this point; and the themes of old age, when success and failure take on altogether different meanings.

The main story is of course that of Hannibal, Fabius, and Scipio, who serve as personifications of the various aspects of triumph and disaster in this book. The story happens to be true, and I stay as faithful to the ancient sources, primarily Polybius and Livy, as I can, taking my dialogues from them where possible and signaling the few places where I conjecture meetings or conversations that might plausibly have taken place.

But in each chapter other stories amplify what is happening to Hannibal, Fabius, and Scipio at that stage in their lives. There will be artists such as Paul Cézanne and Pablo Picasso, writers such as Amy Tan and Tennessee Williams, athletes such as Tiger Woods and Lance Armstrong, thinkers such as Carl von Clausewitz and Carl Jung, businessmen such as Steve Jobs, ambassadors of life such as Eleanor Roosevelt, statesmen such as Harry Truman and my own great-uncle Ludwig Erhard, martial artists such as Morihei Ueshiba, explorers such as Ernest Shackleton and Meriwether Lewis, scientists such as Albert Einstein, and lovers such as Cleopatra. The mystery of triumph and disaster runs through all strands of life, and Hannibal's war serves as a visceral metaphor for all of them.

THE UNIFYING INSIGHT is the one that Kipling expressed: that triumph and disaster, success and failure, are not necessarily what they seem. This idea appears so often in our stories that I believe it to be archetypal. Take, for example, the folktale about an old man and his horse. One day, the horse ran away, and the villagers came over to express their regrets. "Who knows whether this is good or bad?" said the old man, shrugging. A few days later, the horse returned and brought along a herd of wild horses it had met. The neighbors came over again, this time to congratulate the old man. "Who knows whether this is good or bad?" He shrugged. Soon after, the old man's son tried to tame one of the stallions, fell off it, and broke his bones. "So sorry," said the neighbors. "Who knows?" said the old man. Then war broke out, the army drafted all the healthy young men in the village, and only the old man kept his son because the boy was still bedridden. "Lucky you," said one mother. "Who knows?" said the old man.

Thus they show up in their disguises, the ups and downs of life, the turns of good and bad fortune, the whims of the goddess the Romans called Fortuna and the Greeks Tyche, the dramatic reversals the Greeks called peripeteia and built their timeless stories on. Perhaps they disguise themselves to bring something out of us and that something is character, our true self, who we really are. This book is about those moments of impact, when triumph or disaster strikes, and about the aftermath, when the shock fades and lives change forever and character reveals itself.

You won't find any easy answers in this book. It makes no promise that henceforth it will be all success and no failure for you. But you will see a bit of yourself in these stories, and you will empathize and perhaps understand *why* certain things happened in your life, why you responded this way and not that way.

You may even get ideas for a different, a "Fabian" or a "Scipionic" response if you are coping with a setback or loss in your life. You may rethink your situation if you are currently at the top of your game, heeding the lessons of Hannibal. As you will see, the basic conundrum in his life, as in many of ours, was the tension between tactics and strategy, between means and ends. He won his battles but not the war or the peace. Hannibal's most subtle lessons to us today teach us how to think simultaneously large and small so that we can *align* life tactics with life strategy.

If you are in midlife or old age, you may recognize yourself in the later chapters of this book as the various characters redefine what success and failure even are. For the meaning of those words is clear only to the young, who have not been forced to reexamine it. It becomes less clear in middle age. But some people do arrive at a new and higher notion of triumph in later life, when the successes and failures of youth no longer matter so much. In some cases it may even be possible, if not to *defeat* the two impostors, to *transcend* them.

I BEGAN THINKING about these matters that night in the 1990s, slumped in my IKEA chair in my London flat, watching the Hannibal documentary. Soon after, I accepted that I was certain "to fail" at the bank. The beginning of the end took place, perhaps inevitably, during one of those bonus talks in a glass office. My boss put on an earnest demeanor and declared herself disappointed by my recent lack of focus on a particular project. To my boss's surprise, I agreed.

"It's affected your bonus," she said.

"I'm sure," I said, and took the envelope.

"Won't you open it?" she asked.

"Later," I replied.

A couple of onlookers from the cubicles later reported that my boss seemed confused after the meeting. I was not. My days at the bank were now numbered, I knew, and I was looking ahead to what might come next. I left banking and became a journalist, later a husband and father. My ideas about success and failure kept changing and are changing still, but the more they do, the more relevant the story of Hannibal, Fabius, and Scipio becomes.

"The greater a man's success, the less it must be trusted to endure,"[9]

Hannibal said to Scipio the first time they met, on an African plain at a place called Zama, the day before they were to do battle against each other. Scipio, though a decade younger, nodded. He understood completely, although he might have added that failure is to be distrusted just as much. As they knew, there is no escape from the two impostors. The question is what we become when they arrive.

THE INFLUENCE
OF PARENTS

I wished to be left alone to live in a dream world in which I was the heroine and my father the hero.

—Eleanor Roosevelt

I realized that—although it was fiction and none of that had ever happened to me in that story—it was the closest thing to describing my life. Of the feelings that I had, of these things that my mother had taught me that were inexplicable or had no name. This invisible force that she taught me, this rebellion that I had.

—Amy Tan

Once when Hannibal was a little boy, he was playing with his two younger brothers, Hasdrubal and Mago, while their father, Hamilcar Barca, was watching. Hamilcar was himself still a young man, but as Carthage's most successful general he had a powerful presence. Black-haired and sharp-featured, browned by the Mediterranean sun under which he led armies against the Romans, he beamed with pride as he gazed at his rambunctious boys. "These are the lion cubs I am rearing for the destruction of Rome!"[1] he roared with a hearty laugh.

Everyone has a father and a mother, and Hannibal and his brothers and sisters began life first and foremost as Barcids, as children of Hamilcar, the most famous, respected, and feared warrior of his generation. This was a privileged but also a difficult situation to be born into, with pressures and expectations and certain notions about success and failure, honor and duty.

For the three girls, their father's influence was direct and inescapable. Hamilcar married his oldest daughter to an admiral (their son would later serve under Hannibal), his second daughter to a handsome general who would later become Hamilcar's second-in-command in Iberia, and his third daughter to a colorful Numidian tribal chief who promptly galloped onto a battlefield with two thousand horsemen to help Hamilcar win a battle.[2]

But for his boys, his "lion cubs," and above all for his firstborn, Hamilcar had special ambitions. He set up their entire lives as apprenticeships for valor, leadership, and fighting skill. Hamilcar's greatest hope was that his sons would surpass him, that they would achieve the goals that had eluded him. Specifically, Hamilcar dreamed that his sons would one day vanquish Rome as Hamilcar himself might have done had not—or so Hamilcar saw it—the elders of Carthage surrendered before he had a chance.

Like many fathers, Hamilcar saw the meaning of his own life largely in his sons. He said as much even in his manner of dying. His life ended during a campaign in Iberia. He had taken Hannibal and Hasdrubal, by then young men, with his army to fight against a hostile tribe. They were ambushed, and Hamilcar apparently tried to divert the enemy attack away from his sons so that they could escape. His pursuers close behind him, Hamilcar rode on horseback into a stream—the details are not clear—and drowned.[3]

ESPECIALLY DURING THE HEIGHT of his career, Hamilcar had been a talented commander and an astute politician in his own right. When necessary he could be utterly ruthless, as when he subdued a rebellious group of mercenaries by having them trampled to death by elephants, or when he crucified a captured rebel leader in plain sight of the man's comrades. But he could also be charismatic and charming, and he inspired fierce loyalty and adoration in his troops. Once Hamilcar took a town situated between two Roman garrisons. To his soldiers it looked as though they were trapped by the Romans, but Hamilcar convinced them that they were instead holding the Romans on both sides in check. And so they did exactly that.

Hamilcar was more than just a gifted tactician on the battlefield. He could be diplomatic and statesmanlike, as in 241 BCE, when Carthage's Council of Elders chose him to negotiate a peace treaty with Rome to end the First Punic War. Politically shrewd, he made sure that he personally was never blamed for Carthage's defeat and that his own stature instead grew. And he was imaginative, as when he persuaded the Carthaginian elders to let him take an army to Iberia in order to build an entirely new empire for Carthage.

But despite these talents, Hamilcar was ultimately a frustrated and even angry man. Hamilcar believed that he had been betrayed, not only by the Romans but also by their appeasers in Carthage itself, the elders who directed him to end the First Punic War when he believed he still could have won it. It became his mission in life to redeem this loss and to exact revenge on the Roman republic. His sense of humiliation had deep roots, and it is important to understand them.

IN HAMILCAR'S OWN YOUTH, Romans and Carthaginians alike would have been surprised if told that they would soon hate and fight one another. The two states had peacefully coexisted for centuries. Rome was a small but expanding land power in Italy. Carthage was a much wealthier and more powerful maritime empire controlling ports all around the central and western Mediterranean and beyond the Pillars of Hercules, today's Gibraltar, to the Atlantic coast of today's Morocco. Neither Rome nor Carthage interfered in the affairs of the other. They had signed several treaties of friendship. When the Romans defeated their Italian neighbors, the Samnites, the Carthaginians sent a massive gold crown to congratulate them for the victory. They traded heavily.[4]

Carthage was originally a colony of Tyre, a city in Phoenicia, today's Lebanon. In Punic, as the Romans called the Phoenician language, Carthage meant "New City." The Phoenicians and Carthaginians were a Semitic people, with a language related to Hebrew and Arabic. For example, Hamilcar's family name, possibly given to him for his temperament, was Barca, which meant "lightning" in Punic, as *barak* means in Hebrew and *buraq* in Arabic.

The Phoenicians and their Carthaginian offshoots were, along with the Greeks, the great colonizers of the Mediterranean. Greeks and Phoenicians encountered one another almost everywhere in that part of the world and mostly in peace. In places like Sicily, their traditions and cultures sometimes blended. The Greek demigod Heracles, for example, merged with his Phoenician equivalent, Melqart. The Greeks adopted the Phoenician alphabet and naval innovations like the keel.[5] Carthaginian aristocrats in turn spoke Greek and appreciated Greek literature. Hamilcar made sure that his sons were fluent in Greek, and Hannibal later took two Greek scholars, Sosylus and Silenus, along with him on his military campaigns.

The Phoenicians and Carthaginians were traders at heart. Carthage, an independent republic, maintained the largest navy in the Mediterranean, primarily in order to police its merchant empire and keep the money flowing in. Instead of drafting citizens to form armies, Carthage hired mercenaries, since it made good business sense to pay foreign soldiers instead of arming Carthaginians who could be making money instead. In a sense, Carthage was run like a corporation. Once a year, the city totaled its trading profit and parceled it out among its citizens.

Rome, on the other hand, was simultaneously similar to and utterly different from both the Greeks and the Carthaginians. It was similar to Carthage in that it was a republic, with a mixture of monarchy, aristocracy, and democracy that Greek philosophers like Aristotle considered perfectly balanced. Both Carthage and Rome had popular assemblies with limited powers in which all male citizens could vote. Both had senates. And both elected, each year for that year only, two chief executives, whom the Romans called consuls and the Carthaginians suffetes, with the idea that each would keep a check on the power of the other.

But there the similarities ended. At the beginning of the third century BCE, Carthage was a great power, whereas hardly anybody had heard of Rome. When Alexander the Great died in 323 BCE, he had apparently been planning to conquer Carthage while hardly being aware of Rome. For centuries, the Romans had been entirely preoccupied with dominating the cities in their own immediate area, called Latium, and the Italian lands adjoining it. They had never crossed the sea. In fact, they began their first war against Carthage without a single warship.

It was only when the Romans marched into the southern tip of the Italian peninsula, a land dotted with ancient Greek colonies and considered part of the Greek world, that they came into prolonged contact with the civilized—meaning Hellenized—peoples. Those Italian Greeks considered the Romans barbarians (literally, since the Romans, like all non-Greeks, spoke gibberish that sounded like *bar bar bar* to the Greeks). The Greeks wanted to keep the Romans out of southern Italy.

So they invited a swashbuckling Hellenistic king named Pyrrhus from the other side of the Adriatic Sea, today's Albania, to fight the Romans on their behalf. Pyrrhus eagerly obliged and brought an army to southern Italy. A brave and talented warrior, Pyrrhus repeatedly defeated the Romans in battle, but the Romans never gave up. Their resilience was unexpected, and prompted Pyrrhus to lament after a battle, as he contemplated the soldiers he had lost and how little advantage he had gained, "One more such victory will undo me." Pyrrhus, with his "Pyrrhic victories," could have said a word or two about triumphs being impostors. Eventually, he gave up and sailed home, leaving southern Italy to the Romans. It was a lesson some Romans would remember when it was Hannibal who was winning battles against them.

The entire Mediterranean world, Greek and Carthaginian alike, took note. What impressed them about the Romans was their iron discipline and stubborn will. Usually at this time, civilized peoples waged war by

staging a few battles, smashing spears and shields together, and then calling
it quits before too many people were killed. Hellenistic clashes were not
wars of annihilation but higher forms of jousting. But the Romans had
none of that. They never, ever gave up. Every citizen and ally had to be a
soldier, and every soldier had to be ready to sacrifice his life. If a Roman
unit in combat was seen to be weak or cowardly, it was decimated in the
literal sense: every tenth soldier would be beaten to death.[6]

HAVING CONQUERED the boot of southern Italy, the Romans for the
first time stared directly at a land that the Carthaginians considered to be
their sphere of influence: the large and wealthy island of Sicily, both a
stepping-stone and a buffer to northern Africa and Carthage itself. The
eastern side of Sicily had long been settled by Greeks, with famous cities
such as Syracuse. But the western and southern sides of Sicily were Carthaginian. A confrontation with Rome became likely.

The actual trigger for conflict, as so often in life, was an absurd and
tragicomic entanglement better suited to a theater stage than world history.
A large band of originally Italian hoodlums calling themselves Mamertines,
"sons of Mars," seized a Greek town in Sicily, just across from the Italian
mainland, called Messana (modern Messina). They killed the men and
took their wives and families. When the Greek city of Syracuse threatened
them, the Mamertines then appealed to both the Carthaginians in western
Sicily and the Romans across the straits for help.

The Carthaginians obliged by sending an admiral to Messana with a
fleet, intended not only to scare away the Syracusans but also to keep the
Romans from crossing the straits. But the Romans, after a failed attempt,
managed to cross in borrowed boats and skiffs. The Mamertines decided
to throw the Carthaginians out. The Carthaginian elders were so embarrassed by the entire episode that they crucified their returning admiral (not
an unusual punishment at the time). The Carthaginians then attacked the
Romans at Messana, seeking to restore their honor.

And so began, in 264 BCE, when Hamilcar was about eleven, the First

Punic War, which would last twenty-three years, an entire generation. Both the Romans and the Carthaginians quickly lost any interest in the Mamertines. Instead, they now fought a desperate struggle to control Sicily.

At first the Romans won the land battles but, since they had no navy, lost at sea. But the Romans captured a Carthaginian ship, studied it, copied its design, and built their own, again and again, until they had a fleet. And they added an ingenious weapon to their ships. This was the "raven," a large swiveling bridge that the Romans brought crashing down onto an enemy ship when they came within about thirty feet. The two ships were then tied together as a large floating platform, and the Roman soldiers stormed across. In effect, the Romans had found a way to turn sea battles into land battles. After their first naval victory, the Romans brought the prows, or *rostra*, of the defeated Carthaginian ships to Rome and hung them on the speaker's pulpit in the Forum.[7] Ever since, a public speaker takes the "rostrum."

THIS LONG and bitter war had already been raging for eighteen years and Carthage was losing when Hamilcar, only in his late twenties, was given command of an army and set off for Sicily. He had a lot on his mind at the time. He already had his three daughters with his first wife, and his second wife had just borne him his first son, Hannibal. But Hamilcar could not spend much time with the baby, because his place was now with his troops. He was determined to avoid a Carthaginian defeat.

For three years, he used his base in Sicily to raid and harass the Romans in Italy. Then he challenged the Romans in Sicily itself. The Romans learned to fear and respect Hamilcar, although it never came to a decisive battle between them. Elsewhere, at sea and on the rest of the island, the Romans were still winning. The elders of Carthage, exhausted by a generation of war and almost bankrupt, decided to sue for peace and instructed Hamilcar to negotiate a treaty.

This he did with great aplomb, winning for the Carthaginian army the right to evacuate Sicily with their arms and dignity, and for Carthage to pay Rome only modest war reparations. But when the peace treaty was sent to Rome for ratification, the popular assembly demanded much larger payments from Carthage. Carthage's elders, tired of fighting, agreed to Rome's terms. Hamilcar was livid, but he had to follow his orders from Carthage, which were to decommission his army and return home.

BACK IN AFRICA, however, things went from bad to worse for Carthage. Its mercenary armies, while under Carthaginian command in Sicily, had fought as coherent and disciplined units. But now they were milling around the countryside of Carthage, armed and as yet unpaid. They were a polyglot mob of Libyans from east of Carthage and Numidians from the west, of Gauls and Iberians and Greeks, of former slaves and gladiators and vagabonds. They were violent, frustrated, restless, and angry.

The Carthaginians, bankrupt from the war, without their former revenues from Sicily, and hard pressed by the indemnity they were now paying the Romans, could not pay the mercenaries' arrears in full and tried to negotiate. But two of the mercenaries, a runaway slave from southern Italy named Spendius and a Libyan named Mathos, now declared themselves leaders of the mercenary army. Anybody who stood up to oppose them was pelted with stones by their supporters.[8] Spendius and Mathos then attacked Carthage. What had begun as a pay dispute now became a brutal, bloody war for Carthage's survival.

The Carthaginians hurriedly raised a small force of citizens and new mercenaries, but they were outnumbered. So they once again turned to Hamilcar. First he shared command with another general, then he took overall charge. He was now fighting against his own former soldiers, and they against their former commander. At first Hamilcar tried a subtle strategy of selective mercy toward captured mercenaries, so that the others might think there would be no recriminations if they deserted to Hamilcar's side. But Spendius and Mathos understood Hamilcar's plan and, in a calculated way, committed atrocities so vile as to make clemency by either side impossible. They tortured their Carthaginian prisoners, including a general, by cutting their hands off, castrating them, breaking their legs, and burying them alive. All the mercenaries, assuming recriminations, concluded that deserting was no longer an option.

As Spendius and Mathos seemed to desire, the war now became barbaric. When Hamilcar captured rebels, he had them trampled to death by his elephants. He trapped one mercenary force in a valley and starved them until they ate each other. Having captured Spendius and other mercenary leaders, Hamilcar marched on the last rebel holdout and crucified his prisoners in front of the city walls in full view of their comrades. Mathos, watching Spendius die on the cross, in turn captured a Carthaginian general and crucified him on the same cross for revenge. But Hamilcar was already crushing the last remnants of resistance. Mathos was paraded through Carthage and met a cruel end. The mercenary war was over.[9]

But Carthage got little relief from Hamilcar's victory. The Romans, seeing their recent enemies exhausted and weak, broke their peace treaty and seized the Mediterranean islands of Sardinia and Corsica. Besides Sicily, these two islands had been the mainstay of Carthage's trading economy. In a particularly gratuitous gesture, Rome also levied yet another, even bigger indemnity on Carthage.[10]

The Carthaginians, and especially Hamilcar, seethed with anger. But it was an impotent rage because Carthage had no armies, no money, and no will left to resist. The nation-state of Carthage, lord of the seas for hundreds of years, was forced into complete submission. For the rest of his life, Hamilcar remembered this humiliation.

HANNIBAL WAS A BOY when these atrocities and betrayals were occurring. We must assume that he would have seen his father brooding in frustration and erupting in terrifying bursts of wrath. He would have heard his father's bitter monologues about honor, revenge, and the wickedness of Rome. And he must have felt the special and touching pride and hope that Hamilcar held for him, his firstborn son.

Hamilcar formed a new plan for Carthage's future. It was to conquer

Iberia, a savage land in the distant west, north of the entrance to the wider ocean. Iberia had vast mines of silver and gold that could mint the coins to repay Rome and still make Carthage rich again. Iberia's tribesmen were fierce warriors who would make good soldiers for a new Carthaginian army. In short, Iberia seemed an ideal place to build a new Carthaginian empire from which, one day, that empire might strike back against Rome. Hannibal, nine years old by this time, wanted to be part of this adventure.

Hannibal's young personality developed against this backdrop. Long before he could form his own values and worldview, he adopted those of his father. In that sense, Hamilcar and Hannibal were like most parents and children: part of one world, their own world, with a similar outlook on life. Most of us, while young, will define what success means and what failure looks like based on the values and example of our parents.

Some adolescents, like Hannibal and his brothers, try to *emulate* their parents. If their parents are successful, this puts pressure on the children to live up to that high standard. If the parents are *not* successful—if they have "failed" as Hamilcar felt he did when losing to Rome—the children will also feel pressure. This is the anxiety of having to succeed to vindicate their parents.

Hannibal and his brothers would have emulated Hamilcar's valor and martial prowess—and indeed tried to *exceed* it—in order to make him proud. And they would have defined their mission in life as redeeming their father by leading Carthage to victory over Rome. They did not live at a time or in an environment that would have permitted them ever to admit this, but they must have felt a lot of stress.

OTHER ADOLESCENTS, then as now, may grow up not with doting and engaged parents such as Hamilcar but with a parent who is literally or psychologically absent. They may be orphans; their parents may be divorced; or their parents may simply not be very involved in the lives of their children.

But parental *absence* does not mean that there is no parental *influence*. The difference is that these adolescents do not emulate, but rather *search for* their father or mother. This can be metaphorical, as when children look for the *idea* of a parent and the sense of identity that comes with it. A quest to find the missing parent, and his or her values and legacy, can become the mission of adolescence.

A THIRD TYPE of adolescent may feel the attention of parents as overbearing, even suffocating. These young men and women will neither emulate nor search for their father or mother but *rebel.* They will reject their parents' values and expectations. But many youthful rebellions eventually lose steam. And even while rebelling, an adolescent is still reacting against, rather than acting without, the values of his or her parents. One way or the other, parents shape an adolescent's definition of success and failure, just not always in the way they wanted.

The quest to find an absent parent is just as much an archetype in our minds, legends, and myths as the story line of the child who emulates a parent. For example, Theseus, the great hero of ancient Athens in Greek mythology, was motivated to set out on the journey that would eventually lead him to Crete to slay the Minotaur, a monster half bull and half man, only because he originally wanted to find out who his father was.

Theseus was raised not in Athens but in a smaller Greek city, Troezen, by his mother and his grandfather, who was Troezen's king. Theseus did not know who his father was. When he turned sixteen, his mother told him that it was time for him to find out. Years before, his father had hidden something under a huge boulder for his son to find, provided he could lift the stone. Theseus made a lever to move the boulder and found under it a sword. His mother told him that this sword was a present from his father, who was King Aegeus of Athens. Armed with the sword and this knowledge, Theseus set off for Athens to meet Aegeus.

It was a dangerous journey. Theseus ran into bandits and villains along the way but overcame them all, thus continuing the process of proving himself *worthy* of finding his father. When he finally arrived in Athens, the Athenians did not recognize him but understood that he had liberated them from the bandits that made their countryside unsafe. They celebrated with a feast.

The queen, Medea, the king's second wife, instinctively knew that this young hero might become a rival to her own son, so she persuaded King Aegeus to poison Theseus's wine. Theseus was about to drink it when he unsheathed his sword to cut off a slab of meat. King Aegeus at once recognized his own sword, which he had hidden for his heir so long ago. The king knocked the cup of wine away before Theseus's lips touched it and embraced his son in a tearful reunion. Medea fled.

Theseus, having found his royal identity, became heir to the throne of Athens. With this new identity came a challenge. Athens had lost a war against King Minos of Crete, who demanded as an indemnity seven Athenian boys and seven maidens every nine years. A black-sailed ship would carry the fourteen children from Athens to Crete, where they were thrown into a labyrinth from which nobody had ever escaped, to be devoured by the Minotaur.

Theseus volunteered to be one of the youths on the next ship to Crete. With the help of Minos's daughter, who had fallen in love with him, he then entered the labyrinth, unwinding a thread as he walked deeper into its maze. He fought the Minotaur and killed the beast. Then he followed the thread back out. He had liberated Athens.

But on the way back from Crete, Theseus made a mistake. His father had given orders to keep the ship's black sail only if Theseus had failed and was dead, but to raise a white sail if he had succeeded and survived. Theseus returned with the black sail hoisted in error, and his father, looking out from a cliff and thinking that his son had died, hurled himself to his death. Only with this final tragedy does Theseus complete the quest, by succeeding his father and becoming king.

BARACK OBAMA, before he became president of the United States, tapped into that same archetype of the father quest in his memoir, which is the complicated story of his own largely metaphorical search for his father, a Kenyan man whom he had met only once in his life. Like Theseus, Obama was raised by his mother and her parents. And like Theseus, he felt he had to go on a quest to find his father's identity, especially since his mother was white and Obama half black. One day when he was twenty-one, he got a call from an aunt in Kenya who told him that his father had been in a car accident and was dead.

"At the time of his death, my father remained a myth to me, both more and less than a man,"[11] Obama recalled. But "it was into my father's image, the black man, son of Africa, that I'd packed all the attributes I sought in myself."[12] So Obama set out on "a personal, interior journey—a boy's search for his father."[13] It was not unlike Theseus's trip to Athens—lonely, confusing, and difficult.

Eventually Obama traveled to his father's country, Kenya. He visited the small ancestral village where his father and grandfather were buried. There he sat between their graves and wept. "When my tears were finally spent, I felt a calmness wash over me. I felt the circle finally close. I realized that who I was, what I cared about, was no longer just a matter of intellect or obligation, no longer a construct of words. I saw that my life in America—the black life, the white life, the sense of abandonment I'd felt as a boy . . . all of it was connected with this small plot of earth an ocean away, connected by more than the accident of a name or the color of my skin. The pain I felt was my father's pain."[14]

———

WHEN SUCH a quest to find a missing parent fails—by *not* leading to a secure sense of identity—it can rob a young man or woman of the self-confidence needed to succeed. This is what happened to young Eleanor Roosevelt, the future first lady of the United States. Neither her mother nor her father spent much time with her. They were emotionally distant. So Eleanor spent her youth searching for the idea of her mother and father, who died when Eleanor was eight and nine years old.

SHE WAS BORN into an old Anglo-Dutch family of the East Coast aristocracy during the Victorian era. On one side were Roosevelts, including her own father, Elliott, and his older brother, Theodore, the future president. On her mother's side were Halls, Ludlows, and Livingstons. Her mother was the latest in a long line of society belles, flitting from ball to ball and being dazzling and charming.

"My mother was one of the most beautiful women I have ever seen," Eleanor later wrote.[15] She said it with despair, because Eleanor herself was not beautiful, at least not by comparison and not in her own mother's eyes. Her teeth looked too big; her limbs were gangly. "You have no looks, so see to it that you have manners," her mother told Eleanor.[16] As a parental message, it was the opposite of Hamilcar's, which was: Learn from me because one day you will surpass me. What mattered to Eleanor's mother were dances, dinners, and tennis. Eleanor was awkward at all of these and felt worthless.

Reserved toward her mother, Eleanor showered love on her father, Elliott—or rather the *idea* of Elliott, since he, too, was usually absent. He did adore his "little Nell," but he was a tragically flawed man, often drinking himself into oblivion. The young Eleanor once stood outside the elite Knickerbocker Club in New York where her father was carousing. She was holding several of his dogs on their leashes for more than six hours. Finally, she saw her father, unconscious, being carried out. A doorman had to escort her home. With her father thus gone in body or spirit, Eleanor largely created him in her imagination.[17]

Outwardly, Eleanor's parents represented the cream of American society. Inwardly, the family disintegrated. Elliott was sent to asylums to cure his alcoholism, and was sued for fathering a child with a servant. Then Eleanor's mother died of diphtheria. Eleanor at first seemed content "to be left alone to live in a dream world in which I was the heroine and my father the hero."[18] But her father drank himself literally to death, after downing "whole bottles of anisette and green mint—besides whole bottles of raw brandy and of champagne,"[19] as his brother, Theodore, put it. After his death, Eleanor moved in with her maternal grandmother. But her uncles were also drunks, and dangerous. So at the age of fifteen, Eleanor was sent to a boarding school outside London.

THERE, FOR A TIME, Eleanor seemed to find the mother figure she had been searching for, along with an identity. Her boarding school was for the girls of the liberal-minded aristocracy in Europe and America. Instruction was in French, even though the school was in England, rather as the children of the Carthaginian or Roman elite once had Greek tutors. The school was run by a strong, open-minded, and progressive—indeed feminist—elderly French woman named Marie Souvestre, the daughter of a philosopher and novelist.

Souvestre immediately spotted a bright mind in Eleanor, who became her favorite student. For the first time, Eleanor was allowed to blossom. Her chronic colds and coughs disappeared. Encouraged by Souvestre, Eleanor became a leader of the girls and interested in politics. She even traveled with Souvestre to the great cities of Europe, where they "always ate native dishes and drank native wines."[20] These trips were "the most momentous things that happened in my education," Eleanor later wrote. She arranged the tickets and maps and schedules for both Souvestre and herself and felt appreciated for perhaps the first time ever.

But after three years in Europe, it was time to come home and "come out" in New York society. Souvestre, shortly before dying of cancer, warned Eleanor to "protect herself."[21] But in New York, Eleanor was expected to attract eligible bachelors from good families and found herself once again compared—unfavorably—with her late mother. As before, Eleanor was deeply uncomfortable in her tall frame. "I knew I was the first girl in my mother's family who was not a belle," she later wrote, and "I was deeply ashamed."[22] Without Souvestre, the closest thing to a mother figure she had ever had, Eleanor again lost her self-esteem and became lonely.

At least there was a scintillating chemistry between herself and a distant cousin from another branch of the clan, Franklin Delano Roosevelt. He was one of the few men tall enough not be embarrassed next to Eleanor. Franklin filled in Eleanor's romantic mind the role that she had once ascribed to her father. He even called her "little Nell," as only her father had. When Eleanor was nineteen, Franklin, less than three years older, proposed marriage. For Eleanor, it was a triumph of sorts, as though she had at last found the love that her father had not been able to give her.

RIGHT FROM THE START there was a problem, however. Franklin's father had recently died, and he was now under the complete control of his mother, Sara Delano Roosevelt. Sara was an austere and regal beauty, still in black mourning veils. She liked to recite the ancestry of the Delanos back to William the Conqueror and looked down on even the Roosevelts with some disdain: "My son Franklin is a Delano, not a Roosevelt at all,"[23] she told friends. Nobody seemed good enough for Franklin, her only child, whom she had breast-fed, according to rumors, until he was six years old.[24]

As soon as Sara heard of her son's liaison with Eleanor, she tried to break it up. She insisted that the engagement be kept secret for a year. She arranged a six-week cruise in the Caribbean for Franklin and herself, but not for Eleanor, so that he might forget her and discover other interests along the way.

Eleanor reacted as the same vulnerable girl who had once hoped for approval from her mother. She swallowed her frustration and wooed her prospective mother-in-law. She wanted not just Franklin but a harmonious family, *including* a mother. "How hard it is for her and we must both try always to make her happy and I do hope someday she will learn to love me," Eleanor wrote to Franklin, who showed no interest in the tension between the two women.[25]

Eleanor kept fighting her quiet campaign, but the old traumas of her childhood resurfaced. Sara made her feel as rejected and unworthy as her own mother once had. And clinging to Franklin made her feel as vulnerable as when she had stood outside the Knickerbocker Club waiting for her father. "I miss you so much, it really frightens me to see how dependent I am growing and how the whole world turns for me around one person," she wrote Franklin.[26] The confidence she had developed with Souvestre was gone. She deliberately embraced the role of submissive wife and daughter-in-law.

After the wedding, the couple moved into a house that Sara had already furnished. Sara had also hired all the servants. In fact, there was nothing for Eleanor to do. She had yearned for a home of her own, but everything seemed to belong to her mother-in-law. At the dining room table, Franklin sat at one end and Sara at the other, while Eleanor, and later their children, sat along the sides. Franklin had a comfy wing-backed chair on one side of the fireplace, Sara had another on the other side, and Eleanor sat on the floor.[27]

The captivity became quasi-official when the family moved into a Siamese-twin town house on East Sixty-fifth Street that appeared designed to be a prison. Sara had arranged for sliding doors and passageways on all floors of the two houses, so that she could burst in anywhere and anytime. One never knew, Eleanor wrote, "when she would appear, day or night." Once Eleanor was sitting at her dressing table, looked into the mirror, and started weeping. Franklin appeared to ask about dinner. "I said I did not like to live in a house which was not in any way mine, one that I had done nothing about and which did not represent the way I wanted to live." Franklin responded that she was "quite mad."[28]

ELEANOR ROOSEVELT HAD, in so many ways, spent her childhood and youth searching for a mother and a father, and the love and security that only these two can provide. She never found them. The result was the opposite of a stable identity with which to set off on the quests of adulthood and successful life. It was a fragile psyche, ready to shatter at any moment. As indeed it soon would.

A my Tan, a writer born in California as the American daughter of two Chinese immigrants, is an example of the third way of responding to parents: she *rebelled.*

Her mother, Daisy, had left behind a harrowing life in prerevolutionary China. Daisy's own mother had been a concubine and rape victim and had committed suicide. Daisy herself had been abused by her first husband and divorced him, but she lost custody of her three daughters and had to leave them behind when she escaped on the last boat to depart Shanghai before the Communist takeover in 1949.[29] In America, Daisy met John Tan, a Chinese engineer and Baptist minister, and they married and started a new family. They had Amy and her two brothers.

The Tans were now determined to pursue the American Dream with Chinese characteristics. It consisted of rising prosperity ·and frequent moves to better addresses in Oakland and its suburbs, but above all of children who would turn out dutiful, proper, and accomplished. If most Chinese immigrants expect their sons to become either engineers or doctors, Daisy Tan decided early on, and in all seriousness, that her daughter Amy would be a brain surgeon during the week and a concert pianist on weekends.

"I was told what I was supposed to do when I was growing up, so I don't think I ever had a chance to think about what I really wanted to do," Amy Tan recalled years later.[30] Deep down, she fantasized about becoming an artist, but she suppressed that dream. "My parents said, 'You're going to be a doctor.'" And that was it. As in many Chinese immigrant families, she remembers, "my parents had very high expectations. They expected me to get straight As from the time I was in kindergarten."

The atmosphere at home was hypercompetitive, even in the most un- likely contexts. Once, during art class in kindergarten, Amy drew a fine house, with a cute chimney and windows and trees, whereas another girl squiggled something rather more abstract onto her page. Somehow, that other girl's drawing was the one pinned up in the principal's office. "My mother wanted to know: Why wasn't my picture in that window? I was very wounded and frightened. You know? Why wasn't it in the window? I remember feeling that pressure from the time I was five years old."

Daisy Tan expected unquestioning obedience from her daughter. Daisy "had been raised in an atmosphere of fear, that fear was the way to control children for their own good. That's what I grew up with," Amy Tan re- members. There was no room in this world for praise or pride. Daisy and John Tan were quick to scold when Amy fell short of expectations, but they never celebrated her when she succeeded, lest this might spoil her. "They didn't know how much the smallest amount of recognition would have meant to me and how the smallest amount of criticism could undo me. So I grew up thinking that I would never, ever please my parents. That is a difficult thing to grow up with."

These feelings eventually produced a backlash in Amy. From the age of eight she fought with her mother almost every day. She buried herself in books and their fantasy world. "There is one side of me that wanted to behave," she remembers. "On the other hand, I wanted to go out and be a rebel and wind up in jail. . . . I might as well be bad. And that I could succeed in."

A FAMILY DISASTER in Amy's teens provided the opportunity to be bad. In one year, both her oldest brother and her father died of brain tumors— which Amy considered macabrely ironic, given that her parents wanted her to become a brain surgeon. To escape the scene of grief and for superstitious reasons, Daisy Tan moved to Europe, and Amy ended up in a school in Switzerland. Amy chose this setting for her rebellion.

Away from Oakland, in a place where nobody knew her, "I exploded into a wild thing. I shortened my skirts, I put on makeup, I hung out with hippies. I got myself a first boyfriend, who was a German man who was twenty-four. I was sixteen. And it turned out, much to my delight, that he was also the father of an illegitimate child, which made him even more despicable in my mother's eyes. Anything that my mother hated, that was better. He deserted from the German army. I found out later, not simply from its Army but the mental hospital. My mother was convinced that this man was going to ruin me." Her new boyfriend's friends were dealing hashish and marijuana. Amy, who had spent her life up to this point going to church every day for Bible study and choir practice, was now "hanging around with these people in this environment where I know nothing about anything. I start smoking, I start drinking. People roll hashish in their cigarettes and I think that's part of it all and I end up getting arrested."

It "reached a point where I had infuriated my mother so much we nearly killed each other. Literally. And I was sick to my stomach, literally. I had dry heaves, and the pain was so enormous that at one point, when I thought I was going to die, I just suddenly realized that that scared me."

The family moved back to California, but the war between mother and daughter continued. Amy dropped out of the premed course that her mother had prescribed, thus officially rejecting her parents' life plan. She studied English and linguistics instead, as useful in her mother's eyes as a double major in finger painting and cuneiform. The break seemed complete.

BUT IT WASN'T. Amy Tan married. She tried various careers. She achieved a certain success as a technical writer for large companies like IBM, writing text with titles like "Telecommunications and You." For the first time she was making considerable amounts of money. She noticed that her mother understood that currency of success and began to be secretly proud of Amy. At the same time, Amy remembered what she had loved most as a child and began to write fiction.

Around this time, her mother became very ill and Amy feared she was going to die. She vowed that if her mother recovered, she would take her to China to retrace her roots and find the half sisters Daisy had left behind four decades earlier. Daisy Tan did recover, and the two went on their trip.

"I was nervous about it, because it meant three weeks with my mother, and I had hardly spent more than a couple of hours alone with her in the last twenty years," Amy remembers. But once they were in China, she began to see herself and her background in a new way. "I discovered how American I was. I also discovered how Chinese I was by the kind of family habits and routines that were so familiar."

When she came home, she felt that the trip was a turning point. It had made her aware of her heritage and a part of her that she had overlooked. Tan now used this new connection to find an authentic writer's voice within herself. Up to this time, she had tried to write about things unrelated to her own experience, and her fiction sounded inauthentic to people who read it. Now she made up entirely fictional characters who nonetheless lived in her own world. "I wrote about a girl who plays chess and her mother is both her worst adversary and her best ally. I didn't play chess, so I figured that counted for fiction, but I made her Chinese American, which made me a little uncomfortable. By the end of this story I was practically crying. Because I realized that—although it was fiction and none of that had ever happened to me in that story—it was the closest thing to describing my life. Of the feelings that I had, of these things that my mother had taught me that were inexplicable or had no name. This invisible force that she taught me, this rebellion that I had."

The outcome was a series of short stories that eventually became a book, *The Joy Luck Club*, which was a surprise bestseller. Some Asian Americans attacked her for peddling Chinese stereotypes, but many more recognized themselves in her book. Tan, then in her thirties, achieved a triumph bigger than her mother could have hoped for and in a field her mother could never have imagined.

The irony did not escape her. "I said to myself when I was seventeen, 'I'm not going to have anything to do with anything Chinese when I leave home. I'm going to be completely American,'" she recalls. "I was never going to speak to my mother again. She was disappointed in me? Well, I wasn't going to be around to disappoint her anymore." And yet, there she was, in her thirties, wildly successful as a result of her response to her mother and her background.

Her mother had shaped and directed her after all, just not in the way either of them had ever foreseen. "If you were to say to me when I was seventeen, 'You know, one day you're going to write a book about Chinese people and about your relationship with your mother and how much you love your mother,' and all this stuff, I would have said: 'You are crazy. You are absolutely crazy. There is no way I would ever do that.'" But she did.

To understand your life, you have to begin with your parents—just as you need to know about Hamilcar to understand why Hannibal made the decisions that led to his successes and failures. And in your life, the influence of your parents may not fit so neatly into these three categories—emulation, search, and rebellion. More likely, you formed your adolescent identity out of some mixture of the three, as I did.

I grew up in an upper-middle-class family in pleasant German suburbs. My father had followed less in the footsteps of his own father, who died when my father was young, than in those of his godfather and uncle, Ludwig Erhard, or Uncle Lulu. Erhard was an economist, famous for his market-friendly philosophy and his evangelism for freedom. He became the first economics minister of postwar West Germany and fathered its new currency, the deutsche mark. In the 1960s, Erhard became West Germany's chancellor, the equivalent of prime minister. My father followed him into economics, and from there into finance. He became treasurer of a large German company.

But my parents made clear to me early on—as did all the families in our circle—that *Kultur* was the goal to strive for. By this they mostly meant higher culture—ideas, the arts, appreciation of life's finer things. Of course these had to be backed up by solid accomplishments and supported by modesty in physical displays and consumption. The people who came to our house in the evenings after work might be bankers wearing well-fitting Italian jackets, but once they arrived, they would take off their coats and ties and over a glass of wine discuss opera or books.

For my parents, with their background different from, say, Amy Tan's, parenting was about *not* being too explicit in setting directions for me, about letting me discover. So my father deliberately chose not to push finance or economics on me, or any specific vocation. Nonetheless, he did have a goal for me. As Rome was the focus that Hamilcar wanted to bequeath to Hannibal, career *freedom* was what my father wanted for me. If valor was the code that Hamilcar wanted to teach Hannibal, sophistication was what my father thought I needed to live the good life.

Hamilcar's obsession with Rome came out of his own frustration and defeat—it was a score he wanted to settle. My father's preoccupation with career freedom also came out of his own frustration. He hated the corporate hierarchies, the bureaucracy, the petty politics that ensnared him. So his dream was that his son would break free of the definitions of success that reigned in the corporate world. In some of my most vivid memories of him, he came home from work stressed and angry, with the wrath of a Hamilcar. Then, after he calmed down, he would tell me to find some way to become "independent" and to be "my own man" in life. This, he said, was true success.

I WAS USUALLY in no mood to listen to his lectures, because I was often busy rebelling. As Amy Tan chose her move to Switzerland to declare open war, I chose our move to America, which my parents, like Hamilcar when he went to Iberia, undertook in part for my father's career but in larger part for my benefit. They wanted me to be bilingual.

I went to an American boarding school in New England, where I discovered that being foreign, and especially German, made me vulnerable to hazing. Once past the school's lofty motto above the entrance—*Non ut sibi ministretur sed ut ministret:* Not to be served but to serve—I entered a world of lacrosse-stick-cradling Connecticut preppies who distrusted any background other than their own. Whatever was German about me, whatever had to do with my parents, I rejected as Amy Tan rejected anything associated with her mother.

My father and I entered years of tension. Sometimes we barely spoke. When we did, the conversations were awkward and combustible. The years in boarding school were difficult and lonely ones for me, but I deliberately went through them without seeking emotional help from my parents. My parents might drive up to watch my soccer games, but they could not get me to talk to them afterward. I did my best to forget the German language and almost succeeded.

Nonetheless, all during this time, I studied the subjects that belonged to *Kultur* because that is what I had already learned to like. After college in the United States, I went to the London School of Economics for my graduate degree. I made a point not to discuss my studies with my father very often. I pursued whatever interests appeared to have come randomly into my life, a bit as Amy Tan began writing about a place called the Joy Luck Club.

When the time came to write my master's thesis, I chose an extremely obscure aspect of international economics, something about how various currency and trade regimes throughout history affected freedom. I wormed my way deeper and deeper into the ever dustier regions and remoter shelves of the LSE library. I started feeling that I had chosen a lonely subject, but at the same time I discovered that I was enjoying myself, as though my choice had been inevitable.

The obvious books for the topic were soon read. I was now pressing into the arcane layers of research. I started picking up books and periodicals that had probably not been read for decades and were cracking apart on the photocopier. But I felt that I was getting closer to my goal. Near the end, I picked up one more book, yellowed and never checked out from the library. The title was in German but almost the same as the one in English that I was considering.

I opened the book and read the title page. It was the Ph.D. thesis of Gerhard Kluth, my father.

THREE

DO YOU
NEED A GOAL?

In this exercise no season or circumstance could obstruct his purpose, plunging thro' the winter's snows and frozen streams in pursuit of his object.
—Thomas Jefferson, describing Meriwether Lewis

Went into business all enthusiastic. Lost all I had and all I could borrow. Mike Pendergast picked me up and put me in politics and I've been lucky.
—Harry Truman

Hannibal Barca was nine years old when Hamilcar took him by the hand to lead him to Carthage's main temple. They walked partway around Carthage's circular military harbor. After the horrendous losses in Sicily, many of the roughly 170 berths in the harbor were empty, but a few warships were partially pulled up onto their ramps and into the sheds for repairs.[1] They kept going, passed the market, then climbed a steep sandstone hill toward the shrine of Baal.

Carthage had many gods and goddesses, but Baal and his feminine consort, Tanit, were chief among them, roughly like the Greek Zeus and his wife, Hera, whom the Romans called Jupiter and Juno. Like Zeus, Baal was the god of lightning and hurled thunderbolts when enraged. He was a mighty and fearsome god, but Hamilcar Barca had faith that his family, named after the god's lightning, was in Baal's good grace. Hamilcar had named his firstborn son Hannibal, "favored by Baal," and his second son Hasdrubal, "helped by Baal."

Hamilcar and Hannibal pushed through a group of women, who were not allowed past this point, and entered the inner sanctum of the temple. Inside, there were no statues of the gods at all, just an altar and a large pit with a fire that was always kept burning. In the orange glow of the flames, priests were administering rites. They were barefoot and dressed in simple linen robes. Their heads were shaven and covered with a band of woven flax.[2] As they saw Hamilcar approaching with Hannibal, they tensed up in apparent anticipation.

The priests had reason to assume that Hamilcar was about to kill Hannibal and burn him in the fire of Baal. This was an ancient ritual among the Carthaginians, as among their Phoenician ancestors and other peoples of ancient Canaan. They believed that at times of great turmoil, crisis, or danger, the gods needed to be appeased with the sacrifice of those the Carthaginians loved most dearly, their firstborn sons.* Gruesome urns have borne the ashes and charred bones of these boys down the centuries.[3]

Hamilcar poured a libation. Then he asked everybody to step back from the altar and beckoned Hannibal to come forward. But Hamilcar had no intention of sacrificing his beloved son. Affectionately, he asked Hannibal whether he wanted to go with him to Iberia to conquer a new empire for Carthage. Yes, Hannibal beamed. Of course he wanted to go. The boy was beside himself with pride and excitement. Hannibal could think of nothing he would rather do than to follow in his father's footsteps, become a Carthaginian warrior, and salvage the honor of Carthage, which the Romans had stolen.

Proudly and solemnly, Hamilcar took Hannibal by the hand, led him to

---

*Compare, for example, the story of Abraham and Isaac in the Bible.

the altar, and told him to put his hand on the victim he was sacrificing.[4] For Hamilcar had swapped another living being for his son, so that Hannibal might "die" symbolically but be simultaneously resurrected as a hero. The victim may have been a lamb or goat, or even an unfortunate slave boy. Together, Hamilcar and Hannibal touched the quivering body, then put it to death. With their hands bloody, Hamilcar asked Hannibal to swear an oath to be forever "the enemy of the Roman people."[5] Then they shoved the body into the pit of fire. As the victim was burning, Hannibal made his vow.

AND SO HAMILCAR and Hannibal and a new Carthaginian army went off to Iberia. This was a savage place in the third century BCE. It had feuding tribes—some Iberian, others Celtic, and some Celtiberian—and the few cities were mostly Greek or Phoenician colonies along the coasts and rivers. But Iberia had abundant silver mines in its interior that could replenish Carthage's treasury, and it had a long Mediterranean coastline on which Hamilcar Barca was planning to found new ports and trading posts, such as the "camp of the Barcas," which would become Barcelona. Territory, wealth, tribes that would provide mercenaries, power: these were what Hamilcar was looking for, so that he and his lion cubs could take revenge on Rome.

And Hannibal was with him, in campaign after campaign against ferocious Iberian tribes. In those young years, Hannibal saw up close the art and the horror of warfare, the need for discipline and morale in the army, the role of a leader in motivating men of many languages and races to risk their lives for the cause of Carthage.

Then came that day—Hannibal was about eighteen—when Hamilcar sacrificed his own life to save Hannibal and Hasdrubal. Hamilcar's son-in-law, who had married the second of Hannibal's three older half sisters, took over the Iberian command. He founded a new city—Cartagena, "New Carthage"—in Iberia, but was soon murdered in a private vendetta. The Carthaginian army in Iberia now voted for Hannibal, the eldest surviving

Barcid male, as their new commander in chief, and the popular assembly in Carthage ratified the choice.

HANNIBAL WAS ONLY TWENTY-SIX when he took charge, but he soon proved himself to be an exceptionally charismatic leader. He had grown up around the soldiers who were now under his command. "I was your pupil before I was your commander," Hannibal once told his army before a major battle, to remind them that they were fighting as brothers in arms.[6] He never demanded a sacrifice of his men that he himself had not already made. In battle, he risked his own life and remained poised amid danger, "by far the foremost both of the cavalry and the infantry, the first to enter the fight and the last to leave the field," as a Roman historian later described him.[7] He lived as ascetically as an ordinary infantryman in his camp. He ate little. He slept not on a soft bed in an officer's tent but on the hard, cold ground among the soldiers on sentry duty, wrapped only in a cloak, and only when he felt his work was done. He wore the unadorned armor and dress of an officer. His simplicity and discipline earned him complete credibility among his troops.

Initially, it helped Hannibal that he looked eerily like his father so that the soldiers saw "the same determined expression, the same piercing eyes, the same cast of features in the young commander's face," as a Roman historian put it. Many of the Iberian tribesmen in the Carthaginian army knew and cared nothing about the republican protocol of Carthage and had instead developed a personal loyalty toward Hamilcar that they now transferred to his son.

Sometimes there was humor in Hannibal's style. Once, at Cannae in Italy, on the morning before Hannibal's greatest battle against the Romans, he and his officers rode up a hill to survey the huge Roman army as it was lining up for battle. The enemy far outnumbered the Carthaginians, and the sight terrified Hannibal's officers. One of them, Gisco, looked worried as he pointed out the various enemy positions.

Hannibal gave Gisco a mischievous look and said: "There is one thing, yet more astonishing, which you take no notice of."

Gisco, and everybody, looked puzzled. What were they missing?

"In all those great numbers before us, there is not one man called Gisco," Hannibal replied deadpan.

The whole group burst out laughing. The tension snapped, and the Carthaginian officers guffawed like little boys, kidding and ribbing each other. As they rode back down the hill laughing, the common soldiers started laughing, too.[8] Before long the entire army was howling, brimming with confidence in themselves and their leader.

At the same time, Hannibal was careful never to get too close and familiar with his soldiers, for he understood that as leader he had to project a certain mystique. Carthaginian commanders had always lived a precarious existence—the price of failure was often crucifixion in Carthage. Hamilcar had therefore always urged Hannibal to cultivate his own base of popularity, both in the popular assembly in Carthage and among the tribes in their new Iberian dominions.

Hamilcar and Hannibal carefully read the psychology of the Iberians, Numidians, Libyans, and Gauls in their army. These tribesmen fought for money, as mercenaries, but they lived by a code of heroism and honor. The soldiers ignored bureaucratic technicalities—whether the Council of Elders in Carthage, which was days or even weeks away, approved this or that decision—and instead pledged personal loyalty to the leader they considered most charismatic and powerful. Hamilcar and Hannibal, though technically servants of their government in Carthage, therefore deliberately ruled in an almost autocratic style over Iberia.

Hannibal also understood that if he wanted to ask his men to commit to him for years, decades, and maybe lifetimes, he had to capture their imagination. Roman generals had command for only one year at a time and relied on harsh discipline to keep armies of citizens obedient. Hannibal, by contrast, would have to command indefinitely and had an army not of citizens but of volunteers. It included many ethnicities, and Hannibal intended to grow and replenish it by attracting even more as he passed through new lands. All these warriors would have to place and keep their faith in him, Hannibal.

A century earlier, Alexander the Great had become a hero to people of many ethnicities by convincing them that he was divine—divinity was a much more fluid notion for polytheists in antiquity than it is today. Hannibal subtly but effectively planted the same thought in the popular imagination. He equated himself with the hero and demigod the Greeks called Heracles, the Italians Hercules, and the Phoenicians Melqart. Heracles had been—and people at this time did not doubt this—part human and part divine, but had earned immortality through his deeds. He freed cities and tribes from tyrants. And he was strong. Hannibal started minting coins—antiquity's equivalent of mass media—bearing the face of Heracles/Melqart, which bore a striking resemblance to himself.[9]

THERE WAS another reason Hannibal was such a strong leader. He knew exactly what he wanted; he had a clear vision of his goal. In fact, it was more than a goal, it was a *hero quest*, a life dream that became the focus for all his efforts, talents, plans, and preparations.

That quest was encapsulated in his boyhood oath at the altar of Baal. Success for Hannibal would not simply mean pacifying savage tribes in Iberia. Success would mean fulfilling his father's and his dream by avenging Carthage's humiliation and defeating Rome. As he himself later said,[10] Hannibal never forgot the oath he had sworn as a boy with his blood-red hand in the stench of burning flesh.

This focus on his life goal was all-consuming. It took precedence over everything else in his life, even love and family. Hannibal married a woman named Imilce in these years when he was a young leader. Imilce came from an Iberian city named Castulo in what is today Andalusia.[11] Hannibal wanted to cement the loyalty of Castulo to him. But it is likely that Hannibal also genuinely loved Imilce. Nonetheless, he could not spend much time with his bride, for he was often away on military campaigns, his mind fixed on preparations for the ultimate attack on Rome.

———

EVEN WITH SUCH CLARITY of purpose, Hannibal could not simply declare war on Rome. He was a commander, not a king, and Carthage and Rome were officially at peace. For him to embark on his quest, he therefore had to manipulate *Rome* into declaring war—a war that he would then fight and win on Carthage's behalf.

Hannibal spotted an opportunity in an independent town in Iberia called Saguntum. Though not a part of the Carthaginian empire, Saguntum was in the part of Iberia that, as Hannibal's late brother-in-law had agreed with Rome, belonged to the Carthaginian sphere of influence. Yet Saguntum also had a well-known friendship pact with Rome. If the city was attacked, Rome would have to come to its aid. And conveniently, Saguntum was now embroiled in a dispute with a neighboring tribe allied to Carthage. Hannibal supported his allies and threatened Saguntum.

The Romans promptly sent a delegation to Hannibal, warning him to keep his hands off Saguntum. Hannibal, unsurprisingly, gave the Romans a frosty hearing. The Roman delegation then crossed to Africa and went to Carthage to repeat the warning to the Carthaginian senate. But by then Hannibal was already at the walls of Saguntum.

Saguntum was a small city, but sieges were difficult at a time when javelins, arrows, ladders, and catapults were the main weapons available to an attacking army. The people of Saguntum smeared their javelins with sulfur and pitch, lit them on fire, and hurled them at the Carthaginians from the city walls. One javelin pierced Hannibal through the thigh, and the wound festered.[12] Eventually, Saguntum fell, but it took eight long months. The difficulty of taking this small town was sobering to Hannibal and his army.

Rome did not immediately come to the city's aid. Instead, the Roman senate sent another delegation to Carthage. A revered Roman senator and former consul named Quintus Fabius Maximus walked slowly and with dignified poise into the hall of hostile Carthaginian senators. Saguntum was an ally of Rome, Fabius said. Was the attack on this Roman ally the official policy of Carthage or only the transgression of one rogue commander named Hannibal?

What business is it of yours? a Carthaginian senator asked.

Fabius, without flinching, held up one fold of his flowing toga in each hand. In one hand he held peace, he said, in the other war. "Take which you will."

"Whichever you please—we do not care!" came the shout from the Carthaginian senate.

Fabius dropped one fold of his toga. It made a swoosh as it fell and swayed. Fabius said, "We give you war."[13]

AS THE FOLD in Fabius's toga dropped, Hannibal got what he wanted. He was now, at last, ready to set out on his quest. There were immediate sacrifices he had to make. His wife, Imilce, it appears, had given birth to a son during the siege of Saguntum. As Hamilcar had once left his wife when Hannibal was born, to fight the Romans in Sicily, Hannibal now had to leave Imilce and his baby to renew the fight. He took Imilce and the baby to Gades, today's Cadiz, and put them on a ship bound for Carthage to keep them safe during the chaos of war that was likely to follow.[14] As he watched the ship sail away, Hannibal must have wondered whether he would ever see them again.

But he did not lose sight of his quest. Still in Gades, an old Phoenician colony like Carthage, he went to sacrifice at the altar of Heracles/Melqart. For it was from this place that Heracles had once departed, with a herd of cattle, over the land route to Italy.[15] He was the new hero, and the Iberians accepted him as such.

A certain fatalism descended on Hannibal, expressed in the dreams he was now having. One night, Hannibal dreamed that a youthful-looking god—possibly Heracles, or Hermes, the messenger god—came to him and told him that he had been sent to lead Hannibal to Italy. Hannibal was to follow him, but to keep his gaze forward and under no circumstances to look back. Hannibal did as he was told and followed. But then his curiosity overcame him. Hannibal turned around and saw a terrifying scene. A huge and ugly snake, as large as a mountain range, slithered through a devastated landscape. Everything in its path—houses, trees, people, and entire cities—lay in smoldering ruin, covered in a filthy slime. A dark plume rose up from the destruction to form a black cloud in the sky, and this cloud emptied itself in horrendous thunder and lightning, as though Baal were hurling his bolts in fury at the earth.

Hannibal was frightened and asked the young god what was happening.

You're witnessing the laying waste of Italy, came the reply, but now look only forward and keep going.[16] And Hannibal kept going.

D o you need to have a goal in life as clear as Hannibal's in order to achieve success? Hannibal, though young, knew (or thought he knew) exactly what success was: he defined it as the conquest of Rome. Everything else followed from that. He was not confused about what he should do or how he should apply his talents. He was not conflicted about whether he should stay with his wife and baby or leave them behind, or whether he should negotiate with the Roman delegation or ignore them. He had complete focus.

Such focus can be a huge advantage to young adults as they set out to become successful. According to Carl Jung and other psychologists, we have an archetype in our heads of the *hero on a quest*. We have encountered this archetype in so many of the stories we heard while growing up. We recognize that the quest gives the hero his focus.

Having such a quest is often a natural next step in our development after we form a tentative identity by emulating, searching for, or rebelling against our parents. Thus the Greek hero Theseus first had to find out who his father was in order to know that he was meant to be king of Athens, but then, having found his father, he had to go on a quest, which was to free Athens of the Minotaur, which devoured fourteen Athenian children every nine years.

For us today, the very act of dreaming, as one scholar puts it, becomes "a major hero adventure for young people. That is the adventure of finding what your career is, what your nature is, what your source is."[17] The big dream, according to one psychologist, "may contain concrete images such as winning the Nobel Prize or making the all-star team. It may take a dramatic form as in the myth of the hero: the great artist, business tycoon, athletic or intellectual superstar performing magnificent feats and receiving special honors. It may take mundane forms that are yet inspiring and sustaining: the excellent craftsman, the husband-father in a certain kind of family, the highly respected member of one's community."[18]

Later in life, you may have to reappraise your dream and adjust it in a more mature and complex life context, perhaps even drop it altogether if it no longer works. But *at the beginning* of the journey, it helps to start with *something*.

BUT WHAT if you just don't have a specific life dream? What if you don't know what your hero quest is and what you should focus on? Many of us do not have an all-encompassing life dream in our twenties, as Hannibal did. And this, too, seems a familiar story line, like a rival archetype in our minds: the young adult who needs to find himself, the *wanderer* or the *searcher*, often related to the *late bloomer*.

So we might wonder whether wanderers have a disadvantage as they try to find success or whether they merely take a different route. It is even possible that wandering and searching for a purpose have certain advantages in the long run. The dreamers rely on their own imagination to decide on the next step. By contrast, the wanderers find all sorts of unexpected things on their seemingly unfocused search, discoveries that we cumulatively call experience. In time, the wanderers have the opportunity to *know* themselves, both their strengths and their weaknesses, whereas the dreamers must *trust* themselves. Knowledge is harder to break than trust. So wanderers can also

find success, although it tends to come to them differently and probably later, when the world is open to their contribution and they rise to the
occasion.

M eriwether Lewis, the "Lewis" of the Lewis and Clark Expedition of
1803 that explored America's western frontier and planted the idea
of Manifest Destiny in the young nation, is an example, like Hannibal, of
a young man who has a specific dream that becomes his hero quest.

Born in Virginia just before the American Revolution, Meriwether grew
up with a father who was often away on the frontier fighting Indian tribes,
a bit as Hamilcar was often away fighting Romans. Meriwether scarcely
knew him but nonetheless adored and searched for the idea of him. When
Meriwether was five, his father came home to the family plantation for a
visit, but as he left and tried to ride across a river swollen by a flood, he nearly
drowned. Lieutenant Lewis dragged himself home and died of pneumonia.[19]

Meriwether's mother remarried, and the boy grew up in Virginia and
Georgia as a woodsman, hunter, and adventurer. He grew tall, handsome,
and lean. Thomas Jefferson, a fellow Virginian who took a liking to the
boy, later wrote that Meriwether "was remarkable even in infancy for en-
terprize, boldness & discretion. When only 8 years of age, he habitually
went out in the dead of night alone with his dogs, into the forest to hunt
the raccoon & opossum. . . . In the exercise no season or circumstance
could obstruct his purpose, plunging thro' the winter's snows and frozen
streams in pursuit of his object." Once, at about the age when Hannibal
swore his oath to be Rome's enemy, Meriwether was returning from a hunt
with some friends when a vicious bull rushed them. His friends were petrified with fear as they watched Meriwether calmly raise his gun and shoot
the bull dead.[20]

A bit as Ludwig Erhard became the guardian of my father or Marie
Souvestre a surrogate mother for Eleanor Roosevelt after the loss of their
parents, Thomas Jefferson gradually filled Meriwether Lewis's idea of a

father. As mentor and protégé, Jefferson and Lewis developed a vision of and for America. Their dream, the equivalent of Hamilcar's dream of conquering Iberia, was to expand their nation forever westward, to explore its wild and romantic wilderness, and to open it to science, trade, and civilization according to the ideals of the Enlightenment.

In 1801, eleven days before his inauguration as president of the United States, Jefferson asked Lewis, then a twenty-six-year-old U.S. Army captain, to become his personal secretary. At the same age when Hannibal became commander in chief of the Carthaginian army, Lewis moved into the President's House at 1600 Pennsylvania Avenue (later repainted and renamed the White House) as "one of my family," in Jefferson's words.[21]

The new president was a widower, and aside from the servants, Jefferson and Lewis were the only residents. "Capt. Lewis and myself are like two mice in a church," Jefferson wrote his daughter Martha.[22] Together they indulged in their boundless curiosity about nearly everything: botany, biology, geography, ethnology, astronomy, and history. Invariably, their conversations would turn back to that vast and unknown frontier to the west.

Jefferson began actively grooming Lewis for a mission to explore it. Both men had idiosyncratic spelling, but Jefferson, the drafter of the Declaration of Independence, wrote beautifully and taught Lewis as much as he could so that he would be able to keep a semiliterate journal for posterity. Every day for two years, Jefferson also tutored Lewis in history and philosophy, as Hamilcar had once tutored Hannibal in the arts of war and diplomacy.

Jefferson and Lewis's dream was to discover a water route for American trade across the continent, connecting the great rivers of the Ohio, Mississippi, Missouri, and Columbia to the Pacific Ocean and thus Asia. But in the backdrop, there was also an enemy. What Rome was to Hamilcar and Hannibal, Britain was to Jefferson and Lewis. It was the empire that their young country had recently fought and would soon fight again. And this British Empire was now sprawling to their north in Canada and sending its traders into the Indian territories of the west.

Technically, however, it was not Britain that stood in the way. The lands west of the Mississippi still officially belonged to Spain, a decrepit empire that had just been invaded by Napoleon, who installed his brother as king of Spain and thus controlled its dominions. Jefferson informed Napoleon that he would not tolerate any attempt by revolutionary France to land troops in New Orleans and offered instead to buy the city for $2 million, believing correctly that Napoleon was too busy in Europe to have designs on expanding in the New World. Somewhat to Jefferson's surprise, Napoleon countered by offering to sell not just the city but all of "Louisiana," meaning all the lands drained by the mighty Missouri River. How far that drainage might extend nobody knew, since no white man had ever been to its source. On July 4, 1803, America's twenty-seventh birthday, Jefferson announced that the United States had acquired from Napoleon the land now known as the Louisiana Purchase for about $15 million. It was the greatest real-estate bargain in history.

On that same day, Jefferson gave Lewis a letter authorizing him to demand from any agency of the U.S. government anywhere in the world anything he wanted for an expedition to explore the new territory, define its actual boundaries, and find a river route to the Pacific. He also gave him an unlimited letter of credit. Lewis set off the very next day.[23]

Lewis made his way west, walking, riding, and floating by boat down the Ohio River, en route to meet up at the frontier with his friend William Clark, whom he had decided to take on as co-captain of the expedition, and the rest of the party. Like Hannibal when Rome declared war on Carthage, Meriwether Lewis felt that he was embarking on a quest.

Harry Truman, who would become one of America's greatest presidents, is one example of the opposite archetype, the searcher, wanderer, and dabbler, the man who does not have a quest to set out on but rides the ups and downs of life and accumulates experience until he is ready to rise to the occasion of success, should it present itself.

His cousin Ethel Noland once said that Harry "didn't do anything early."[24] He married at thirty-five, late by the standards of his time, and did not enter his ultimate profession, politics, until he was almost forty. In his youth, he had interests—Roman and American history, especially—but no goals as such. For a time he was a farmer on his family property in Missouri. He tried his luck at business by investing in a zinc mine in Oklahoma when he was thirty-two. The mine was a failure and Truman's savings were wiped out. "There was never one of our name who had sense enough to make money. I am no exception," he wrote in May 1916, the year the zinc mine closed, to Bess Wallace, his sweetheart and future wife. "You would do better perhaps if you pitch me into the ash heap and pick someone with more sense and ability and not such a soft head."[25]

Truman first espied the hero in himself the following year, at thirty-three, when he enlisted for duty in World War I and led an artillery battery against the Germans. To his men he became "Captain Harry." But that was not a dream or a quest, merely an episode. Truman came back from the war, married Bess on the day of the Versailles Peace Treaty, and then had to look for something else to do with his life.

With a friend, Eddie Jacobson, he started Truman & Jacobson in Kansas City, Missouri, selling gentlemen's shirts and ties. They invested their own money, took out a bank loan, and were open from 8:00 A.M. to 9:00 P.M. Within three years, that store also failed. To a friend whose father had invested in the store, it was a case of "There goes Harry again."[26]

Thirty-eight now, and still without discernible focus, Truman befriended the Pendergasts, a clan of old-time Democratic Party bosses in Missouri. The Pendergasts pushed him into small-time local politics. It was not, at this point, because he showed any sign of political talent or any sense of calling. It was simply because he was a friend of a Pendergast, and the Pendergasts needed to fill a position. As Truman put it: "Went into business all enthusiastic. Lost all I had and all I could borrow. Mike Pendergast picked me up and put me in politics and I've been lucky." Truman was still not on a quest, but at least he had found a mentor.[27]

As protégé of the Pendergasts—including the family's patriarch, Tom Pendergast—Truman stayed in county politics until term limits forced him again to look for something else. He was fifty now, and had occupied himself mainly with improving local roads and the courthouse. He would have a future in politics only as "long as the Big Boss believes in me," he said.[28] Fortunately, Tom Pendergast decided that Truman should run for the U.S. Senate in 1934—though only after Pendergast had asked three others who had turned him down.[29] With Pendergast's backing, Truman won.

But when he arrived in the Senate, Truman later remembered, "I was under a cloud." The other senator from his state was spoken of as the senator from Missouri; Harry Truman was known derisively as "the Senator from Pendergast."[30] The Pendergast political machine, as everybody knew, was corrupt and venal; by being associated with it, Truman had no credibility in Washington.

Arguably, Harry Truman only genuinely became his own man, even going on a sort of quest, when he was already nearing sixty. During World War II, he had taken the chairmanship of what became known as the Truman Committee in the Senate, which investigated America's defense contractors to keep down waste and fraud. Truman was fair and professional and worked diligently, winning the respect of his colleagues and the public. In March 1943 he made the cover of *Time* magazine, which called him the "watchdog, spotlight, conscience and spark plug to the economic war-behind-the-lines."[31] To his own surprise, Truman became one of those talked about by Democratic Party elders as a candidate for vice president to run with President Franklin Delano Roosevelt for his fourth term in 1944. Chosen in what were at that time literally smoke-filled rooms, he ended up on the Democratic ticket at age sixty.

THE REST, of course, is history. Truman, who had struggled all his life to make little dreams come true rather than pursuing one big dream, now found himself vice president of a superpower at war. This he remained for exactly eighty-two days. Then Roosevelt died suddenly of a cerebral hemorrhage in Warm Springs, Georgia. Truman and the world were stunned. When Truman learned of the president's death, he ran through the Senate halls and hurried to the White House. Two ushers were waiting at the door. They took him to an oak-paneled elevator and up to the second floor, where First Lady Eleanor Roosevelt was waiting. She stepped forward and put her arm on Truman's shoulder. "Harry, the President is dead," she said.

"Is there anything I can do for you?" Truman asked.

"Is there anything *we* can do for *you*?" Mrs. Roosevelt replied. "You are the one in trouble now."[32]

Thus responsibility, a quest, and success burst through Truman's front door at the age of sixty-one. What people know about Harry Truman began on that day. Having been kept in the dark by Roosevelt about the progress of World War II and everything else of consequence, the new president had to go to Potsdam to face two larger-than-life statesmen, Winston Churchill and Joseph Stalin, and negotiate the world order to emerge out of the ruins of war. While in Potsdam, Truman made the single biggest decision any president has ever made: whether to drop a mysterious new weapon, the atomic bomb, on Japan to accelerate the end of the war. He set the rules of the newly freezing cold war, recognized the new state of Israel, fed Berlin with a defiant airlift, reconstructed Europe with the Marshall Plan, and contained Communism in Korea.

ANOTHER WANDERER and searcher was my great-uncle Ludwig Erhard, whose life overlapped with Truman's. I remember Uncle Lulu from my toddler's perspective in the 1970s as a huge man with many flapping chins and no neck, a deep voice, and a permanent cigar in his mouth. Most other Europeans remember Ludwig Erhard as one of West Germany's, and Europe's, greatest postwar leaders. But that is not what anybody who knew him would have thought possible until the man was in his forties.

Uncle Lulu was born in 1897 in Fürth, a small city in an area of Bavaria called Franconia, lampooned by other Germans for its backwoods local dialect. His middle-class family was noteworthy for being optimistic when life was hard and for being tolerant when society was not. At age two, Uncle Lulu caught polio, which left him with a deformed foot and a limp for the rest of his life. Though a lifelong soccer fan, athletic success was now out of the question. The family suffered more tragedy when two of his siblings died in infancy.

Uncle Lulu started keeping to himself a lot. He loved classical music and dreamed of becoming a conductor, but he realized at an early age that he was not gifted enough to make this a life dream or quest. His grades in school were mediocre. Everything suggested that he would take over his father's small textile business, not so much out of commitment but necessity. Like young Truman, Uncle Lulu had no big dream.

When World War I broke out in 1914, Uncle Lulu, at the age of nineteen, enlisted. He was no Hannibal. With his clubfoot, he wasn't going to do much running, so he was trained as a gunner. The stories he told my father about this time focused on the comic aspects of his experience in the Kaiser's army. Once, or so he claimed over a whiskey and cigar, he was sent to comb through a wheat field in eastern Europe looking for the enemy. Inconveniently, he actually found one. For an awkward instant, Uncle Lulu and his counterpart stared at each other from behind their bayonets. Then, with a wink, a tacit agreement was struck, and both Uncle Lulu and the enemy passed nonchalantly by each other to keep dutifully combing their wheat field for enemies.

Uncle Lulu's real enemy on the eastern front turned out to be a typhus epidemic. Uncle Lulu became sick and was given up for dead. In the tale he later gave my father, he was lying in a hospital where nurses were moving up the aisle, pulling blankets over the dead soldiers. One nurse looked at Uncle Lulu, decided that this one was clearly gone, and pulled the blanket over his face. Uncle Lulu considered this an exaggeration and pulled the blanket down again, a moment he would turn into family comedy forever after.

He eventually recovered and was sent from the eastern to the western front, to Ypres in Belgium, a bit north of where Captain Harry Truman was bombing the Germans. An artillery shell exploded near Uncle Lulu and ripped his entire left side to shreds. He was carted off to a hospital again and, in seven rounds of surgery, saved. But his left arm atrophied and remained shorter and hardly usable for the rest of his life. My father remembers not a single instance of Uncle Lulu ever complaining or even dwelling on his clubfoot or his war wounds.

UNCLE LULU'S next problem, quite like Harry Truman's at the same time, was what to do with his life after the war ended. Even though chaos reigned in Germany, he started preparing to take over his father's textile shop in Franconia. But as my father recalls him saying, he was never all that interested in a "career" in the conventional sense, or even success. Instead, Uncle Lulu was always intensely curious about ideas for their own sake. This drew him to academia, but he did not have the top high school degree required to enter university. Fortunately, a new business college that had an easier admissions policy opened near his hometown. He matriculated and, after struggling with accounting and math, became passionate about economics.

With the help of an economics professor named Wilhelm Rieger, his first mentor, Erhard built on his deeply optimistic convictions about human nature to form his own view of the world. He believed that people were mostly good in the right circumstances and that these circumstances were freedom, dignity, and tolerance. With Rieger, Uncle Lulu explored liberal political economy.[33] Together, they refined their ideas about free markets, free prices, free competition, and freedom in general.

These were exotic ideas in continental Europe at the time. Many Germans and other Europeans in the twenties fell prey to simpler and darker ideologies, based on envy (communism and socialism) or anti-Semitism (Nazism and fascism). Many Germans, like the Carthaginians after the First Punic War, were just plain bitter, resentful, and confused by Germany's defeat in the war and the hyperinflation that stole their savings and made their lives miserable.

Uncle Lulu had none of this bitterness. Instead of wallowing in his own or Germany's problems, he decided to study and explore the tolerant, optimistic, and liberal alternative he had experienced in his own family.

At the age of twenty-two, he went on to a university in Frankfurt to study with the man he respected most, a Jewish professor and liberal economist named Franz Oppenheimer.

Oppenheimer and Erhard became genuine soul mates, rather as Marie Souvestre and Eleanor Roosevelt or Thomas Jefferson and Meriwether Lewis did. With a small group of like-minded scholars, they lived secluded in their world of ideas. When the time came for Uncle Lulu to pass the oral part of his Ph.D. thesis, Oppenheimer told him to come to Switzerland, where Oppenheimer was on vacation. There, Uncle Lulu passed his exam with flying colors—probably literally, because Oppenheimer conducted it on a gondola at nine thousand feet.[34] The two became close intellectually and emotionally. Uncle Lulu was devastated when Oppenheimer, being Jewish, had to acknowledge the poisonous turn in German society and emigrated, eventually ending up in the United States. "He pulled me into his soul and his life," Uncle Lulu said.[35]

AS THE NAZI YEARS descended into ever darker evil, Uncle Lulu was living with his wife and family in the house of my grandfather, Dr. Wilhelm Kluth, at Forsthausstrasse 49 in a suburb of Fürth. The Erhards lived upstairs, the Kluths downstairs. My grandfather was a left-leaning intellectual, doctor, and psychiatrist. Fürth's small population had one of the highest concentrations of Jews in Germany, and many people in town were either my grandfather's patients or friends or both.

But the Nazis spread a blanket of terror over the town, and my grandparents' house did not escape it. At home, the Kluths and Erhards were taking great risks—by listening to the BBC on shortwave radio, for instance, which was a crime. Any cleaning lady or repairman overhearing their conversations might report them. My grandmother lived in constant fear that they would be arrested.

Once the SS came by on a tip, confiscated my grandfather's car, and crashed it into a nearby tree. Why? Because they could. On flag day, when all houses were required to fly the Nazi swastika, my grandfather refused, and the Gestapo came and forced him at gunpoint, in front of the family and neighbors, to hoist the flag.

The Kluths and Erhards became ever more private, secluding themselves the best they could in the safety of their immediate family. They went swimming in the nearby creek, played cards, and listened to music. "The internal and external simplicity of my life then was an effective weapon for me to defend myself against the barbarian and brutal affront of Nazism," Uncle Lulu later recalled.[36]

But any notions of goals, quests, dreams, or success were completely gone. Survival, existence, sanity, and decency were all Lulu could hope for during that dark time. To feed his family, he wrote articles for journals with titles such as "The Finished-Goods Market" and "Economic Policy Newsletter of the German Finished-Goods Industry"—not exactly *Time* magazine.[37] Because the family refused to join the Nazi Party, including the academic associations linked to it, German academia was now completely shut off from Uncle Lulu and any hope of a conventional "career" was dead. Because the family refused to pay lip service in public—for instance, by not giving the mandatory greeting of *"Heil Hitler"* when they met people in the street, but doggedly saying instead *"Grüss Gott,"* "God be with you"—the household lived under constant threat and harassment.

UNCLE LULU took it dangerously close to the edge. He was in contact with Carl Friedrich Goerdeler, a former mayor of Leipzig who plotted to overthrow Hitler and was associated with the men who eventually tried to assassinate the Führer. With the help of a wealthy relative, Uncle Lulu went into what he later called an internal exile, keeping a low profile in a tiny town under the guise of a "market research company," which consisted of himself and his secretary. There, he wrote for Goerdeler, who was assumed to become the leader of a new and free Germany after Hitler's assassination, an economic plan to reconstruct destroyed and defeated postwar Germany. Uncle Lulu assumed as a matter of course that Germany would lose the war, which was itself treason punishable by death.

The assassination attempt failed on July 20, 1944. That same month, as a nationwide hunt for Goerdeler was on, Erhard's manuscript was on its way to Goerdeler in the ordinary mail. The family feared the worst, but nobody knows what happened to the packet. In August, the Gestapo caught Goerdeler, and with him a text that he had written with instructions to his coconspirators. In it, Goerdeler mentioned Erhard by name ("Dr. Erhard . . . will give you good counsel."[38]). Goerdeler was tortured and hanged in early 1945.

After the assassination attempt failed, and with the letters between Erhard and Goerdeler still unaccounted for (and possibly in the hands of the Gestapo), Erhard and the family had reason to fear for their lives. But chaos reigned in Germany, as the Allies were bombing its cities to smithereens—the earliest memories of my father, who was a small boy at this time, are of nights spent in air-raid shelters. It appears that Uncle Lulu simply flew below the radar, muddling through for a few more months until the Allies swept into Germany—an event the Kluths and Erhards celebrated as a liberation.

THE AMERICANS pulled into Fürth on April 18, 1945, which was the birthday of Uncle Lulu's wife, my great-aunt Lu, and the family was toasting both occasions. The next day, April 19, an American major named Cooper was driven through the bombed-out rubble that used to be Fürth to one of the few houses that was neither destroyed nor occupied by the Americans, which was my grandfather's. He asked for Dr. Erhard and told him that he was now in charge of the town's economy, or whatever was left of it.

The Americans and their allies were scouring Germany for people who had been certifiably anti-Nazi and were simultaneously experts in fields such as economics. The alliance with the Soviet Union, which occupied eastern Germany, was turning into confrontation and a cold war, and the Americans, British, and French wanted to rebuild with haste the parts of Germany that they occupied. There were few Germans who fit either category, and even fewer who met both qualifications. Uncle Lulu was one.

A few months later, another American jeep showed up at the Kluths' house, and this time a Major Wilson demanded that Dr. Erhard get in the car for a ride to Munich. My grandparents, after years of terror, were afraid that they'd never see him again, but Uncle Lulu was cracking jokes. The next day he was back home to tell the family—who, given their breed of humor, must have been guffawing—that he was now the economics minister of all of Bavaria.

True to character, Uncle Lulu stubbornly refused to join any of the newly emerging or reemerging political parties. But he was thrilled to be in a position at last to shape economic policy as he had studied it all these years. When the British and American zones of Germany merged to form one economy, excluding only the French-held southwestern parts of what would later become West Germany, he became its economic administrator.

In this role Uncle Lulu achieved his greatest success in 1948, when he took the lead in creating a new currency for Germany. (Because he was considered the Deutsche Mark's father, his jowly face later graced the two-DM coin.) The following year, West Germany became a new country, and Uncle Lulu its first economics minister.

"As far as my political career is concerned, I am an American discovery,"[39] he later said, as Harry Truman might have said he was a Pendergast discovery. Uncle Lulu was already in his fifties when he *began* the life and work for which Germans and Europeans today know and remember him. It had never been his goal. Instead, he had been wandering through life, accumulating experience and self-knowledge, until he was ready when opportunity knocked.

I s it preferable to be a hero on a quest like Hannibal or Meriwether Lewis, or a wanderer like Harry Truman or Ludwig Erhard? Personally, in my twenties, I always envied the young heroes. They seemed to have it so easy, with their clear and specific goals. They were excited about something and seemed focused, whereas I was not.

Instead, I was experimenting, searching, and wandering—although at the time it felt more like drifting. Once, during a trip to Prague with friends from the LSE, a few of us were sitting in a Bohemian (in the literal sense) pub when someone suggested that we play a game in which we each had to choose one adjective to describe ourselves. I chose "confused."

Only with time did I appreciate, even savor, what that confusion did for me. It forced me to come to terms with whatever life brought me, as Truman and Uncle Lulu had done. It forced me, while waiting for a dream to emerge, to form *values*. As I went through my twenties, I told myself that it was perhaps all right to be a little confused for a while longer. Gradually, through trial and error, a dream did form. It was journalism, and when I was twenty-seven, *The Economist*, a quirky British magazine full of eccentrics like me, gave me a chance to explore that path by hiring me. It is a path that I am still exploring.

THE GENIUS of a Hannibal or a Meriwether Lewis wants to burst out and change the world. If you are that type, your success, if it comes, is likely to be explosive. The temperament of a Truman or an Uncle Lulu slowly and gradually matures to become integrity. If you are that type, success, if it comes, probably arrives more gradually and later in life.

These two temperaments tend to lead to very different life trajectories. Those pursuing their big dream may achieve spectacular success early in life; those wandering through their early years may find a more gradual recognition later in life. You might call the first trajectory one of towering peaks, the other one of gently rising hills. As it happens, towering peaks can be deadly.

FOUR

TOWERING PEAKS

No part of earth reaches the sky; no height is insuperable to men.

—Hannibal

You, not to be successful, I think you deceive yourself! I have already told you: in the artist there are two men, the poet and the workman. One is born a poet, one becomes a workman. And . . . you complain when all you need to succeed is to exercise your fingers, to become a workman!

—Émile Zola in a letter to Paul Cézanne

A range of towering peaks stood between Hannibal in his Iberian base and the Romans on the Italian peninsula: the Alps. Hannibal knew that the Romans thought that no army could cross these mountains. Yes, the great hero Hercules had once crossed the Alps when he was returning with a herd of cattle from Iberia, via Italy, to Greece. But Hercules was the son of Jupiter and became immortal. And yes, there may have been some wild, barely human Gauls living in the foothills. But the Romans were sure that for civilized and mortal people, not to mention entire armies with supply trains, the Alps were an impenetrable barrier. No maps existed of the glaciers, peaks, and passes. Above the timberline, there was little to eat and no shelter, only deadly crevasses and ice polished blue by whipping gales.

To Hannibal, focused on his goal of conquering Rome, these same peaks, long before he saw them, formed the ideal threshold—physically and psychologically—for his quest. The fact that only Hercules had crossed them before made him even more eager. He would take the same route that Hercules had taken to demonstrate to all the Mediterranean peoples that he was their new hero. After all, Hercules, having crossed the Alps, had gone to the exact site where Rome would later stand and killed a vicious ogre.[1] Now Rome itself had become that ogre, and Hannibal would liberate the Italians from its tyranny. He would do something so bold that the Romans could not imagine it and therefore were unlikely to plan for it. His feat would be literally Herculean. Hannibal decided to take his army across the Alps.

HANNIBAL'S MOTIVATION in hatching this plan was certainly in part romantic: he was twenty-nine and saw himself as Hamilcar's lion cub turned Carthage's roaring lion with a full-grown mane like the one Hercules had worn as a helmet. But Hannibal was not delusional. He had often discussed his strategic options with his late father and brother-in-law and with his brothers, Hasdrubal and Mago. They always led him to the same conclusion—that he had to invade Italy rather than defend Iberia and Africa, and that he had to invade by land rather than sea.

His thinking would have gone roughly as follows. In the First Punic War, whose lessons Hamilcar had taught him in detail, the Romans displayed a unique style of warfare—perpetually aggressive, always taking the initiative. In part, this was due to their structure of government. Carthage had professional generals who served for many years. By contrast, Rome's generals were its two consuls, elected each year for one year only. A consul who wanted to distinguish himself—and every consul did—would have only one fighting season, usually the summer, to achieve victory. Almost every Roman consul therefore went on the attack.

Hannibal assumed that the Romans would wage this new war—the Second Punic War, which the Romans called the Hannibalic War—in the same way, by attacking. They had two consuls, so they were sure to send one consular army by sea to attack Hannibal's base in Iberia and the other consular army toward Sicily, the theater of the First Punic War, as a stepping-stone to invade North Africa and attack Carthage itself. As it soon turned out, this assumption was correct. Hannibal therefore left some troops in Iberia, where he put his brother Hasdrubal in charge, and some troops in North Africa.

But Hannibal decided that his main strategy should be to turn the assumptions of the Romans upside down. If the Romans assumed that *they* would again take the initiative, Hannibal would make sure that the opposite was the case now. *He* would seize the initiative and force the *Romans* to react.

This meant that he had to invade Italy. But how? The way most armies would have done it at this time was to attack by sea. But rowing and sailing to Italy were now out of the question. The Romans had forced Carthage to give up most of its war fleet after the First Punic War. And, of course, they had stolen Sardinia and Corsica, the two large islands between Iberia and Italy that used to be Carthaginian. The Romans also had allies all along the coastline of what is today southern France, such as Massilia, modern Marseilles. Ships at this time had to be rowed, and oarsmen had to be fed, so ships had to pull into port every few days. Without friendly ports and without a large fleet, a sea invasion from Iberia to Italy seemed impossible.

This is why Hannibal decided to invade by land. He believed it was possible. The lands on both sides of the Alps, in what is today France and Switzerland *and* in what is today northern Italy, were settled by Gauls. These tribes, like the Allobroges on the western side of the Alps and the Taurini on the eastern side, near today's Turin on the Po River, were each distinct and rivaled one another. But they had in common that they hated Rome. The Romans had recently subdued the Gauls in northern Italy, yet the plain of the Po was far from pacified, and the Gauls were likely not only to let Hannibal's army pass but even to join it.

PEOPLE WHO HAVE a clear goal are often meticulous planners, because they know exactly what they want to achieve. And Hannibal was meticulous. He sent spies and envoys ahead to reconnoiter the entire route from his base in Iberia over the Pyrenees and into today's France, then into and through the Alpine valleys and passes that led to the plain of the Po River in northern Italy. Their mission was to make maps and to befriend the Gallic tribes so that they would support Hannibal.

In the spring of 218 BCE, Hannibal set off from Iberia with an army of about one hundred thousand. He knew that his first enemy was not Rome but time: he had to reach and cross the Alps before the winter snows. If he arrived at the foothills too late for a crossing, his army would be stuck in Gaul during the entire winter, perhaps unable to feed itself and leaving the initiative to the Romans.

The difficulties started at once. An army of this size did not march in one piece. Rather, it snaked through the countryside in separate lines that stretched for many miles and often lost communication with one another. Communication was bad even when the units were together—the officers were Carthaginian and spoke Punic, but the soldiers came from many lands and spoke many languages.

There were the Numidians, the ancestors of today's Berbers, who came from the Atlas Mountains and the northern coast of Africa and who were such skilled horsemen that they rode without stirrups or bridles. There were Libyans, armed like the Romans with large oval shields and spears and famous for their endurance as heavy infantrymen. There were the Balearic warriors from the islands of Majorca and Menorca, who were so accurate with their slingshots that they could shoot birds out of the sky. There were the various Iberian and Celtiberian tribes, whose fighters wore white tunics with purple borders and carried short, curved stabbing swords. There were Gallic mercenaries, who fought almost naked and wielded long slashing swords. And there was that most fearsome and exotic cohort: twenty-seven war elephants from the northern African forests.[2] Tagging along with all these fighters and beasts were mobs of craftsmen, prostitutes, and stragglers, perhaps as many again as there were fighters.

Such an unruly human mass did not behave itself. The army was like a moving city, eating and ravaging everything in its path. The Carthaginians consumed the fields and slaughtered herds along the way and everywhere left a fetid wake of sewage. Invariably, they must also have raped and spread disease. There were casualties and defections, and Hannibal had to leave some warriors behind to guard his rear. The huge army began to shrink.

HANNIBAL PRESSED ON, still hoping to reach the Alps before winter. The Pyrenees proved easy to cross. But as the Carthaginians entered Gaul, Hannibal had to use his diplomatic finesse. Using the envoys and translators he had sent ahead, he charmed and bribed some of the local Gallic tribes into letting him pass in peace. But the dark faces and otherworldly elephants affronted some chieftains.

One tribe of Gauls, the Volcae, challenged Hannibal. They waited on the far bank of the Rhône River. Hannibal sent his cavalry one day's gallop upstream, where the river was shallow and they could wade or swim across. Those horsemen then stealthily rode back downstream on the far bank, behind the Volcae. Once this cavalry was in place, they sent Hannibal a smoke signal so that he knew to begin the crossing. Hannibal gave the order and the Carthaginians started rowing and punting in boats and on rafts toward the far bank where the Volcae had lined up, naked and howling and swinging their long swords. Just as the first rafts prepared to debark into this onslaught, the Carthaginian cavalry broke out of its ambush and galloped at the Volcae from behind. The Volcae panicked and ran.

Hannibal now faced an equally challenging task: how to bring the rest of his army across the gushing river. It took days. The elephants were especially frightened by the torrent. So the Carthaginians built rafts and made them look like floating islands, padding them with mud and shrubs, and then led two elephant cows on, luring the males to follow. Then they cut the rafts loose and began to cross the river. Some of the elephants panicked and toppled their rafts, and their drivers drowned. But the elephants used their trunks as snorkels and swam across. On some other rafts, the elephants became paralyzed by fear and stood perfectly still on their swaying platforms until they reached the far bank. All the elephants appear to have survived the crossing.

It was around this time that the Romans first learned that Hannibal was no longer in Iberia. As Hannibal had guessed, one of Rome's two consuls was sailing with his army to Iberia and had stopped for food in the Greek city of Massilia. Massilia was near the mouth of the Rhône, and reports came down the river that Hannibal was nearby. This came as a surprise to the Romans. Roman scouts rode inland, where they bumped into Carthaginian scouts. A bloody skirmish took place. It was the first direct clash of Carthaginians and Romans in the Second Punic War.

The Romans immediately prepared for battle, determined to defeat Hannibal in Gaul and end the war. But Hannibal knew that a battle, even a victory, on this side of the Alps would only be a distraction from his goal. At this stage, the Alps were a more dangerous enemy than the Romans. So he turned inland, away from the Roman army and toward the Alps, hurrying along as the days got shorter and cooler.

The Romans still did not believe that an Alpine crossing was feasible. So the consul Publius Cornelius Scipio took only a small force back to Italy by ship but sent his brother, Gnaeus Cornelius Scipio, to continue to Iberia with the bulk of the army, according to their original plan, which was to attack and win the war outside of Italy.

WHEN THE CARTHAGINIANS, this army of brave warriors from Africa and Iberia, finally reached the Alps and looked up to the white peaks in front of them, their faces turned ashen with fear.

"What sudden panic is this, which has entered those breasts where fear has never yet been?" Hannibal said, mocking his generals. "What do you think the Alps are?" he shouted, and laughed, doing his very best to show disdain for the mountains. "No part of earth reaches the sky; no height is insuperable to men."[3]

But even Hannibal dreaded what lay ahead. He knew that they might never come out of these mountains again.

As the Carthaginians began to climb, local tribesmen gathered on the heights above them. These Gauls had no idea who the strange-looking men and beasts were. They watched from their perches as this alien army wound itself through their valley floors. When the tribesmen spotted a weak part of the column below, they rolled boulders and hurled rocks down the steep slopes. When the Carthaginians below had to traverse alongside a vertical cliff, the Gauls shrieked their war cries into the echoing gorges and fired their javelins at the mules. Some of the Carthaginian pack animals panicked and fell over the edge to their deaths. The Carthaginians had no choice but to keep marching, but the harassment took a toll in casualties and morale.

During the night, Hannibal took a few scouts, scaled the heights, and waited for the Gauls to return the next morning. He put them to a swift end, then traced their tracks to their village. To his surprise, he found a lot of Carthaginian baggage and supplies that the tribesmen had raided in the preceding days and even a few Carthaginian prisoners, who had been tortured. Hannibal took the villagers' cattle and grain to feed his hungry army and allowed a few of them to escape so that they might spread the word to the tribes in the neighboring valleys that it was in their interest not to cause trouble.

As the army climbed to ever steeper, higher, and colder heights, other tribesmen did indeed come forward. Hannibal did not trust them and demanded hostages and guides. For two days, the army marched unperturbed and, after days of getting lost in the mountains and wasting time, finally seemed to make good progress. But it was a trap. The new Gallic "guides" were leading the Carthaginians into an ambush.

They brought the Carthaginians into a long, deep, and narrow gorge where the column had to march in a thin line. On the cliffs above them the Gauls lay in hiding. Once the Carthaginian army was stretched out inside the gorge, the Gauls above rained boulders down upon the Carthaginians. Bodies were crushed and piled up, blocking the path of the column. Hannibal, bringing up the heavy infantry in the rear, realized that he had no choice but to prod the entire army onward, over the corpses and through the hail of rocks. Eventually, the Carthaginians broke out of the gorge at the other end, turned around, and scattered the Gauls.

It was a sobering setback. This mighty Carthaginian army, marching to destroy Rome itself, had nearly succumbed to a horde of savages using nothing but their own terrain as a weapon. Hannibal took note and would use the guile of these tribesmen in his own battles to come.[4]

Exhausted, the men kept climbing toward the pass, probably what is today the Col de Clapier, near the French–Italian border.[5] They had wounds, cuts, and oozing blisters. The ones walking in the back waded through a sludge of snow and human and animal feces. Morale was down as the men started feeling, as one historian put it, that if hypothermia didn't get them, the Gauls would; if the Gauls didn't get them, dysentery would; and if dysentery didn't get them, typhus would.[6]

The Carthaginians had thus been climbing the Alps for nine days when the first parts of the long column reached a good place for the base camp before the final ascent. Once the whole army had caught up, they rested for two days to dress their wounds. Many of the men had frostbite and their leather gear and wool clothes were wet and clammy and would not dry.

THE NEXT MORNING Hannibal scaled the last slope and stood at the top of the pass. As exhausted as he must have felt physically, it was an exhilarating sight, for he could make out, far in the distance, the green plain of the Po River in northern Italy. He walked among his officers, pointing to the horizon and promising them the warmth and food of the lowlands, and the eternal glory they would earn once they sacked Rome.

"My men," Hannibal said, "you are at this moment passing the protective barrier of Italy—nay more, you are walking over the very walls of Rome."[7] There they stood, these Carthaginian aristocrats, on an icy ridge worlds away from the Mediterranean port that was their home, howling at the top of their lungs like boys or madmen at the white peaks around them. They may have grabbed a few of their half-starved animals and sacrificed them to Melqart and to Baal.

BUT THE DESCENT was much steeper and harder than the ascent had been. As they started down, men and horses slipped on the sheer ice sheets and slid off steep rock ledges, dragging other soldiers and animals with them. Hannibal was losing as many men going down as he had lost coming up.[8] Slowly and painfully, the soldiers and animals made their way down.

Then, suddenly, they reached an unexpected barrier. By all appearances it was their death sentence. A landslide had swallowed the narrow track they were walking on, and boulders as large as ships lay in the way. To one side was a steep slope; to the other, a nearly vertical drop into a crevasse.

Hannibal conferred with his engineers. Going back up the slope was not an option because new snow had fallen and the thousands of feet and hooves had turned the old snow underneath into a treacherous sheet of ice. Instead, Hannibal and his aides staked all on a risky idea. They would try to blast through the boulders.

In a remarkable display of discipline for an army that was now out of physical and psychological reserves, the men made a long and orderly relay stretching back up to and over the pass and down on the other side to the timberline, which was higher in those times.[9] The men started chopping down trees as fast as they could and passed the trunks along the entire column, over the pass and to the site of the fallen boulders. There, the engineers kindled huge fires under the rocks and stoked them until the boulders were glowing red hot. Then the soldiers passed their remaining rations of vinegar—wine that had gone sour and was meant as disinfectant—up to the front, where it was poured and sprayed onto the glowing boulders. The acid seeped into the pores of the stone and fissures opened with loud cracks.[10] The engineers did the rest, perhaps by using the elephants to pull or push the broken rocks apart.

It was excruciating work. The men were simultaneously scorched by the fire from one side and frozen by the icy wind from the other. But after four days they widened the opening just enough so that the army, its animals, and its supplies could squeeze through and on down the path.[11] Their ingenuity had saved them.

BY THE TIME they arrived in the lush Italian countryside, the Carthaginians barely looked human. Starved, frostbitten, and filthy, they resembled madmen more than an elite fighting corps. In the fifteen days that it took to cross the Alps, about half of Hannibal's soldiers had died. Only twenty-six thousand were left.[12] Astonishingly, most of the elephants seem to have survived, although they looked mangy.

Word of Hannibal's crossing soon spread among the Gallic tribes of northern Italy, then to the peoples farther south in Italy under Roman domination, and of course to the Romans themselves. It was an epic feat. Hannibal seemed to be a new Hercules.

The Romans were in utter shock. In great haste, they recalled their second consul from Sicily and ordered him to drop all preparations for an invasion of Africa and instead to march all available soldiers north as fast as possible and to join forces with his colleague, who was now encamped near Hannibal's army.

That consul, Publius Cornelius Scipio, did his utmost to rally his troops for the imminent battle against the invader. "I want to know if this man Hannibal can substantiate his claim to be the rival of Hercules," Scipio told his troops in a mocking tone, seeing that they were worried. Are these Carthaginians supermen? "Nonsense!" Scipio thundered. "They are ghosts and shadows of men; already half dead with hunger, cold, dirt, and neglect; all their strength has been crushed and beaten out of them by the Alpine crags. Cold has dried them up, snowstorms have frozen their sinews stiff, their hands and feet are frostbitten, their horses lamed and enfeebled."[13]

Much of this was true. And yet, there was desperation in the way Scipio repeated it again and again to his legionaries. There remained the stunning fact that Hannibal, against all odds, was now in Italy. He had crossed the Alps. He had done the unthinkable.

Who in his twenties does not dream of scaling towering heights of success? Hannibal was twenty-nine when he crossed the Alps. In his own eyes and in those of history, he became the quintessential youthful hero on a quest. He had a big dream, and he had set out to make it real, defying all odds and succeeding.

Young heroes who go on a quest—the *dreamers* such as Hannibal and Meriwether Lewis—tend to think outside the proverbial box because, being young, they have spent so much less time inside that box. Their *in*experience is an asset because they do not yet know enough *not* to try something bold that older, more experienced people would find harebrained. And because they see their life dream so vividly in their imagination, they know how to prepare, planning meticulously and diligently as Hannibal did when he reconnoitered the route from Iberia to Italy, or as Meriwether Lewis did when he prepared with Thomas Jefferson to explore the Louisiana Purchase.

One problem for these young heroes is that there are only so many truly big quests to go on—only so many Alpine ranges to cross, so many frontiers to explore. Once a young hero has completed one quest, he might discover at an awkwardly early age that his best moments already lie behind him. How will he react then?

Another problem is that, even if young heroes have more big ideas later in life, their former asset of *in*experience will be gone. They have grown older, they are now aware of the complexities underneath any simple vision, they are likely to get discouraged as they never were in their younger years. It is hard to be a young hero and then an old hero, to dream, dare, and succeed on a large scale more than once. Some young heroes find that crossing peaks early in life brings danger because, as in the Alps, a steep climb often leads to a steep descent.

THERE IS, of course, an alternative trajectory of success. It rises gradually, slowly, and much less spectacularly, but often keeps rising throughout life and into old age. This is the trajectory that is more common for the wanderers, searchers, and late bloomers like Harry Truman and Ludwig Erhard. While they are young, they have no clear idea what they want to achieve, so they cannot really prepare or plan as the young heroes do. This might make them appear less energetic or driven, when in fact they are accumulating what will later be their biggest asset: experience.

Whereas the young heroes often start having a hard time after their early successes as they enter middle age, the wanderers only really come into their own around that time. In contrast to the young heroes, they thrive on nuance, subtlety, and complexity. The wanderers may not achieve one big success, but they are quite likely to score many incremental ones, as Truman and Erhard did, that add up to a legacy of success.

Their disadvantage is that they often have to suffer through many years of frustration and self-doubt. Their advantage is that they can continue their trajectory indefinitely, possibly until the very end of their lives.

One of the starkest contrasts between these two trajectories comes from the world of art, where Pablo Picasso epitomized the young hero on a quest and Paul Cézanne the wanderer, searcher, and late bloomer who succeeds as an old man. Using them as archetypes for many other painters, poets, and writers, one researcher, David Galenson at the University of Chicago, calls Picasso the quintessential "young genius" and Cézanne the "old master."[14]

———

PABLO PICASSO was born in 1881 in Málaga, a city in southern Spain, to a father, José Ruiz, who was a painter, a professor of art, and a museum curator. At the age when Hannibal swore his oath to his father, Picasso was learning drawing and oil painting, in a very traditional style, from his father. Later the family moved to Barcelona, where Ruiz helped his son, only thirteen years old at the time, to enroll at the School of Fine Arts. Picasso, like Hannibal, not only emulated his father but had a very precise dream, and it involved art.

As Hannibal dared to cross the Alps, Picasso at the age of twenty-six had the idea for a painting that was iconoclastic and shocking, that was sure to provoke huge controversy, either changing the world of art forever or flopping disastrously. Because Picasso saw this painting in his mind so clearly, he was able to make precise preparations for it, with more than four hundred sketches. Once he felt ready, he painted it in a relatively short time. When it was done and Picasso beheld his conceit on the canvas, he knew that no additional brushstroke was needed. He signed and dated the painting, and it was finished.

"I have never made trials or experiments," Picasso once said. "The key to everything that happens is here," he explained, pointing to his forehead; "before it comes out of the pen or brush, the key is to have it at one's fingertips, entirely, without losing any of it."[15]

It was 1907, and the painting, called *Les Demoiselles d'Avignon*, depicts five Barcelona prostitutes in saucy but strangely distorted outlines. It became Picasso's equivalent of Hannibal's Alpine crossing. It launched the Cubist revolution in art and influenced virtually every painter who has come since. It is one of the most important paintings in all of history.

Picasso would produce one other painting—*Guernica*, thirty years later, depicting the bombing of a city during the Spanish Civil War—that would equal *Les Demoiselles* in importance and power. But although Picasso kept painting for decades, the work he did in his sixties is worth one fourth of the work that he created in his twenties, and it rarely appears in art history books.[16] His success was front-loaded toward his younger years, and he found it hard to follow up with equally important paintings later in life.

PAUL CÉZANNE grew up in the sunny and languid city of Aix-en-Provence in southern France. His father, Louis-Auguste, had made some money as a hat trader and become a prominent local banker. The locals regarded him as a nouveau riche. He was stingy and had a rigid view of the world. The thought of his son becoming an artist horrified him the way it horrified Amy Tan's mother that her daughter might become a novelist instead of a brain surgeon. Louis-Auguste Cézanne was determined that his son should become a lawyer or a banker.

But nothing about young Paul said "banker." With his two best friends—Émile Zola, the future writer, and Baptistin Baille—Cézanne spent his youth hiking through Provence. Cézanne and Zola were especially close. Physical opposites—Cézanne was big and burly, Zola small and delicate—they were soul mates. A typical day might start at three in the morning, when the first of the three friends to wake up threw pebbles at the shutters of the other two. Before dawn, they would set off for the countryside. When it got hot, they found a shady spot and made lunch. Ostensibly, these were hunting trips, and they took guns, which they occasionally pointed and fired at moving things—apparently without much danger to any wildlife—and then put away for the greater pleasure of reading poetry and the classics to one another.[17]

Success came easily to Zola. He had a gift for words. And he won prizes for drawing. Cézanne, meanwhile, did not stand out in drawing or painting. Nor was he optimistic that he ever would. "The sky of the future is very dark for me!" he once said.[18]

The clash between Paul and Louis-Auguste Cézanne was as inevitable as that between Amy Tan and her mother, Daisy. Louis-Auguste decided that his son would study law. Paul hated every minute of it and scribbled drawings into his notebooks. He began to suspect that he was meant to be a painter. His father kept telling him to "think of the future, for one dies with genius but one eats with money." Zola wrote that Cézanne Senior "cannot understand that it is possible to prefer painting to the bank and the air of the sky to his dusty office." After a long struggle, Louis-Auguste finally gave up and allowed his son to go to Paris to study art.[19]

BUT CÉZANNE was no Hannibal or Picasso. He did not think of himself as the artist's equivalent of a conquering hero. He rarely socialized and was painfully awkward with women. Out of insecurity in group settings, he was often gratuitously vulgar, farting, belching, or cursing. He dressed like a pig, and his studio was a filthy sty. He did not even like what he painted. Once, when Zola came over and asked about the portrait that Cézanne had just painted of him, Cézanne said that he had smashed it, because while he was finishing it, it just kept getting worse.

Another time, Zola replied to a letter from Cézanne, saying that "one sentence in your letter made a bad impression on me. It was this: 'Painting, which I love, even though I am not successful, etc., etc.' You, not to be successful, I think you deceive yourself! I have already told you: in the artist there are two men, the poet and the workman. One is born a poet, one becomes a workman. And you who have the spark, who possess what cannot be acquired, you complain when all you need to succeed is to exercise your fingers, to become a workman!"[20]

It was not so much advice as description, for Cézanne indeed approached his art as workmanship, as constant improvement with gritted teeth through never-ending cycles of setback, self-doubt, and progress. In one down cycle, he was so frustrated that he quit painting and pleased his father by taking a job in his bank. But as soon as he was there, he remembered his dream, scribbling on the ledger of the Banque Cézanne & Cabassol a verse:

> *The banker Cézanne does not see without fear*
> *Behind his desk a painter appear.*[21]

So it was back to painting, and onto the trajectory that would see him through the end of his life. He began a perennial war with the art establishment of France. Again and again, the Paris Salon, France's formal art academy, rejected his paintings. And yet, year after year, Cézanne kept submitting canvases. He fraternized with a group of painters including Camille Pissarro, Pierre-Auguste Renoir, and Claude Monet, who were derisively dubbed Impressionists, after a painting called *Impression: sunrise* by Monet. But Cézanne was never quite one of them, always searching for his own style and trusting his own direct observation of nature.

All through his twenties and thirties, he experimented. He painted many canvases, and they were all different. If he used thick and bold brushstrokes in one, he layered paint on another. It is fair to say that he was awful at drawing in the conventional sense. But perspective, proportion, and line did not really interest him. Gradually, he discovered that he was most interested in color. "I try to render perspective through color alone," he once explained. "I proceed very slowly, for nature reveals herself to me in very complex form, and constant progress must be made."[22]

His proceeding "very slowly," in fact, may have been an understatement. Once, when he was painting in the countryside with his friend Pissarro, a peasant came up to Pissarro and said, "Well, boss, you have an assistant over there who isn't doing a stroke of work!"[23]

Nor did Cézanne ever really finish a painting. There was always another touch of paint to add. There was always something not good enough. In this as in every way, Cézanne was the exact opposite of Picasso. If Picasso knew what he wanted and how to prepare for it, Cézanne was searching without a plan. Whereas Picasso signed and dated his paintings, Cézanne usually did not, because he considered them works in progress.

AND THUS CÉZANNE gradually improved his skills. He painted still lifes, landscapes, portraits—often the same subject, over and over again. He captured color as few painters had before or would ever again. People began to take note. Cézanne earned the respect first of his fellow painters, then of the critics, and finally of the public. His canvases made it into exhibitions in Brussels and Berlin. A new generation of young painters started coming to him for inspiration.

Although he was as cranky as ever—especially when, at the age of about sixty, he became diabetic—even Cézanne himself occasionally had to admit that he was good. He told Renoir, "It took me forty years to find out that painting was not sculpture." At the age of sixty-four, he told another friend, "I am working obstinately; I am beginning to see the promised land. Shall I be like the great leader of the Hebrews or shall I be able to enter it?"[24]

ALWAYS THE WORKMAN, as Zola had advised, and ever a searcher, Cézanne kept growing in his art. When he was sixty-seven and it was October, he went, as usual, to the countryside to paint a landscape. A thunderstorm broke out. The old man kept painting. He got drenched. A few hours later, a laundry cart picked him up and drove him back to his house. Two men carried him to his bed. The next day, he got up at dawn and went to his garden to resume work on a portrait of his gardener, but he collapsed. Brought back to his bed again, he wrote a letter ordering more paint. So it went until, a few days later, he died.[25]

At his death he had already become a legend. Picasso would, a generation later, become known for specific paintings that changed history. Cézanne is not known for any one painting, but for the entire body of his work, especially his later work. Whereas Picasso climbed a towering peak in the history of art at the age of twenty-six, Cézanne trudged steadily and was still climbing when he died. A canvas Cézanne painted during his last year is worth fifteen times the price of a painting he did when he was twenty-six.[26] In his own way, Cézanne had become one of the most successful painters in history. Pablo Picasso himself would call Cézanne "my one and only master" and "the father of us all."

Meriwether Lewis illustrates the great danger to the young heroes, the dreamers on a quest, *after* they succeed. Like Hannibal and Picasso, Lewis achieved towering peaks of success early in his life. But in his case, the descent from those peaks was so steep that it killed him.

As a young man, Lewis was like Hannibal and Picasso in that he knew exactly what he was trying to do and therefore was able to prepare in meticulous detail for his great adventure, the exploration of the Louisiana Purchase and the breakthrough to the Pacific. Once President Jefferson saw him off, Lewis had a special riverboat made. He drew up lists of supplies, including blue and white beads that he planned to offer the Indians as presents, and whiskey, medicine, and salt to keep his men in good spirits. He thought of everything from the gunpowder for the rifles to the ink for the journals in which he planned to record his scientific discoveries.

Like Hannibal, Lewis discovered that he was a charismatic leader, able to command the utmost loyalty of his men. Self-assured, he was not threatened by the presence of another leader, but understood that he could benefit from help. He invited another frontiersman, whom he trusted completely, William Clark, to be his co-captain with equal authority, even though Clark, a second lieutenant, was technically of lower rank than Lewis.

In May 1804, Lewis and Clark met up in St. Charles, Missouri, with their carefully chosen corps of, at this point, twenty-seven men, including Lewis's personal slave, a man named York. Lewis also had with him his dog, Seaman. They left St. Louis, the last outpost of white civilization, such as it was, and made their laborious way upstream against the mighty Missouri into the new territory.

On one of their boats, a mounted swivel gun was ready to fire at hostile Indians. But Lewis was hoping that he would never have to use it. His goal was to make trading partners out of the Indians and to announce to them that they had a new "father" in the east, named Jefferson.

Clark was the better waterman, so he tended to command the boats.

Meanwhile, Lewis, with Seaman and a few men, walked along the riverbank to collect specimens of plants and insects for his scientific notes. He wore moccasins of buffalo hide, a fringed deerskin jacket, and a three-cornered leather hat. Looking and feeling like the archetypal explorer, he celebrated his thirtieth birthday as they moved deeper into uncharted Indian territory. Lewis was almost exactly the same age as Hannibal when he began his climb into the uncharted Alps.

Like Hannibal, Lewis made himself simultaneously loved and respected by his men. When they got sick, he was their doctor, dressing wounds and prescribing laxatives against most ailments. (Medical knowledge had barely progressed since Hannibal's time.) When discipline lapsed—which occurred only a couple of times during the entire trip—he punished with the lash. His communication with William Clark was harmonious. Lewis's expedition quickly became a superb force for exploring, enduring, and, if necessary, fighting. Lewis wrote in his journal what Hannibal might have said, that "all appear perfectly to have made up their minds to succeed in the expedition or perish in the attempt."[27]

Some tribes greeted the expedition in peace. Others, such as the Sioux, staged tense standoffs. But Lewis kept his cool, remembered his mission, and averted bloodshed. They moved upstream on the Missouri as Indians stared in amazement at York, the first black man they had seen. By October 1804, they reached the villages of the Mandan tribe in today's North Dakota. There they built a small fort to spend the winter.

For the next few months, they were stuck in a frozen landscape with nothing to do except drink. The Mandan warriors, believing that the power of the white men could be transferred to them through their wives, merrily offered their squaws for entertainment, so the men had a lot of sex. In return, the men got venereal disease. Most of them developed what was probably syphilis, and Captain Lewis dutifully treated them with pills of mercury.[28]

IN APRIL 1805, they finally got into their canoes again to continue following the Missouri to its source, as ever in search of a water route to the

Columbia River. Soon there was the first sighting of the Rocky Mountains. Lewis and Jefferson had always assumed that the Rockies would look like the Appalachians, gentle and low. But Lewis now felt as Hannibal must have felt when he first beheld the Alps. "When I reflected on the difficulties which this snowey barrier would most probably throw in my way to the Pacific, and the sufferings and hardships of myself and party in them, it in some measure couterballanced the joy I had felt in the first moments in which I gazed on them."[29] Beauty came mixed with terror.

Then came a crushing disappointment. From the Shoshones they learned that there was no water route to the Columbia, and thus the Pacific. This shattered one of the main objectives of the entire trip. Nonetheless, they were determined to complete the mission.

For a while the only things they found to eat were bitter roots, which they boiled to be somewhat digestible but which tore apart the men's guts. Taking frequent breaks to vomit or alleviate their dysentery, they kept trudging through the snow. Lewis's fighting force now resembled a hospital ward.

On they moved, through the lands of the Nez Percé and down the Columbia River. The Indians gathered on the banks to watch the white men drown as they put their canoes in the river and pushed off to run the rapids. Somehow, they didn't drown. Instead, they made it past the rapids and then drifted down the river to the Pacific Ocean, where they spent a damp, soggy, sickly, and boring winter near what is today Astoria, Oregon. They were halfway toward triumph—the first white men who had crossed the continent.

IN MARCH 1806, they set out for the return journey. As Hannibal discovered when descending from the Alpine pass on the Italian side, the worst was yet to come. Lewis and his expedition had to wait for the snow to melt but they were impatient and attacked the Rockies too early. Stuck in the snow, they had to retreat. The second attempt took them across the mountains.

Lewis and Clark now split up, each with a few men, to explore different tributaries of the Missouri to find its source. Lewis, accompanied by only three men, encountered a band of hostile Blackfeet. Two of his men stabbed one Indian to death. Lewis shot another through the belly and left him to die. This meant that they would soon have the entire Blackfoot tribe coming after them, so they raced back to the Missouri and down the river to catch up with Clark's party.

They escaped the Blackfeet, but soon after, as Lewis went ashore to hunt an elk, a bullet hit him in the buttocks. Assuming they were under attack, Lewis struggled back to the boats. Most likely, one of his own men had shot him by mistake. Either way, Lewis now continued the journey downriver in a canoe lying facedown, buttocks up, and in constant agony. In a sorry but triumphant state, they finally floated back into St. Louis.

RATHER AS the Romans had written off the Carthaginians after they entered the Alps, most people in America, including Jefferson, had all but given the expedition up for dead. Its safe return therefore became the biggest news in America, and Lewis and Clark became heroes. There was some disappointment that the Missouri did not extend even farther north into British Canada and that there was no water route to the Pacific. But the bigger news was that Americans had triumphed over the continent. Lewis and Clark now had maps, journals, specimens, and knowledge. Indian tribes were sending emissaries to Jefferson. Lewis's dream had come true. He had returned from his quest successful.

On December 28, 1806, Lewis arrived back in Washington a celebrity. He toasted the new year in the President's House with Jefferson, whom he had not seen for three and a half years. The two men spread out Lewis's maps and got down on the floor on hands and knees to pore over them.[30] A poet proposed renaming the Columbia River the "Lewis River." Jefferson nominated Lewis to become governor of the new territory. Plans were made for the publication of Lewis's journals, which were sure to become a bestseller. Everything pointed to continued success for Lewis.

—————

BUT SOMETHING had changed. Lewis himself seemed different. For the first time, he showed a surprising mean-spiritedness and pettiness toward the other members of the expedition. He was not the only one who had kept a journal, and he had already given permission for others to publish theirs. Besides, there was a genuine question about whether these journals were private property—in which case, who was Lewis to give or withhold permission?—or public property—in which case, why should Lewis "own" even his own journals? When one of his men wanted to publish his journals, Lewis wrote an open letter to a newspaper disparaging him. He made himself look cheap, greedy, and disloyal to his men. Most bizarrely of all, even as he tried to stop others from publishing their journals, he made only a token effort to publish his own.

Lewis should have been America's most eligible bachelor. He was feted in Pennsylvania, Virginia, and Washington, going from one ball to another. But although he wooed several women, they all rejected him. By contrast, Lewis's best friend, William Clark, proposed to his sweetheart upon his return and married her, becoming genuinely happy. Lewis became bitter and lonely. He wrote to Clark, "I am now a perfect widower with rispect to love. . . . I feel all that restlessness, that inquietude, that certain indiscribable something common to old bachelors, which I cannot avoid thinking my dear fellow, proceeds, from that void in our hearts, which might, or ought to be better filled. Whence it comes I know not, but certain it is, that I never felt less like a heroe than at the present moment. What may be my next adventure god knows, but on this I am determined, to get a wife."[31] He never would.

Instead of love, he found liquor. He got drunk every night, cursed himself the next morning for doing so, then got drunk again that same evening. In this state he set off on the long journey to St. Louis to take up his new position as governor. But for the next eight months he did nothing noteworthy. He still made no effort to edit and publish his journals. He seemed bored and depressed, pining after the adrenaline-filled exploration he had led, after the absolute power he had wielded, the epic feats he had accomplished. Now he had only his slaves to order around. The world he lived in seemed both messier and more banal than the one he had explored for three years.

Installed in St. Louis in 1808 and turning thirty-four, he began speculating in land deals and the fur trade. He moved in with his friend Clark, but Clark's new wife made it known that she considered the house too cramped with a bachelor in it. So Lewis moved out but still came for dinners. At about this time, Lewis received the news that one woman he had wooed back east had married another man. This depressed him even more. Perhaps in pity, Clark and his wife named their first son, born the next year, Meriwether Lewis Clark. But Lewis drank even more, and now he also took "medicine," probably opium or morphine.[32]

Politically and financially, Lewis was digging himself into a hole. He was deep in debt. In his own territory of Louisiana, he made political enemies. His deputy described Lewis as "over whelmed by so many flattering caresses of the high & mighty, that, like an overgrown baby, he begins to think that everybody about the House must regulate their conduct by his caprices."[33] He neglected his superiors in Washington. "It is astonishing we get not one word from him," Jefferson told his secretary of war. Diplomatic and generous toward the Indians during his expedition, Lewis now turned bloodthirsty and fanatical. He told a subordinate dealing with a restive tribe "to exterpate that abandoned Nation if necessary,"[34] in effect calling for genocide.

And during all this, he still did nothing to publish the journals, which were staring at him from his desk.

FIRST GRADUALLY, then suddenly, Lewis's life deteriorated. In March 1809, a new president, James Madison, took office, and Lewis no longer had a protector in the capital. In August of that year, as he was turning thirty-five, Lewis received a letter from an obscure clerk in the State Department questioning Lewis's drafts on the Treasury and his expense accounts and cutting off his credit. Later that month, Lewis got an icy letter from the new secretary of war informing him that no additional funding would be forthcoming. Lewis had officially fallen out of favor in Washington.

Lewis panicked. Desperate to clear his good name, or what remained of it, he set out to travel to Washington to defend himself. His creditors were now calling in their debts, and Lewis had to sell his lands and assets. Only his journals he was not prepared to sell.

As Lewis was traveling back east, he was a sorry sight: sick, drunk, and depressed. Twice he tried to kill himself and had to be restrained. On September 11, 1809, he wrote a last will and testament. Coming through Tennessee, at the site of today's Memphis, he met the local commander, who feared that he was suicidal and ordered a twenty-four-hour watch on him. Lewis kept going east and got to Grinder's Inn, a run-down tavern southwest of Nashville, where he checked in for the night. He started pacing outside the cabin, smoking pipe after pipe, telling Madam Grinder what "a sweet evening" it was.

Lewis paced in his room for several hours and Mrs. Grinder could not sleep because she heard him talking to himself. In the middle of the night, she heard the first shot. Lewis had fired at his head but only grazed it. He got up, took his other pistol, and shot himself in the breast. Even that did not kill him. He called for water. He staggered outside, fell, crawled, clutched a tree, and crawled back to his room. The servants found him "busily engaged in cutting himself from head to foot" with his razor. It took hours, until sunrise, for him to die.

A broken shaft, authorized by the Tennessee legislature in 1849, now marks the spot as a symbol of the "violent and untimely end of a bright and glorious career."[35]

Pablo Picasso found it hard to follow up his early triumphs with more success later in life. But his triumphs were not impostors, as Rudyard Kipling might say, for Picasso's contributions to art are timeless and they secure his legacy. For Meriwether Lewis, however, early triumph was an impostor, and he was duped by its disguise, losing his discipline, focus, and even character to the trappings of fame until his life unraveled.

Hannibal, however, was of a different caliber. He may have understood the danger inherent in his stunning triumph over the Alps, which raised expectations almost impossibly high. So Hannibal treated his victory over these towering peaks as only the prologue to the larger quest that still lay ahead. He knew that success for him would henceforth mean above all one thing: winning.

FIVE

THE ART OF
WINNING

The more power the opponent uses, the easier it is for
you. . . . It's not that I am so strong—they were wres-
tling with themselves, and spending their energy on
the air.

—Morihei Ueshiba to a student of aikido

As his soldiers were recovering from crossing the Alps at their campsite in northern Italy, Hannibal staged an unusual diversion. The Carthaginians had come out of the Alps with prisoners from the tribes who attacked them. Hannibal gave these captives a choice. They could either remain prisoners or volunteer to fight for their freedom. Those who chose to fight would be paired up in combat, and the winner of each pairing would earn his freedom, a horse, and weapons, while the loser would die with honor. The proud Alpine tribesmen chose to fight.

So the Carthaginians stood in a large circle and watched. The prisoners drew lots to determine the pairings of gladiators and stepped into the ring with a proud and defiant swagger. Then they tore into each other—brothers, cousins, and friends fighting one another to the death.

The Carthaginians cheered the good moves, oohed and aahed at the reversals, and rooted for the underdogs. And they felt a surprising and deep bond with the prisoners in their midst. They saw nobility in them. And they recognized themselves. When the time came for the victors to ride away in freedom, the Carthaginians celebrated them and sent them away with gifts and good wishes, as though they were old friends.

It seems barbaric today, but at the time it was a moving moment, and Hannibal used it to address his men. We are like our own prisoners, these noble and brave men, he told them. We are in the same situation, with the same existential choice: victory or death. We cannot go back, because we barely crossed the Alps in October, when we were fresh and the snow was thin, and now it's winter, we are tired, and the snow is thick. We can't march to the coast and sail home because there are no ships waiting for us. So we must advance to confront the Romans and when we "come face to face with the enemy, you must conquer or die."[1]

CONQUER OR DIE. Rarely in life are choices that stark. But Hannibal's strategy had brought him into exactly this situation. He had decided not to be a defender but an invader. From this point on, his dream, his quest, and his life depended on one thing: winning.

Projecting invincibility—not only to Rome but to Rome's enemies and, even more, to Rome's allies in Italy—was the premise of his entire plan. If those allies abandoned Rome and threw their lot with Hannibal instead, Rome would be left isolated and would have to surrender to Carthage. This was a plausible expectation. Rome had only recently, and precariously, subdued the Gauls in northern Italy, who had sacked Rome in 390 BCE and were always ready to take up the fight again. The ethnic Greeks in southern Italy, the Samnites of the central mountains, and the Capuans might also turn against Rome if it was shown to be weak.

But for all this, Hannibal needed to win and then to *keep* winning. If he lost only one major battle, his invasion would fail and his army, unable to retreat, would almost certainly be exterminated. So he really was like his Alpine prisoners. He had volunteered to win or die.

A SMALL SKIRMISH by a river called the Ticinus confirmed Hannibal in his overarching strategic calculation. In this encounter, the Carthaginian cavalry chased away the Roman cavalry and even wounded Publius Cornelius Scipio, one of the two Roman consuls, who would have died had not his own teenage son, also named Publius Cornelius Scipio, daringly galloped to his side and saved him. Hannibal may have taken note of this young Roman, whom he would meet again. But for now, he was more interested in the effect that even such a minor victory was having on the Gauls in the area, who immediately volunteered to join Hannibal's army. Even the ethnic Gauls who were fighting in the Roman army as mercenaries came to his side. That same night, two thousand of them, inside the Roman camp, got up and killed a few Romans in their sleep, cut off their heads, and brought them to Hannibal as tokens of their newfound loyalty to him.

But the first real battle was yet to come, and the stakes would be much higher this time. The consul Scipio, suffering badly from his festering wound, broke camp and retreated to the Trebia, a tributary of the Po River, where he met the other consul, who was force-marching his legions up from Sicily. This meant that Hannibal was now facing the entire Roman fighting force, with both consuls and their armies. He was, as he would be from now on, badly outnumbered. And yet he had to win.

Hannibal studied his enemies meticulously. He sent out spies and interrogated prisoners to learn everything he could about the characters and psychology of the two consuls on the other side. Roman custom said that when both consuls campaigned together, they should take turns in command on alternate days. Scipio, Hannibal learned, was a cautious man, doubly so at the moment because of his wound. But the other consul, Sempronius, was rash. He hungered for the glory of being the one to defeat the invader, and he needed to do so before his term in office ran out, which was imminent. Hannibal understood that it would be easier to goad the Romans into a battle on a day when Sempronius, rather than Scipio, was in command.

Hannibal took equally great care in studying the surrounding countryside. It was deep winter now, right around the solstice. It was freezing cold and about to start sleeting. The Romans were camped on the far side of the shallow but frigid Trebia. On Hannibal's side of the river was a large plain. Hannibal knew that the Romans preferred fighting on plains because they assumed that they could not be ambushed on flat and clear ground. He also noticed that the banks of the river were so overgrown with trees and bushes that an ambush force could hide there. So he chose a hundred horsemen and a hundred foot soldiers and told each of them to choose the ten bravest fighters he knew. He then put his youngest brother, Mago, in command, and these two thousand warriors, shivering but eager, hid by the riverbank during the night.

The next morning Hannibal woke his army early, told them to eat an extra ration, to keep warm by the fires, and to rub oil into their muscles to stay lithe. Then he sent out bands of horsemen to cross the river and ride up to the Roman camp, throwing javelins and taunting the Romans, and calling Sempronius dirty names. Sempronius was so furious and insulted that he immediately gave orders for the entire Roman army to march out, caring little that the soldiers had not eaten yet.

The Romans staggered out, disheveled and in bad order. The Carthaginian horsemen retreated, then attacked again, then retreated, goading the Romans and their commander into crescendos of wrath. Then, suddenly, the Carthaginians turned and seemed to flee back across the river. The Romans assumed that they were winning. Cheering, they waded into the icy river in pursuit, then advanced across the open plain.

By now the Roman soldiers were hungry and shivering. Their clothes and armor were clammy, and their fingers so stiff that they could barely hook into the little leather loops on their javelins. But Sempronius himself was beaming with confidence.

Hannibal now lined up his own infantry on the far side of the plain, letting Sempronius see his target. In contrast to the Romans, these Carthaginian foot soldiers were warm, supple, and fed. Sempronius, seeing his chance for glory, ordered a charge. Just as the two armies prepared to clash, a downpour of sleet and hail started.

At this precise moment, Mago and his thousand horsemen and thousand foot soldiers broke out of their ambush by the riverbank, now behind the Romans, and with terrifying howls tore into the Roman rear. Simultaneously, Hannibal unleashed his war elephants with archers mounted on top.

The young Roman soldiers had never seen such beasts before. The Roman ranks dissolved in chaos. One batch of Romans escaped, but most were butchered or trampled by the elephants. The rest plunged back into the icy river to try to get back to their camp, but froze and drowned or were speared by Mago's horsemen.

It was the first major battle in history to be fought on the winter solstice, the shortest day of the year and one of the coldest. Even the Carthaginians were suffering from the cold, and all the elephants but one froze to death. But the Carthaginians had won. The battle at the Trebia was a disaster for Rome and a triumph for Hannibal.

HANNIBAL WAS a big step closer to his goal. He immediately turned his victory into a propaganda tool. About half of the Roman soldiers he had taken prisoner were Roman citizens, whom he fed just enough to keep them alive. But the other half were men from Italian cities allied to Rome, and he treated these Italians as guests of honor in great comfort. Then he summoned them and told them that he had come as Rome's enemy but Italy's friend, and that he was in fact fighting on their behalf to liberate their cities from the oppression of Rome. To cheers of relief and celebration from these prisoners, Hannibal sent the Italians home without ransom, asking only that they spread the word all across Italy that Hannibal, not Rome, was their new friend and overlord.

When the people of Rome learned of the disaster at the Trebia, they were mortified. The city mobilized every available man in Rome and in every allied city. Then two new consuls were elected and sent into the field. Hannibal was still in the northern and Gallic part of Italy, so the priority now was to stop him from marching into the Italian heartland. There were two easy and obvious passes over the central Italian mountains that Hannibal could take, and one Roman army went to block each one.

As spring came, Hannibal indeed left his winter camp to penetrate central Italy. But he decided to take neither of the obvious and easy routes, correctly assuming that the Romans were waiting for him there. Instead, he marched his army straight through a swamp. It turned out to be a nightmare.

For four whole days and three nights, the huge army waded through shallow and fetid water, the mud turning softer and slimier as thousands of hooves and feet kneaded it into a stinking brown sludge. Nobody could sleep, because there was not a dry spot of land to rest on. When mules and asses died, the men, in their desperation, made piles out of the carrion and lay on top of them to take short naps. Men and horses urinated and excreted into this giant sewer, and infections and dysentery started spreading.

Hannibal himself caught a painful case of conjunctivitis. His eye oozed sticky slime and soon he could not open it. It throbbed and burned, and Hannibal knew that this eye would be blind forever. Stoically, he climbed on top of Sirus, his last remaining elephant, and kept leading the army through the swamp.

WHEN THEY MADE IT through the swamp, Hannibal discovered that one Roman army, under a consul named Flaminius, was close by. Once again, he lost no time collecting every scrap of information about this man and his mind-set. And again Hannibal learned that Flaminius was irascible. He was a demagogue whose real priority was to silence his political enemies in Rome with a quick success in the field. Underneath his bravado, Flaminius was insecure. An insult or a perceived slight would lead to an overreaction. Hannibal decided that a slight was called for.

He also wanted to find a place where the topography would complete his next trap, as it had at the Trebia. So he marched his army right past Flaminius's camp and onward, thus dishing out the first insult to Flaminius. As Hannibal searched for the perfect spot, he plundered and ravaged the countryside of Etruria, in today's Tuscany, making sure that the smoke plumes of the burning farms and fields were visible to Flaminius and his Roman soldiers. Hannibal was sending a message to the Etruscans—a people ruled by, but distinct from, the Romans. Here I am, Hannibal signaled, laying waste to your land, and the Romans who are claiming to be your protectors are standing by helplessly.

Flaminius, as predicted, was livid. He raced after Hannibal, determined to charge into him as soon as he caught up.

Hannibal then came to a place that suited his purpose. He still remembered how the Gauls in the Alps had forced him to run a deadly gauntlet through a gorge, using the topography as their best weapon. Now, at a lake called Trasimene in central Italy, Hannibal visualized in his mind just such a gauntlet for the Romans.

Arriving at the lake, one could see across it to a plain on the far side. But to get to that plain, an army would have to march around the lake on a very narrow path, with the water on the right and a steep, wooded slope rising up immediately on the left. The marching army would have to walk in a long, thin line, without any battle formation, as the Carthaginians had done in that Alpine gorge. Hannibal at once marched to that plain, so that he would be in plain view when Flaminius arrived at the lake. Then he sent his Gauls to hide along the wooded hillside next to the narrow trail that led from Flaminius to Hannibal. And he placed his crack cavalry behind the hills, ready to close off the chute behind the Romans once they were in it. Then he waited.

Flaminius arrived in the last light of a beautiful evening and immediately saw the Carthaginian camp on the other side of the lake. He camped for the night, but set out first thing in the morning to attack. A thick fog was still hanging over the hillside beside the lake where the Gauls were hiding. As the Romans marched through the narrow path, they stretched into a thin line, only a couple of men wide. Just as the first Romans were emerging at the far end and preparing to get into battle formation, Hannibal gave his signal.

Out of the fog and down the slope echoed a horrid roar of Gallic war cries. The Romans were petrified, not knowing what was happening. Then the Gauls, naked from the waist up, their hair spiked with mud, swinging their long slashing swords, threw themselves down upon the Romans, cutting them limb from limb and pushing them into the lake. The consul Flaminius was killed, along with some fifteen thousand other Romans, whose blood colored the lake red.[2]

For three hours of slaughter, Hannibal's men butchered the Romans. Some Romans drowned in the lake, pulled down by their own armor. Others died from the spears of the Carthaginian cavalry that chased them down. When it was over, Hannibal searched among the corpses for Flaminius's body to give him an honorable burial, but body parts were strewn or floating everywhere and he never found the consul.

When news of the slaughter reached Rome, the city was stunned with fear and grief. Women stood by the city's gates for days, interrogating passersby about news of their loved ones. In their desperation, the Roman senate appointed a dictator, something they did only in extreme circumstances, to lead them at this perilous time. But Rome, even at this moment of panic, was a proud republic, and the dictator, Quintus Fabius Maximus, would have a fixed term of only six months. He would then be expected to call a new election for two consuls and to step down. One of those two consuls was yet another demagogic hothead.

THAT CONSUL'S name was Varro, and he was a political upstart, a populist and firebrand who liked to whip up crowds by decrying the cowardice of Rome's elite and bragging that he would make short shrift of Hannibal if given a chance. That chance he would soon get. But the Romans paired Varro with another consul, Paullus, who was known to be more cautious. This was very Roman: they liked the idea that each consul was a check and balance to the other. But it was also impractical. An army can have only

one commander at a time, so the consuls once again had to take turns
leading on alternate days.

Hannibal made sure that he knew exactly when Varro was in charge.
Since his last victory, Hannibal had marched to the Adriatic Sea and around
the countryside, letting his men recover; many of them were suffering from
wounds and scurvy. Hannibal then made his way to a huge grain depot
near a village called Cannae. He placed his camp so that the Romans coming after him would be facing into a wind that whipped the dust of the
plain into their eyes. Then he waited, letting the two Roman consuls
bicker. On a day when Varro was in command, Hannibal provoked.

The Romans had assembled their largest army ever, some eighty-six
thousand men. Every freeborn man of fighting age was there, almost all of
Rome's aristocracy, many of its senators, and both consuls. Varro, excited
that it was his day to lead, ordered his army to march out and line up. In
an awe-inspiring spectacle that took several hours, the vast Roman army
got into formation, as its long columns jogged out and then turned hard
right to form one rectangle of men, then the next and the next.

The Carthaginians facing them were also a sight to behold. Right in the
middle and slightly in front stood the Gauls, as ever mostly naked and with
spiked hair or winged helmets and long swords, howling at the top of their
lungs. Next to them were the crack Iberian troops, who wore their traditional white tunics with purple borders and carried short stabbing swords.
At the end of each wing, Hannibal placed his Libyans, the ferocious and
dependable heavy infantry, a lot of whom were now carrying Roman
shields or helmets taken from the corpses at Trasimene. The Romans exploded with rage when they recognized their own weapons. Both armies
kicked up tall plumes of dust.

The Romans outnumbered the Carthaginians two to one,[3] so that
Varro's plan was simply to attack and punch through the Carthaginian
middle, then turn both ways and mop the enemy up. It was simple, typically Roman, and typically Varro, and Hannibal knew exactly what was
up. But this time he did not have topography to help him. He was on a

plain. There was nowhere to hide an ambush. Hannibal somehow had to create an ambush dynamically, by letting the Romans themselves do it for him.

Hannibal began by sending his cavalry to overwhelm the Roman cavalry at the extreme wings. With the horsemen chasing each other off the battle-field, both cavalries were temporarily out of the picture, although they would return. The cavalry was the one part of Hannibal's army that was numerically superior, so Hannibal was confident that his own, rather than the Roman, riders would return to join the fighting.

Now the infantry battle began, with the vast Roman force crashing into the Carthaginian line. But Hannibal had placed his army in a peculiar order. In the middle and in front, jutting out in a strange bulge, were the flamboyant but untrained Gauls, who, as Hannibal knew, would make a lot of noise but then lose discipline and retreat. This is exactly what happened.

But because the Gauls were jutting out, the Roman center was the first to engage, and those Roman legionaries just to the right and left of center naturally and instinctively turned toward the middle to attack the retreating Gauls from the sides. The Romans behind them followed, without even meaning to. The entire Roman army was thus punching and stabbing its way into the soft center of the Carthaginian line, which gradually gave way.

But on the wings, it was a different scene. Here Hannibal had placed the toughest warriors, his Libyan and Iberian veterans. When the Roman line finally touched them, the Carthaginian line held firm. Over several hours, the engaging armies thus bent into what looked from above like a half moon or a horseshoe, as the Romans pushed into the middle and the Carthaginians almost enveloped them on the left and right as though they were a huge pocket.

Patiently, Hannibal waited, knowing that timing would now decide the battle. Then, in the distance, Hannibal saw his cavalry returning and gal-loping straight for the Roman rear. Hannibal gave the order to his trum-peters at the extreme flanks to close the circle around the Romans.

Very quickly, the Romans were completely surrounded. Suddenly, their numerical superiority didn't matter, because most Roman soldiers were now standing in the middle of other Roman soldiers, unable to move and waiting their grim turn as those facing out from the circle dropped, like layers of an onion being peeled.

From this point, the battle of Cannae turned into pure and dreadful slaughter. The Romans were pressed together like herrings in a can, and the Carthaginians butchered them methodically. Limbs, skin, flesh, and blood formed a viscous lake on which the remaining Romans slipped and fell, never to get up again. Most died slowly, from cuts and slashes that bled them dry in hours or even days.

SOME SEVENTY THOUSAND Romans died that day at Cannae,[4] about one in five Roman men. Among the dead was almost the entire aristocracy of Rome and about one in three of Rome's senators. The Carthaginians were stepping over the heaps of corpses to cut the family rings off the fingers of these aristocrats, in order to send them in a big casket as a present to the senators of Carthage.

Also among the dead was the prudent consul Paullus. He had not been in command that day, but he had done his duty by executing the orders of his co-consul and fighting bravely. One of the few Romans who escaped was the other consul, Varro, the one who was in command that day and who had been so eager for his chance.

Hannibal's victory at Cannae was one of the most crushing victories in military history. His own losses were minor; Rome's were devastating. Three times in a row—at the Trebia, at Lake Trasimene, and at Cannae—Hannibal had demonstrated to all Italy that he was superior to Rome and that the Italians should cast their lot with him.

And now they did. Many of the towns and cities of southern Italy abandoned Rome and came to Hannibal's side. In Rome itself, there was only wailing. Every family had lost sons, fathers, brothers, and husbands. The Romans expected that at any moment Hannibal would turn up at the city gates. They, like everybody else in Italy, assumed that the war was over. It seemed that Hannibal had won.

W inning is not the same as success, but sometimes you have to win in order to be successful, or at least in order to avoid failing. Your struggles are likely to be less violent and to involve smaller stakes than Hannibal's. But whether you are pursuing success in a company, in sports, in politics, or even in love, you are certain sooner or later to encounter a rival, an enemy, or someone who appears set on blocking your dream, your quest, your journey. Theseus had to win his fight with the Minotaur. Ludwig Erhard and Harry Truman had to win elections—one of the most poignant pictures of Truman shows him holding a premature issue of the *Chicago Daily Tribune* in 1948 with the headline "Dewey Defeats Truman," when in fact it was the other way around.

Hannibal proved that winning is not always about brute strength, since the Romans outnumbered his Carthaginians in all three of his great victories. Instead, Hannibal perfected a *style* of winning in which he used the very strength of his opponents to overcome them. He made his enemies *defeat themselves*. Here are four lessons from Hannibal's victories that together amount to that distinctive style of winning:

1. Fix the attention of your opponents on a point of your own choosing.

As seducers use suggestion to plant amorous or erotic ideas, which then take on a life of their own in their victims' imaginations,[5] Hannibal chose a place, a point, or a part of his own army that the Roman commanders fixated on. Merely by choosing what his opponents paid attention to, he already seized the initiative. His opponents became predictable, they stopped paying attention to other things, and their blind spots became vulnerabilities.

At the Trebia, Hannibal directed Sempronius's attention to the taunting, then fleeing, Carthaginian riders, who drew his army across the freezing river and to the main Carthaginian force visible on the far side of the plain. Sempronius was so focused on these targets that he ignored the more ominous and overgrown riverbank and the river itself. At Lake Trasimene, Hannibal fixed Flaminius's attention on the Carthaginian camp in plain view across the lake, making him forget the dangers of the narrow path that led to it. At Cannae, Hannibal focused Varro's attention on a protruding bulge of Gauls in the middle of his line, making the Romans forget their flanks and the rest of the battlefield.

2. Make your own weaknesses irrelevant.

Hannibal's foot soldiers were always his weakness—not because they were bad but because they were outnumbered. But Hannibal had better and sometimes more numerous cavalry than the Romans did—that was his strength. So he designed battles, at the Trebia and at Cannae, in which the cavalry played a disproportionate role. And he chose places and situations that enlisted nature as an ally, making the land itself a Carthaginian division. At the Trebia he used a river and its overgrown bank; at Trasimene he used a lake and a hillside. He chose sites in such a way that the Romans could not use their numerical strength.

Before his battles, Hannibal walked and rode through the Italian countryside, gazing at plains, mountains, valleys, forests, rivers, and lakeshores and visualizing in his mind how masses of men and horses might move across, through, and around them. In the same way, you might visualize the setting, ambience, and other surroundings of your confrontations with rivals to constrain them but leave you free to maneuver.

3. Throw your opponents off balance by surprising them.

Hannibal planned his surprises in parts of the battlefield to which his enemies *no longer* paid attention, in the blind spots that he had created. At the Trebia, the surprises were Mago's attack from the riverbank and the elephant charge. At Lake Trasimene, the surprise was the terrifying attack by the Gauls from the foggy hillside by the lake. At Cannae, it was the closing of the circle by Hannibal's cavalry and elite troops on the flanks. In each case, the surprise worked because of precise timing. The same maneuver too soon or too late would have failed; at the right moment, it was deadly.

4. The greater *your opponents' momentum,*
  the more easily *they will defeat themselves.*

All the preceding stratagems served this overarching insight. The Roman force and thrust were strongest at Cannae, and Cannae was their most devastating defeat. The more momentum they brought to bear, the more they, rather than Hannibal, were off balance. Hannibal never tried to block a Roman attack head-on. Instead, he always encouraged the Romans to charge with full force, then swooped in from *another* direction to make the Romans lose their balance. In a way, Hannibal had the instincts of a black-belt master in the Japanese martial art of aikido, standing calmly in the middle of a group of attackers and hurling them through the air with no apparent exertion at all.

Morihei Ueshiba, the founder and master of aikido, known to his students as O Sensei, was invincible in thousands of fights spanning decades, until he died, undefeated, at the age of eighty-six. But he was pathetically weak and small as a boy. That weakness taught him how to win.

Born in 1882 into a family of Japanese farmers, he was the only boy among five children. His father, Yoruku Ueshiba, adored his son. Throughout his life, "the tolerance and generosity Yoruku showed to O Sensei almost defy understanding," Morihei's own son would remember.[6] But a father's love alone could not make Morihei strong or tall.

Young Morihei often felt impotent. One night, "a group of hooligans showed up at the Ueshiba house while the family was asleep. Yoruku managed to fight them off. But this event had a profound influence on O Sensei; he was never the same afterwards," his son later said. "He began to realize that power was necessary to defend oneself against lawless violence. Later on, he told me how much he wished he had been able to help his father that night."[7]

FOR A LONG TIME, young Morihei did not know what to do with his life. He was a wanderer and a searcher, not a hero on a quest. When he was eighteen, he moved to the big city, Tokyo, and tried his luck in business by selling school supplies door to door. The job bored him. He got sick with beriberi from a lack of vitamin B, dragged himself home, and told his father, "I went to Tokyo with one suit of clothes, and that's how I came back."[8] His first attempt at success had failed.

There were more failures. It was early in the twentieth century, Japan was getting closer to war with Russia, and the young men of Japan wanted to enlist and become heroes. But Morihei was only 1.55 meters tall (five-foot-one) and missed the minimum height requirement for recruits by one centimeter. The rejection humiliated him. So he tried to change his height. "He would go up to the mountains and hang from the branch of a tree," his son later wrote. It became a joke around town, but eventually he was accepted into the military, where he kept "hanging from a steel bar" whenever he had time, often until midnight.[9]

After the brief excitement of a short and victorious war against Russia, the twenty-something Ueshiba, rather like young Captain Truman or Ludwig Erhard after World War I, fell into another crisis when he returned home with no idea what he should do next. For five years, he "struggled to find a path for his life, and an outlet for his overflowing energy. He yearned to discover his true purpose," his son later said. He was often angry and unbearable. "Sometimes he would blow up at [his wife], at other times retreat to the mountains and embark on periods of fasting."[10]

Yoruku decided to give his son an outlet for his frustrated energies and turned their barn into a judo dojo, or training room. "It started out as a corner of the barn that was a dojo in name only, but gradually the number of tatami mats grew larger," Ueshiba's son remembered. Ueshiba's younger sister recalled that "these energetic young people broke countless *shoji* screens and *fusuma* partitions. Not content with Judo, they were also trying out sumo wrestling."[11]

But Ueshiba was still not content. "I like to create something where there wasn't anything before. Otherwise, I'm not really interested," he said.[12] So he gathered a group of volunteers and, with their families, moved to a remote wilderness in northern Japan. They cut trees and cleared land for a new village, ate wild plants, caught fish, and grew mint. For a while this new settlement promised to become his life dream.

THEN HIS FATHER DIED. In an instant, O Sensei's perspective changed, as his son later said. "With the news of his father's death, and a sense of rebirth, he quietly departed from [the village], leaving his possessions behind."[13] In his new and open state of mind, Ueshiba met a charismatic religious leader who became his mentor. They believed that all religions were fundamentally the same and could live together in harmony, and they decided to travel to Mongolia to spread this idea. With a small group, they arrived there in 1924, at a time when warlords and bandits ruled the place. They were there for only four dangerous and nearly fatal months. But this trip would change Ueshiba forever.

Everything went wrong, and the small group found itself under almost permanent attack from Mongolian nomads. Like Hannibal, Ueshiba had to fight and win just to survive. Something inside him now revealed itself. His group came under fire as they were traveling through a gorge. Bullets flew toward them, and O Sensei stood in front of their cart, trying to protect his mentor by drawing the fire toward himself. "I couldn't move away, so when bullets came toward me, I would twist my upper body away to avoid being hit. As I sharpened my vision, I became able to sense clearly the direction from which the bullets would come. A split second before the bullet, I would see a white flash—and if I moved away from the white flash, I could avoid the bullet. This happened every day, and in a natural way I was able to unfold the innermost secret of the martial way: the more you can maintain a calm and empty mind, the better you can reach out to sense the intention of your opponent."[14]

When they finally made it back to Japan and safety, Ueshiba was a different man. A friend remarked: "I was amazed that someone's personality could be so transformed by living under the threat of death. . . . So considerate, so empathetic, as if he could see through surface appearances to another person's real position of feelings."[15] Before long, Ueshiba's mentor told him to go and do what he appeared destined for: to open a new dojo, or school, and teach the style of winning he had discovered. It would be called aikido.

AIKIDO, O Sensei's son once said, is "Zen in Motion," or the combination of movement and stillness.[16] There are no punches or kicks in it, as there are in other martial arts. Instead, the method relies entirely on using the opponent's own energy, or *ki*, to overcome him. An aikido master is constantly in subtle and dynamic motion that responds to and channels the movements of the opponent. Because every opponent is different, every aikido move will be different, just as Hannibal adjusted every tactic to the mind of the enemy he was confronting on that day. But always the aikido master, like Hannibal, grasps how the opponent's center of gravity is shifting as the opponent lunges in attack. Once the opponent's center of gravity is in flux and momentarily unstable, the master merely tips him with what may look like an effortless flick of the wrist.

The first requirement is the complete stillness and serenity of the master, no matter how chaotic the fighting. The ideal is a mind as clear as unruffled water that reflects images like a mirror. In that state, "one has the insight to perceive clearly the slightest move of one's opponent," Ueshiba said. "As one stands at the center of the universe, whatever persons or things are outside that center can be easily observed."[17] The aikido master is then able to become "one with an opponent, in *ki*, in mind, and in the movements of the body. The one who was enlightened would be, as we call it, the winner. But this would be a victory without 'winning'—real victory, winning over one's self. . . . This would be the victory of merging with one's opponent."[18]

Ueshiba told another interviewer that aikido is about using "the power of the opponent completely. So the more power the opponent uses, the easier it is for you."[19] Once, standing all of his five feet and one inch, Ueshiba confronted a well-known sumo wrestler named Mihamahiro, a huge and bulky man who could lift enormous weights. "Why don't we test our strength," suggested the sumo wrestler. "All right. Fine. I can pin you with my index finger alone," answered Ueshiba. Mihamahiro slammed his large body toward Ueshiba. But "I redirected his power away from me and he went flying by," recalled Ueshiba. "As he fell I pinned him with my index finger, and he remained totally immobilized. It was like an adult pinning a baby."[20]

Ueshiba repeated this sort of feat again and again. Once, during World War II, when he was teaching Japan's military police, a group of new students decided to test him with an ambush. "I was walking in the training ground one evening," O Sensei recalled, "and I sensed something that was not quite right, so immediately I was on my guard. Lo and behold, some thirty people who had been hiding in the grass suddenly jumped up and charged at me, carrying wooden swords and wooden rifles used for training. Ambushes are nothing new to me, so I wasn't much disturbed. They attacked from every direction, but all I had to do was step off the line of attack and gently push them away. They were flying all over the place! If people try to swing a wooden sword or wooden rifle around without hitting anything, the weight of the weapon alone takes up a lot of their energy, and when there are so many people, things become quite chaotic for the attackers. After five or six minutes, they were out of breath and lost their will to fight. It's not that I am so strong—they were wrestling with themselves, and spending their energy on the air."[21]

In the same way, Hannibal made the Romans "wrestle with themselves." Hannibal was less gentle than O Sensei in dealing with his attackers. But even O Sensei's opponents, when reflecting on their defeats, spoke as thoughtful Romans would have felt after a battle against Hannibal. "He had an eye for the openings created by my ego—the exposure of my own cruder strength would trip me up, and without meaning to, I would throw myself," said one. "When you faced the Founder on the mat, in effect you confronted yourself instead of him," said his son. "You would fly through the air without ever being touched."[22]

T his subtle art of winning as practiced by Hannibal in war and Ueshiba in martial arts works in almost all areas of life. Seduction, for example. It usually begins as a drawn-out game, an eroticized battle, in which two (or more) people face off, resist, advance, parry, evade, overcome, and succumb. Winning at this game by using the ego and psychological momentum of her victim was the specialty of Cleopatra.

CLEOPATRA WAS a Greco-Macedonian heiress of the Ptolemies, who ruled Egypt for almost three centuries until her own death in 30 BCE, two centuries after Hannibal's time. Cleopatra was distantly related to Alexander the Great and lived in the city that he had founded, Alexandria. Famous for its lighthouse and its library, it was the richest and most cultured city of the Mediterranean at the time. It was a Greek city whose people barely mixed with the native Egyptians who farmed the lands flooded by the Nile every year. Cleopatra lived a luxurious life. But she had problems.

Her family was dysfunctional, to say the least. Her Macedonian ancestors, the Ptolemies, had presented themselves to the Egyptians as gods and adopted the bizarre Egyptian custom of marrying a brother and sister as divine co-rulers. The brother played the part of the Greek Dionysus or the Egyptian Osiris, his sister-wife that of the Greek Aphrodite or the Egyptian Isis. The practical result was incest. Several of Cleopatra's ancestors were grotesquely fat and apparently psychopathic, with a worrisome tendency to murder family members. Cleopatra herself appears to have been genetically lucky, but she also married—formally if not sexually—her two brothers in succession, and would merrily see her sisters and brothers dispatched.

Cleopatra's other problem was that Egypt was increasingly a puppet state of Rome and utterly at its mercy. Cleopatra knew that she would need Rome to survive and to succeed.

She became co-ruler of Egypt when she was nineteen, first with her father and then with her thirteen-year-old brother and first husband. Her little brother, however, had powerful and wily councilors who pushed Cleopatra out. Fearing murder, Cleopatra fled up the Nile, then out of the country. Her reign and her life were in grave danger. And just at that moment, a Roman landed in Alexandria who, as Cleopatra realized, might be able to help her. But first she had to win him.

GAIUS JULIUS CAESAR arrived in Egypt having just prevailed in Rome's bloody civil war. Cleopatra studied this complex and sophisticated man as meticulously as Hannibal researched his Roman opponents. She knew all about his stunning military success in Gaul, his womanizing, his tastes, and his vanity. She learned that Caesar was obsessed with comparisons to Alexander the Great. Once, when Caesar had seen a statue of Alexander, he wailed that he had done so little at an age when this great Macedonian had already conquered half the world.[23] Cleopatra, aware of her femininity, sophistication, and connection to Alexander, formed a plan for entrapment.

Cleopatra was in her youthful prime, although she knew that she was not a classical beauty. As depicted on coins, she had inherited her father's long, pointed, and hooked nose, and was apparently rather dark for a Macedonian girl. A bit of makeup—black antimony to emphasize the striking eyebrows and lids; ocher lips; nails, soles, and palms dyed orange with henna[24]—could make her look striking. But looks alone were not her strength. Charm, sophistication, and imagination were. She spoke Greek, Hebrew, Aramaic, Egyptian, and some African tongues, and knew the ways, erotic and otherwise, of those exotic cultures. She was able to entrance with her voice, and to plant thoughts without having to say them out loud.

Cleopatra also knew that even, or especially, a great womanizer and conqueror such as Caesar had a lot to prove with women. She was twenty-one and looked it; Caesar was fifty-two and looked it. He was balding and self-conscious about it. And there had always been a question about his sexuality. As a young man visiting the Hellenistic East, Caesar had once been the guest of a king named Nicomedes. The rumor was that Caesar had been Nicomedes' lover.[25] Ever since, Caesar made sure that he was extra-vigorous around women. Cleopatra decided that she would use the forceful ego of this man to throw him off balance.

But first she had to emerge from her hiding place in the Egyptian countryside and slip into Alexandria, then into the palace and in front of Caesar. A friend rowed her in a small skiff into the harbor of Alexandria. He then wrapped her in a sumptuous carpet and went to the palace to deliver it as a present to Caesar. Caesar was in a meeting with his advisers when the bundle was brought in. The deliveryman took the rolled-up carpet off his shoulder and unfurled it.[26] Out rolled a scantily clad, beautifully scented young woman, Cleopatra. In one fluid motion, she rose to her feet and was inches before the great Caesar, who was stunned speechless. Her large eyes gazed up toward his. Her insinuating voice murmured her name and status. She slept with Caesar that night.

CLEOPATRA'S APPEARANCE out of nowhere, as intended, fixed Caesar's attention on her and threw him off balance. He knew it and liked it. Cleopatra had taken a liberty with him that nobody else dared. She was making him feel risqué for sleeping with the very queen ousted by the ruler in whose palace he was staying. She was making him feel young and manly.

Every morning and night, she was in a different dress and different mood. Caesar never knew what to expect. She was hot one minute, cool the next.[27]

Within days, Caesar became as helpless before Cleopatra as the huge sumo wrestler who found himself pinned to the floor by O Sensei, or as the mighty Roman army that advanced into Hannibal's center at Cannae to find itself entirely surrounded. Caesar thought he was conquering; instead, he was enveloped.

Under Cleopatra's sway, Caesar discovered a keen interest in Ptolemaic paperwork, in particular a will left by Cleopatra's late father, which stipulated that she and her brother were to rule jointly. Caesar had come to renew Rome's alliance with the young Ptolemy, but he now explained to the boy and his councilors that the throne was Cleopatra's, too. When Ptolemy walked in on his sister and Caesar making love, the boy ran out of the palace and into the streets, tore his royal diadem off his head, and started screaming. Caesar's legionaries dragged him back into the palace and placed him under house arrest. De facto, Cleopatra was now the sole monarch.

But Ptolemy still had an army, which rose up against Caesar's small Roman force. War broke out. Once Caesar even had to jump into the harbor and swim to a ship to save himself, all while holding important papers in one hand and paddling with the other. But somehow the danger only added to the frisson of being with Cleopatra, who diligently stoked his virility whenever he returned from the fighting. She soon discovered that she was pregnant.

Caesar put down the rebellion and young Ptolemy was found floating in the Nile. For appearances, Cleopatra married her even younger second brother as co-ruler, but Caesar and Cleopatra in effect reigned as a pair.

Cleopatra could have let it rest at this. But she wanted to consolidate her victory. To seduce means "to lead astray" in Latin, and as Hannibal led astray Roman consuls—across a freezing river, around a treacherous lake, into the center of his own army—so Cleopatra decided to lead Caesar far, far away from the Mediterranean world that he knew, into a fairytale land where his imagination and ego would roam free.[28]

Cleopatra took Caesar up the Nile in the most extravagant boat cruise in history. A fleet of some four hundred ships moved upriver. Caesar and Cleopatra lounged in a floating palace of cedar and cypress, with statues of Dionysus and Aphrodite that resembled themselves. All along, Cleopatra staged diversions for Caesar so that he never knew what the next day would bring. He was being revered as a god, inhaled exotic perfumes and ate sumptuous food, conversed in Greek about philosophy and history. And Cleopatra was visibly pregnant now. Caesar, his only daughter having died in childbirth, looked forward to a son.

All this time, Cleopatra was allowing Caesar to believe, with every gesture and allusion, that he was a new Alexander and thus worthy—*worthy*—of being the consort of Cleopatra, Alexander's heir, in Alexandria, his city. Here were the peoples that Alexander had once conquered, and they were now worshipping Caesar. Here, in Cleopatra's womb, was a child who had the blood of both Caesar and Alexander.

And so, on the Nile, Caesar's ego lunged forward into Cleopatra's embrace. Even as he felt like a god, he became her slave. Only when his own soldiers, following along on the riverbank, threatened to mutiny did Caesar turn back from his honeymoon cruise toward the treacherous politics of Rome. Soon after he left Egypt, Cleopatra bore a son, whom she named Ptolemy Caesar. The Alexandrians called him Caesarion, little Caesar.

IN ROME, as Cleopatra realized, Caesar would again be around aristocratic ladies and former and new lovers. She soon heard that he was having a new affair with a Mauritanian queen. And she knew that Caesar had a wife, Calpurnia. It occurred to her that Caesar might free himself from her ensnarement and fall prey to senators who were hostile to Egypt and Cleopatra. She felt she had to win Rome's leader anew.

So she and her entourage followed Caesar to Rome. Roman law did not recognize marriages between Romans and foreigners, so neither Cleopatra nor Caesarion was officially considered his family. But Caesar was again as besotted with Cleopatra as ever. He put her up in his villa across the Tiber, placed a gilded statue of Cleopatra in the temple of Venus, the Roman version of Aphrodite and Isis. And Cleopatra secured an official treaty to protect Egypt. Her life plan seemed to be working.

But then it collapsed, and through no fault of her own. A group of senators who had long thought of Caesar as a tyrant stabbed him to death inside the Roman senate. With Caesar dead, Cleopatra was suddenly vulnerable. She sailed back to Egypt with Caesarion, miscarrying another pregnancy by Caesar during the journey.[29] Her future was again in jeopardy.

CAESAR'S DEATH renewed the brutal Roman civil wars. The most prominent contender for power was Mark Antony, a brave warrior who had been Caesar's deputy. But there was another, more surprising arrival on the scene. In the will that was discovered only after his death, Caesar had officially adopted his grand-nephew Octavian as his son and heir. Octavian now formally took his new father's name, Gaius Julius Caesar. Cleopatra immediately realized that this Octavian, the only man alive who could compete with her Caesarion in claiming to be Caesar's heir, would be a mortal threat. To protect herself, her son, and her reign, she had to win over Antony and ensure that he prevail over Octavian.

Antony and Octavian officially began their relationship as allies. Caesar's murderers were still at large and Antony and Octavian defeated them together. Soon they carved the Mediterranean up between themselves. Octavian got the western half, including Rome. Antony got the eastern half, which was richer, more cultured, more exotic, and altogether more to his liking.

Cleopatra, watching these events from Alexandria, waited for Antony to arrive. She had arranged for her brother-husband to be poisoned and now placed Caesarion on the throne with her. She was preparing to ensnare Antony as she had won Caesar so that Rome would again be her protector. And again, she began by studying her target.

————

ANTONY WAS DIFFERENT from Caesar. He was ruggedly handsome, looking a bit like statues of Hercules. And he was vulgar, telling ribald jokes, carousing and whoring with his legionaries. But he had a rough charm and an un-Roman ability to laugh at himself. His ego was huge, but he was at heart a simple man. He was also, despite his womanizing, a very married man. His wife, Fulvia, was herself a prominent Roman and a headstrong woman, and Antony liked that about her. For all his swagger, he found it thrilling to be dominated by certain women, and Cleopatra took note.

To win Caesar, Cleopatra had gone to him. To win Antony, she decided to make him come to her, even while letting him think the exact opposite. Antony had taken up residence in his half of the empire in a place called Tarsus, in today's Turkey. He wanted to show the subjects, kings, and queens of the East who was in charge, so he summoned Cleopatra. Cleopatra ignored him. Antony summoned her again. Cleopatra waited. Showing no urgency at all, she leisurely sailed up the coastline from Egypt and into the river that led toward Antony.[30]

Slowly, she floated toward Antony in a gilded barge with billowing purple sails. Silver oars were beating time to the flutes and harps that were playing exotic music. Cleopatra herself lay languorously and suggestively under a canopy, dressed as Aphrodite. Beautiful boys, dressed as Cupids, were fanning her. Her maids were dressed as sea nymphs. Perfumes wafted from the barge with the breeze toward the Romans and Antony himself.

Antony was sitting on a sort of throne, with his mouth open. Slowly, this spectacle moved toward him and, like Caesar, he was speechless, trying to take it all in. He had been surrounded by a fawning crowd. But these people started running down to the riverbank to gape at the barge. By the time Cleopatra docked, Antony was sitting completely alone.

The crowd was already whispering that Aphrodite had arrived to sup with Dionysus. Antony was giddy. What would happen next? From a distance he watched Cleopatra's suggestive moves. He sent a messenger to invite her to dinner. Cleopatra barely noticed. Then she suggested that Antony might instead like to join her. He was already on his way. He walked toward her in the sultry evening air through what seemed an endless sea of lights. Then he stood before her. Reclining, Cleopatra gestured for him to join her. He was transfixed. The delights began showing up. Foods he had never tasted, aromas he had never smelled. He felt like a simple grunt out of the trenches who had suddenly gone to heaven to be with a goddess who would make him a god, too.

Nothing sexual happened that night, except in Antony's mind. Cleopatra was in no hurry. Antony invited her to his tent the next evening, and she accepted. He joked about the comparatively simple food and setting, and Cleopatra laughed at his jokes. This night, as every night, she was different. She appeared transfixed by his tales of mud and blood and Gauls. He felt not only at ease but once again Herculean. He performed for her—and splendidly, he thought—and she was his best audience. They became lovers, and he her slave.

Cleopatra soon got everything she wanted. She disliked her sister, a potential rival, so Antony had her executed. She mentioned another political enemy, and Antony had him killed, too. Her alliance with Rome, in the person of Antony, was as strong as it had been under Caesar.

Cleopatra took Antony to Alexandria, where they lived in decadent splendor. But Cleopatra never allowed the fun to become stale or predictable. Every day, every hour, there was a new diversion—a cross-dressing game, an excursion, a sexual technique, or a public appearance. Antony was living his every fantasy. Cleopatra was the woman Fulvia could never be; Alexandria was the city Rome could never be; Antony himself was now the man he never could have been with anybody else.

CLEOPATRA AGAIN became pregnant, and Antony, like Caesar, was dreaming about founding his own dynasty. But there were distractions. In the east, the Parthians were making trouble. In the west, Antony had to patch things up with Octavian. He left Cleopatra for what would be three years.

Once again, Cleopatra knew that she had to consolidate her victory or she would risk losing it. Fulvia died, and Antony and Octavian reaffirmed their tenuous alliance with Antony's marriage to Octavian's sister Octavia. It was an act of diplomacy, but Octavia was young and pure in a Roman way and soon became pregnant, even as Cleopatra bore Antony twins, whom she named Alexander and Cleopatra. Cleopatra placed a spy—officially an astrologer—in Antony's entourage to keep her informed of what was going on in Rome.[31]

When Antony returned, Cleopatra immediately seduced him again. This time she asked for more. Antony ceded parts of Roman territory to her Egyptian kingdom. More shocking to the Romans, Antony bequeathed entire kingdoms to his children with Cleopatra, who were now renamed Alexander Helios, the sun god, and Cleopatra Selene, the moon goddess. Once again, Cleopatra became pregnant.

Like Hannibal, she kept winning by using the ego and momentum of her targets against them. Cleopatra's ultimate goal was to install her heirs as secure and powerful rulers over strong and growing empires. Everything suggested, as it did for Hannibal, that the victories would lead to that ultimate goal—everything, that is, up to this point.

SIX

TACTICS AND STRATEGY IN LIFE

Most golfers play tee-to-green; Tiger Woods plays
green-to-tee.

—Steve Miller, consultant

Again and again, Hannibal had prevailed—first over the Alps, then against one Roman army after another, at the Trebia River, at Lake Trasimene and, most devastatingly, at Cannae. Just as he expected, the other parts of Italy were now recognizing him, rather than Rome, as the most powerful force in the land and coming to his side. The most illustrious of these new allies was the rich and beautiful southern city of Capua, the capital of Campania, a land of lush and easy living.

Hannibal promised the Capuans that he would make their city the new regional capital of Italy. He wanted to call a meeting of the Capuan senate as soon as he entered the city. But the senators laughed and said that this was not a day for work, and that instead they should have a celebration. Like a modern tourist, Hannibal spent his first day in Capua "seeing the sights of the town."[1]

Meanwhile, his brother Mago sailed to Carthage to deliver the happy news of the latest victory at Cannae. Mago swaggered into the Carthaginian senate and reported that his brother had beaten, in total, six consuls and their armies; that he had killed more than two hundred thousand Romans, about a quarter of all the free men in Italy; and that the cities of Italy were accepting Carthage as the victor. Mago then had the casket brought into the courtyard before the senate. Out poured a huge pile of gold rings, with the signets of the patrician Roman families whose names the senators still remembered from their last war against Rome.

Mago then asked the senate to send more troops, elephants, and supplies to reinforce Hannibal's victorious army. Most of the Carthaginian senators enthusiastically granted the request.

But not all. A senator named Hanno, who had long been a political enemy of the Barcid clan, spoke up. If Hannibal had indeed just scored such an enormous success as Mago reported, Hanno said, then surely this was "the moment when we are in a position to grant terms of peace." If, on the other hand, we are not in a position to grant terms, he continued, then "what, precisely, have we to rejoice over? Hannibal says he has killed whole enemy armies—and then asks for reinforcements. What else would he have asked for if he had been defeated?"[2]

AT WHAT POINT did Hannibal himself first pause to reexamine his own strategy in this war and in his life? When did he ask himself the question that I regard as the eternal riddle of his life, its warning to posterity? That question was this: Was Hannibal winning the *right* battles? Did his victories advance his goals? Or were his triumphs impostors? Should he have done something *other* than take his army over the Alps to invade Italy? Now that he was here, what should he do next?

Unfortunately, the ancient sources are silent on what must have been a constant and recurring conversation that Hannibal had with himself, his brothers, his officers and advisers. But here is how such a conversation *might* have gone. Traveling with Hannibal was his Greek tutor, Sosylus, and I imagine that he would have been Hannibal's intellectual sparring partner.

"*Strategos,*" said Sosylus as he entered the Capuan chambers of Hannibal. It was the Greek word for "general." Hannibal was a general, but he nonetheless smiled at his tutor's wit, for Sosylus liked to use his words carefully, almost as puns, to help him set up philosophical arguments.

"Sosylus, I'm glad to see you," said Hannibal, also speaking Greek and gesturing toward an amphora of wine and two couches.

"You've done well, Hannibal," said Sosylus, reclining on one of the couches and taking wine from a slave as Hannibal leaned against a wall, deep in thought. "Your men are carousing as victors with the women of Capua, praising you in everything they say. Your enemies are frightened behind the walls of Rome, fearing you."

"Do you really think that I've done well?" asked Hannibal.

"Yes, I do," said the Greek. "You are a genius at what we Greeks call *taktike techne,* the art of maneuvering troops in battle for victory. I have never seen anybody command his army as lethally and calmly in the chaos of an unfolding battle as you did at Cannae. They say that Alexander was the greatest commander ever, but he never fought against enemies as disciplined as the Romans."

Hannibal nodded at the compliment but did not dwell on it. He knew that his tutor was not prone to empty flattery, but he also suspected that Sosylus was preparing to say something else.

"*Taktike techne,* the art of tactics," repeated Hannibal pensively. "Yes, I am good at that. But you never fail to remind me that my first task as general is strategy, not tactics."

"I never said that," corrected Sosylus. "It is both. As general you need the right strategy and then the right tactics to execute your strategy. The two must be aligned, the means pointing to the ends you want to achieve. May I ask: Are you nervous?"

"I don't show it around my brothers and the officers," answered Hannibal, "but I have been anxious, yes, and thinking. You heard what Hanno said when Mago went to Carthage and asked for reinforcements. Hanno is shrewd, and he hates me. But what he said is what I have secretly been wondering myself."

"And what is that?" asked Sosylus.

"Hanno was insinuating that I am not actually winning the war, even though I am winning the battles. He was casting doubt on my strategy."

"And now you yourself doubt your strategy," said Sosylus.

"I want to know what *you* think, and *how* you think, about my strategy, Sosylus," said Hannibal.

"We talked about this before you attacked Saguntum," said Sosylus.

"Yes, I was sure that the plan I had made with my father and brother-in-law was the best plan," said Hannibal, recollecting. "Hamilcar always told me about the last war, about how the Roman style was always to be aggressive, to charge, to attack, to take the initiative, and how our Carthaginian style used to be too passive. In my father's war, the Romans invaded Africa and threatened Carthage. We threw them out, yes, but we were always the ones *re*acting, and Hamilcar told me never to let that happen again."

"Probably good advice," said Sosylus. "But you never win a war by re-fighting the previous one, Hannibal. And in any case, there is nothing wrong with *re*acting, nor is initiative necessarily good if the action is stupid. The point is to achieve what you want."

"And I want to defeat Rome," Hannibal shot back. "And this is how I have to go about it. I could not wait in Iberia till they sent one consul to me and the other to Africa to attack Carthage again. I had to take the fight to them, to Italy, to Rome."

"But you do recall that I told you in Iberia my view that *defending* is always easier than attacking and invading," countered Sosylus. "Whoever defends can fall back and feed himself in his own land, whereas the enemy must keep attacking and feeding himself in a hostile land. The defender can afford to lose a few times. The invader cannot."

"And that is why I decided to invade," said Hannibal. "Because I knew that I could keep winning."

Sosylus nodded.

"And you know perfectly well, Sosylus, that I could not invade Italy by sea," continued Hannibal. "We had too few ships, and to row them to Italy we would have had to trace the coastline of Gaul and pick up food at Massilia—"

"My Greek brethren," interrupted Sosylus.

"Your Greek brethren who are allied to Rome and who would have fought us before we even got to Italy!" Hannibal said. "And we could not sail across the open sea to pick up food at—"

"Sardinia or Corsica." Sosylus completed Hannibal's sentence. "I know it hurts. I know that Hamilcar never forgot how the Romans stole your islands."

"So it had to be the land route," said Hannibal.

"Yes, it did," said Sosylus. "And everything is going the way you planned. The Romans have barely anybody left to keep fighting. Tell me, have they made any gesture of surrender?"

"None," said Hannibal with a frustrated sigh. "And this is what surprises me. If not now, when?"

"Remind me of your grand strategy in Italy," said Sosylus.

"It was—it *is*—to defeat the Roman armies so that all the other cities of Italy join me, leaving Rome isolated and forced to surrender," said Hannibal.

"Fair enough," nodded Sosylus. "A century ago, Alexander crushed the Persian armies, and Persia did indeed submit to him. Persia *was* its armies, so by defeating the armies Alexander conquered Persia."

"So you still think that my strategy is right, that my battles will bring me victory?" asked Hannibal.

"There was that other great warrior, Pyrrhus of Epirus, whom you admire so much for his prowess and heroism," responded Sosylus.

Hannibal began pacing the room, knowing where Sosylus was leading.

"Pyrrhus invaded Italy to fight the Romans, and he won his battles, as you did," continued Sosylus. "But where did it get Pyrrhus? Nowhere. With each triumph he lost a lot of his own men, but he could not get the Romans to surrender. Then he left Italy to fight other wars, which meant that the Romans, strategically speaking, had won simply by not being defeated."

"So Pyrrhus could not defeat Rome by defeating Rome's armies, even though Alexander had defeated Persia by defeating Persia's armies," summarized Hannibal.

"Exactly," said Sosylus. "This tells you that Pyrrhus overlooked something, something that was different, and this led him to make a strategic mistake. You might say that in Alexander's case Persia's *center of gravity* was its army. But in Pyrrhus's case, Rome's center of gravity was not its army, otherwise Rome would have surrendered to him."

"What do you mean by 'center of gravity'?" asked Hannibal.

"I have a friend in Syracuse, Archimedes, the best mathematician among the Greeks. He once showed me how to move any object, no matter how large, by identifying its center of gravity and then shifting it by use of a lever. But you need to be able to locate the center of gravity in order to apply the lever at the right place."

"So what do you think Rome's center of gravity is, if *not* its army?" asked Hannibal.

"Well, it could be Rome's allies. That's what you seem to be implicitly assuming, by trying to make them come to your side."

"But they *have* come to my side, which is why we are here in Capua," said Hannibal, gesturing to the town outside his window. "And yet Rome has not surrendered."

"Which raises the possibility that Rome's center of gravity is something different. Perhaps it is Rome itself, the city behind the walls," said Sosylus.

For a moment, the two were silent. Hannibal had thought countless times about how to take Rome, but each time he had concluded that he could not.

"What good would genius battle tactics do if I placed my army outside the gates of Rome?" asked Hannibal, frustrated. "It took us the better part of a year to take that small town of Saguntum," he continued, touching the scar on his thigh from a Saguntine spear. "In a siege the Romans could feed themselves from within their walls, whereas we would have to forage for food outside the walls. The Romans might have allies attacking us from the outside while they simultaneously attack from the inside. The risk of failure of a siege is too high. And as you said, Sosylus, I as the invader have to keep winning to keep appearing invincible."

"And so you knew all along that you had no intention of attacking Rome?" asked Sosylus, somewhat surprised.

"I was hoping that the Romans would give up and turn the city over to me," said Hannibal. "So yes, I was—I *am*—planning to win the war without a siege."

"Then implicitly you have calculated that the city of Rome is not the center of gravity of the Roman republic," Sosylus responded.

"Yes, and that is not unreasonable," said Hannibal. "Just think of how the Persians invaded Greece more than two centuries ago. They were marching on Athens—"

"That rival of my native Sparta," interrupted Sosylus.

"Athens, which was not *yet* a rival of your native Sparta," continued Hannibal, catching Sosylus's humor, "and the Greeks debated whether or not to save Athens. The oracle at Delphi told the Athenians that only their 'wooden walls' would save them, but the Athenians evacuated their city anyway and the Persians sacked and destroyed it. Then the Athenian ships waited for the Persians in the Bay of Salamis, and when the Persian ships came for them, the Athenians sank them. So the 'wooden walls' were the *ships*, not the city."

"You're absolutely right." Sosylus nodded. "The center of gravity of Athens in those days was not the city but the Athenian navy. As long as the Athenian navy was at large, Athens was undefeated, even if the city lay in ruins. In fact, the Persians came back the next summer and sacked the city a second time. But the Greek army, led by my Spartans, then defeated the Persian army and won the war."

"So why should the city of Rome necessarily be the center of gravity of the Roman republic?" asked Hannibal.

"We do not know that it *is*, but we have to be open to the possibility," said Sosylus. "It makes me think of Troy, Hannibal. For ten years, the

Greeks and Trojans fought, and it did not matter who won the battles, because Troy itself had to be taken. And the Greeks just could not take it, except by a ruse that the Trojans fell for. Had the Trojans not brought that wooden horse into their walls, the Greeks would have lost that war."

"And the Romans think that they are descended from those same Trojans," said Hannibal with a mischievous smirk.

"They do," said Sosylus, winking. "Sons of Aeneas the Trojan, he who jilted Dido, queen of Carthage."

"Well, if necessary, I could wait ten years to think of a ruse to enter Rome," said Hannibal.

"But could you stay invincible in Italy that long?" asked Sosylus. "What if your mercenaries mutiny? What if Carthage cuts off support as they did to your father? What if Capua and the other cities have doubts about you and support Rome again?"

"I know, Sosylus, I know," said Hannibal.

For a while, Hannibal and Sosylus stayed silent. Then Sosylus said, "Hannibal, I have a much bigger question for you: What do you want from this war?"

Hannibal gave his tutor a surprised look.

"I know you intend to win," elaborated Sosylus. "But *then* what? What sort of *peace* do you want?"

Hannibal thought for a moment. "I want revenge, Sosylus, and I want justice for what they did to my father and Carthage in the last war."

"Yes," said Sosylus, "but what would justice look like? Will you declare victory if Rome gives Sicily, Sardinia, and Corsica back to Carthage? If Rome cedes Iberia to Carthage forever? Would you demand, as the Romans demanded of Carthage last time, that they destroy their fleet?"

Hannibal and Sosylus looked at each other. Sosylus raised his eyebrows. "Or do you intend to raze Rome altogether, to annihilate it, to sell the Romans into slavery or kill them?"

Hannibal stayed silent.

"I am asking—I am *demanding*—that you define success, *strategos*," said Sosylus.

"Success will be the redemption, prosperity, and glory of Carthage," said Hannibal.

"Well said, *strategos*," said Sosylus. "No matter what happens next, let us always keep that in mind."

S osylus and Hannibal, as I am describing them here, were thinking deeply about strategy, even after Hannibal's ability to win battles was established beyond all doubt. The context of their strategizing was war, which continues to be a primal metaphor even in modern and peaceful times. But strategy extends to sports, business, love, and all of life, which is why Hannibal's strategic choices and dilemmas offer such rich lessons today. And to make these dilemmas intelligible I took the liberty of making Sosylus articulate concepts—such as the asymmetry between defense and offense and the importance of understanding the enemy's center of gravity—that were laid out two thousand years later by perhaps the greatest strategist ever to live, Carl von Clausewitz.[3]

Clausewitz was an introverted, shy, and bookish Prussian officer who lived through the Napoleonic wars. In his youth he dreamed of becoming a hero and leading men into glorious battles, but he never became more than a midlevel officer. But like Sosylus, he was an eyewitness to a great European war. Its dominant figure was a man who, like Hannibal, was for years considered invincible and who personally admired Hannibal: Napoleon Bonaparte.

Clausewitz, from his vantage point as an enemy, observed Napoleon's victories and later the human tragedy that was Napoleon's invasion of Russia. He was in Russia when Napoleon took Moscow and then abandoned it again in ruins, having *mistaken* it for Russia's center of gravity. He saw firsthand the agonizing retreat of the French and their catastrophic crossing of the freezing Berezina River, which only a pitiful remnant of Napoleon's army survived. Later, Clausewitz was at Waterloo, Napoleon's ultimate defeat. And when Clausewitz died of cholera at the age of fifty-one, he left behind mountains of notes about his observations. Under the title *Vom Kriege* (*On War*), these writings have become the most studied, if enigmatic, text on strategy ever.

BEFORE CLAUSEWITZ, nobody had thought systematically and deeply about strategy as opposed to tactics. Theorists such as Heinrich von Bülow, a contemporary of Clausewitz's, pontificated that tactics was "the science of military movement in the presence of the enemy" whereas strategy was "the science of military movements beyond the range of cannon-shot of either side." Clausewitz considered this nonsense. To him, it was always clear that "the object of war, as of all creative activity, was the employment of the available means for the predetermined end."[4]

By equating strategy in war with strategy in the rest of life and defining it as the alignment of means to desired ends, Clausewitz made himself relevant to all of us. He was the first to see that war was not an exception to ordinary life but a part and continuation of it. Like Sosylus, Clausewitz knew that tactics was about winning battles, but strategy was about something much, much larger. It was about winning wars and, beyond that, about winning the peace that was to follow a war, about achieving the ultimate objective, whatever that may be.

In theory, Clausewitz said, there are two kinds of war, two ends of a spectrum. One kind is a "limited war"—to regain some territory, say, or to secure a trade route. The other kind is "absolute war," in which two enemies fight to annihilation. But in practice, Clausewitz then said, all real wars fall somewhere between these two extremes, or they may start as one and become the other. The strategist first must be clear about which sort of war he wants to fight.

This was the reason for Sosylus's final question to Hannibal. What was Hannibal's *overall* purpose in waging the war? Did he want to annihilate Rome, or did he want specific, and therefore limited, concessions? Sosylus was challenging Hannibal to become clear about the world as he wanted it *after* the war. *That*—meaning the ultimate as opposed to the immediate goal—had to be the premise of strategy. It was Sosylus's way of reminding Hannibal, as Clausewitz would remind generations after him, that war was *not* an end, but a means to an end.

Clausewitz's most famous, as well as most notorious, assertion was that "war is nothing but the continuation of politics (or policy) with other means."[5] This is often misunderstood to be a cynical endorsement of war. In fact, it is the exact opposite. Clausewitz was saying: Know what you're getting into when you go to war. Figure out what you want, and then make sure that you fight the kind of war that will bring that about. If you want a world in which, one day, you live side by side with your enemy, then wage a humane war that can be ended in dignity. Restrain your soldiers; allow your enemy a way to surrender on terms that let you thrive *and* that are sustainable.

Sosylus in the imagined dialogue forced Hannibal to remind himself that his strategic objective had to be more than the negative goal of annihilating Rome: it had to be the positive goal of making Carthage prosperous and free. Whatever strategy Hannibal chose, Sosylus suggested, it had to serve *that* end.

All of these strategic concepts translate perfectly into all other contexts of life. Success requires good strategy, and good strategy is about setting the appropriate ends and not losing sight of them, then choosing the tactics that will lead to those ends and none other.

Let's look at one example of strategy in sports and life, one example of bad strategy in love and power, and a third example of a direct clash of the tactical and strategic ways of thinking.

I n March 2007, I was in Monterey, California, at an eclectic conference for big thinkers called TED (which stands for Technology, Entertainment, Design). Celebrities such as Al Gore and Bill Clinton were in the speaker lineup, but the session that was most enlightening to me was a small gathering where a marketing consultant I had never heard of, with the nondescript name Steve Miller, was giving a twelve-minute talk titled "How to Play Golf Like Tiger Woods."

When Miller later told me his personal story, I came to think of him as a sort of Clausewitz of golf. As Clausewitz in his youth had dreamed about being a commander in glorious battles, Miller once dreamed about being a golf hero. So, in the 1970s, he became a golf pro. As Clausewitz got stuck in a mediocre rank, Miller languished near the bottom of the rankings and struggled just to qualify for tournaments he was supposed to be winning. To pay the bills, Miller became a salesman and consultant on the side, and soon he exited the sport of professional golf altogether.

But like Clausewitz, he never lost his fascination with his subject. And like Clausewitz, he became obsessed with studying and analyzing the titan in his field. This was long before Tiger Woods became the butt of late-night television jokes about his sexual escapades. Woods was known for only one thing, his utter mastery of the sport of golf. What Napoleon was to Clausewitz, Tiger Woods was to Steve Miller.

"You study the best in all fields," Miller told me. And "if there is anybody who has *clarity of objective*, it's Tiger." What impressed Miller most about Tiger Woods was not his coordination, stamina, or swing but his perfect grasp of strategy and the alignment of his tactics with the chosen strategy. When Tiger Woods was at his best on the golf course, the means were in perfect harmony with the end. This relentless focus on the *ultimate*—as opposed to the immediate—purpose, Miller told me, is more than just goal setting. In Woods's case, it was "goal setting squared."

HERE IS HOW ordinary golfers, and even very good golfers, such as (by his own admission) Miller, play: They hit the biggest shot every time they approach the ball. When they step up to the tee, they pull out a driver. They don't look at the pin on the green, because it is out of reach and therefore does not seem relevant yet. Instead, they peer at an ambitious spot on the fairway. Then they whack the ball. If they are "good," they whack it harder than others. If they succeed, the drive is a beauty and evokes oohs and aahs, in which case they proudly walk up to their ball and *then* look ahead to the green to plan the next big shot. If they fail, they head into the rough, try to find their ball, and then—again—plan the next big shot.

By contrast, here is how Steve Miller remembers Tiger Woods playing the 2006 British Open, which he won. It took place on a golf course that is notorious for its treacherous sand traps and that practically begged for the long hitters to whip their drives over the bunkers. Most of the players did exactly that, recalls Miller. They played what the pros call a "bomb game." Tiger Woods is one of the longest hitters out there—he hits the ball so far that many course designers are making some of their holes longer, a trend known as "Tiger-proofing." So Miller was naturally expecting some *big* tee shots from him.

Woods did nothing of the sort. In fact, he left his driver in his bag. In the entire tournament, Woods pulled out his driver only twice, Miller counted. Instead, Woods teed off with puny four and five irons, clubs that are meant for precise shots at medium range. Woods hit these tee shots to particular spots on the fairway, not necessarily the middle. For a while, this seemed strange and counterproductive. On this fiendishly difficult course, Woods, one of pro golf's longest hitters, was deliberately leaving himself in a position where his second shot onto the green was much longer than those of his rivals.

When Miller finally figured out what was going on, he was in awe. Tiger Woods, he realized, had *inverted the mental process* of the ordinary golf player. As Woods stepped onto a tee, he looked *beyond* the fairway to the pin—not the green, but the pin. With his caddie, he compared notes to figure out in which quadrant of the green the pin stood and what the curvature of the green was around the cup. He worked out in his mind where the ball had to be for the easiest putt into the hole—short, straight, and either flat or uphill. Then he thought backward. To put the ball into that spot on the green, what would be the ideal angle and trajectory of an incoming stroke? This led Woods to a spot on the fairway—optimal to him, seemingly random to everybody else. His final step was to think which club he should take to lob the ball from the tee to that spot on the fairway. It so happened that in almost every case, the answer was a four or five iron, boring to watch on a tee but cumulatively lethal in the hands of Tiger Woods.

Fascinated by this display of tactical discipline in the service of a larger strategy, Miller fixed his gaze on Woods the entire time. As soon as that tee shot was in the air, Woods seemed to forget about whether it was good or bad. As he walked up the fairway to his ball, he was again looking only at the pin and the spot on the green for the short, straight, uphill putt. Whatever had happened to his previous shot, whether it had been good or bad, it was as if he were starting the hole over, always working backward in his mind from the pin to his ball. "Every step of the way he starts over again," Miller told me. Woods is constantly fine-tuning, but always toward the same precise objective.

MILLER CALLS THIS "green-to-tee" thinking. And, like Clausewitz, he thinks his insight applies to a lot more than its immediate context. It is really about life strategy. Ordinary golfers, and ordinary people in life, play "tee-to-green," says Miller. They hit the "best" shot every time, which they assume to be the longest and most impressive drive, or the job with the highest pay and most power, or the rhetorical victory during a conference, or perhaps an Alpine crossing. Afterward they sometimes find that their big shots have led them into a "bad lie"—in the rough, where they can no longer see the pin—and they get frustrated and fail. But strategists like Tiger Woods during his best years train their minds to work in the opposite direction, and they succeed.

Psychologically, it takes a healthy mixture of confidence and humility to follow a green-to-tee strategy. The humility is necessary when comparing the odds of a precise five iron to the correct spot on the fairway against the odds of a huge drive close to the green. Miller told me, "Tiger always put the odds in his favor and didn't attempt a shot that he shouldn't be trying. Tiger [at that British Open] had a *controlled ego*. Our egos prevent us from being like Tiger."

Confidence is necessary because you might be the only one following or even understanding your strategy. All the other guys whipped out their drivers on hole after hole, and only Tiger stuck with his humble five iron. He was the exception. Most people would start having doubts or worrying how they looked to the spectators. "Tiger doesn't give a crap what others think when he tees off," Miller told me; he could afford to be *humble* in the face of the odds because he was so *confident* that he could win the entire tournament.

But above all, Woods seemed to have clarity of vision, a constant focus on his *ultimate* objective, which then dictated the appropriate tactics. "Every goal is part of a goal which is part of a goal and so on," Miller told me, and "everybody knows that Tiger's career goal is to win nineteen majors, to beat Jack Nicklaus's record." Woods did not define success by money or fame but by this simple yardstick, Miller thinks. "His ultimate pin is nineteen majors," the equivalent of what should have been the prosperity of Carthage for Hannibal.

Working backward from that pin, Woods knew that he had to win tournaments, and working backward from there, Woods arrived at the conclusion that made him different from other golfers. To other golfers the basic unit, the atom, of success might be the *stroke*—as in: hit great strokes and you win tournaments. Woods stopped one level higher and regarded the hole as the unit of success. To Tiger Woods, strokes were the equivalent of tactical maneuvers, holes were battles to be won in order to win the tournaments, which were analogous to wars, and nineteen majors was the peace, the objective.

Sosylus was urging Hannibal to clarify what people in most areas of life today would do well to contemplate: What is the equivalent of nineteen majors? What are the equivalents of tournaments, holes, and strokes? Which quadrant is the pin in? And what do I need to do to get there?

THESE BIG and simple questions of strategy are, paradoxically, *easier* to lose sight of than the smaller questions of tactics. And nobody illustrates this better than Tiger Woods himself. His very success, by making him famous, offered him erotic opportunities along the way that made him *lose* the strategic focus that had made him successful in the first place.

Perhaps he had limited his strategic thinking to golf, as opposed to life. Perhaps he forgot that the goal of winning more than nineteen majors ought itself to be subservient to an *even* larger goal, the overall life success of raising a daughter and son in harmony with his wife, Elin Nordegren. For years he seems *not* to have included them in his life strategy, which started to become clear at two-thirty one morning in November 2009, when Woods crashed his SUV into a fire hydrant and tree outside his Florida home. His injuries were minor. But the accident lifted the veil on a wrenching personal drama: Nordegren had been furious and hurt after discovering her husband's serial adultery.

One after another, women came forward to acknowledge or claim that Tiger Woods had been sleeping with them. His focus and humility on the golf course, his self-control off the course—all of this suddenly appeared to have been a sham. His main corporate sponsors dropped him. His wife threw him out. On December 11, 2009, Woods acknowledged "the disappointment and hurt that my infidelity has caused to so many people, most of all my wife and children." He took a break from golf and entered therapy to "focus my attention on being a better husband, father, and person."[6] But his personal and golfing lives were in crisis. Nine months after his car accident, he and his wife divorced. On the golf course, he seemed distracted. It was an open question whether Woods, still young, would in time reexamine and change his life strategy, just as he might have walked toward a bad lie on the course and mentally worked backward again from the pin.

Like Hannibal and Woods, Cleopatra had proven beyond any doubt that she could win the battles she chose, which happened to be neither military nor athletic in nature but erotic. She had seduced Julius Caesar, after identifying him—correctly—as the most powerful Roman of his day, and thus the most able to reinstall her as queen of Egypt and to give her a viable heir.

For she was clear about her ultimate objective, her "peace." It was, first, her own and her son's survival and, second, her own and her son's continued reign. Because she was weak within Egypt and Egypt was weak within the Mediterranean world, she needed the support of Rome as a means toward her end, and to have the support of Rome, she needed to seduce Caesar. Like Tiger Woods on the golf course, Cleopatra thought strategically, meaning "backward" from her goal.

The strategy was working until Caesar was murdered—just as even Tiger Woods's tee shots sometimes ended up in the rough. So Cleopatra had to do what Tiger Woods did when a drive went wrong: to forget about it and to keep looking toward the goal and working backward in her mind to a *new* means of reaching it.

And so she seduced Mark Antony, whom she identified—correctly, at first—as the most powerful Roman, the most likely to prevail in a new round of civil wars, to protect her as queen of Egypt, to give her more heirs and to protect them, too. But after this second tactical victory—her seduction of Mark Antony—her strategic genius began to weaken. She was still confident. But she was losing some of her old humility when calculating the odds of different scenarios. She lost control of her ego.

AND SO SHE MADE her first big miscalculation. This was to underestimate the wily and cold political genius of Octavian, the future emperor Augustus and the man who was now the biggest threat not only to Mark Antony, his co-triumvir, but to herself and her son by Caesar. Octavian had become, through the dead Caesar's will, the legal heir to Julius Caesar and knew that only Caesarion, Cleopatra's son with Caesar, could rival him for this title. It was therefore in Cleopatra's interest not only to keep Antony beholden to her, which she was good at, but to strengthen Antony politically in Rome in order to weaken Octavian. At the very least, she should do nothing to weaken Antony in *his* struggle against Octavian for control of Rome, since Rome, rather than Antony, was the necessary means for her strategic ends, the equivalent of the pin on the green.

But she did weaken Antony, while inadvertently strengthening her enemy, Octavian. The tales of Antony and Cleopatra's sensuous life in the east were received with prurient interest back in Rome, which was still straitlaced in the late republic. Rome's patricians, egged on by Octavian, disapproved. Antony had become soft in the east, they said, and was peeing into golden chamber pots. He was alleged to have lost his Roman virility and to have betrayed Rome's republican values by becoming an eastern king. He had stolen Roman territory to give to his brood, sired with Cleopatra. He had abandoned his wife, Octavia, who was a virtuous Roman wife as well as the sister of his co-triumvir, for the embrace of that eastern temptress.

Octavian's propaganda fed the Roman notion that Antony was not really to blame for his waywardness because it was really *Cleopatra's* fault that he had gone astray. Cleopatra became, to the Romans, a sultry and sinister concubine. It was rumored that she was scheming to take over Rome itself, then move the empire's capital to Alexandria and install Caesarion as Caesar's heir and make him a tyrant over the Romans.

It was Antony who realized that the mood in Rome was going in the wrong direction and wrote a letter to Octavian, who was still officially his brother-in-law and co-triumvir. Antony said: "What's come over you? Is it because I got to be with the queen? But she isn't my wife, is she? And it isn't as if it's something new, is it? Haven't I been doing it for nine years now? And what about you, is Livia the only woman you go to bed with? I congratulate you, if at the time you read this letter you haven't also had Tertulla or Terentilla or Rufilla or Salvia Titisenia or the whole lot of them. Does it really matter . . . who the woman is?"[7]

But Antony was now misreading the situation. Octavian had never taken any interest in the marriage between his sister and Antony except as a political tool, an alliance while it was useful and now a propaganda weapon. Octavian *needed* Cleopatra to keep making strategic mistakes, to act like an exotic, sinister, and sultry harlot.

Cleopatra piled on more tactical mistakes. Still believing that she primarily had to win over Antony, she convinced her lover to divorce Octavia formally. Did this make Cleopatra safer? On the contrary. The link between Octavian and Antony, between Rome and Cleopatra's protector, was now severed. Octavian took the opportunity to declare war—not on Antony but on Cleopatra, the foreign harlot who had corrupted a brave Roman soldier.

The fleets of the two enemies—Octavian and his general Agrippa on one side, Antony and Cleopatra on the other—met in Greece. Cleopatra had accompanied Antony with her own Egyptian ships. She had always excelled at winning amorous battles to secure her bigger objectives, but now her fate was riding on a *military* battle, something that she had not chosen and that was beyond her ken, a bit as Tiger Woods had always excelled at winning battles on the golf course until he found his fate riding on a personal dilemma.

Octavian won the battle, and the war. Cleopatra and her lover Mark Antony escaped on separate ships to Alexandria and waited. Within a year, in 30 BCE, Octavian arrived. Neither Antony nor Cleopatra wanted to give him the pleasure of gloating. Antony, thinking that Cleopatra had already killed herself, rammed a sword into his belly. Two slaves carried his body to the mausoleum where Cleopatra had taken refuge with a eunuch, a hairdresser, and a servant. Cleopatra had two poisonous asps delivered and held out her arm to be bitten—or perhaps she stabbed herself with a poisoned hairpin—and died.[8] Octavian's soldiers hunted down Caesarion and killed him, too. Cleopatra, one of history's greatest winners, lost everything in the end.

Clausewitz's ideas about strategy as opposed to tactics and the tension between the two were perhaps best illustrated by the events that began to unfold in June 1950, when Communist forces from North Korea poured south across the 38th parallel in an all-out attack on South Korea.

Harry Truman, having come to power late in life, was the American president and commander in chief and had already made history by dropping the first and only two atomic bombs on Asian cities just five years earlier. He knew immediately and instinctively that this Communist attack had to be reversed or contained. And there, in theory, to achieve this objective was Douglas MacArthur, the commander of the United Nations forces in the region, as well as a certified American hero from World War II and a well-known prima donna of a character.

MacArthur began, true to form, by amazing the world with a daring landing at Inchon in South Korea. He took the enemy by surprise, liberated Seoul in eleven days, and, by October 1, 1950, brought UN forces—primarily composed of Americans—back to the 38th parallel, which the North Koreans had crossed. MacArthur wanted a "hot pursuit,"⁹ and Truman authorized him to cross the 38th parallel. Truman, however, added two crucial conditions, one tactical, the other strategic: The tactical warning was to avoid getting caught in the North Korean winter. The strategic warning was not to provoke the Chinese to enter the war, lest that should spark World War III and possible nuclear Armageddon.

Things quickly became problematic, not only in the war effort but in the relationship between MacArthur and Truman. MacArthur appeared to be thinking purely tactically—in terms of winning *this war*—whereas Truman was thinking strategically—about this war and its role in *the wider world conflict* between communism and capitalism. Their disagreements were all the more flammable for the clash of egos. Truman summoned MacArthur to a meeting, but tactfully met his general halfway on a tiny coral islet in the Pacific Ocean called Wake Island. MacArthur's plane touched down first, then Truman's. MacArthur greeted the commander in chief but failed to salute, which did not go unnoticed by witnesses.¹⁰

The two men then met alone, before inviting others to join them. Truman made clear his overarching concern, one that Clausewitz would have approved of: to keep this a "limited" war,¹¹ meaning a war to meet one objective—rebuffing Communist aggression in Korea—without risking an escalation into what Clausewitz would have called an absolute war. After an hour and thirty-six minutes, Truman called a break and suggested lunch. MacArthur declined, saying that he had urgent business back in Tokyo. "It was insulting to decline lunch with the President, and I think Truman was miffed, although he gave no sign," said Omar Bradley, one of the top generals in attendance.[12] Truman and MacArthur would never meet in person again.

The following month, Truman's fears came true and the Communist Chinese attacked with huge force. Suddenly, MacArthur, who had been dreaming of another glorious military victory, was trying to avoid a humiliating defeat. He demanded huge reinforcements, a wholesale naval blockade of all of China, and immediate bombing of the Chinese mainland. MacArthur wanted to broaden the war, to burst any remaining "limits" on it. For MacArthur, there was only one objective: victory. At all costs.

Truman thought the exact opposite. His first fear had already come true, and he now worried that the Chinese were the advance guard of a Soviet Russian intervention, what he called "a gigantic booby trap"[13] that could lead to the explosion of World War III. Truman and MacArthur started issuing competing press releases. MacArthur began publicly blaming Washington for everything that was going wrong. He disobeyed specific orders. He called on Truman to drop thirty to fifty atomic bombs on the cities of China, then to "sever" Korea from China by laying down a field of radioactive waste all along the Yalu River.[14] To Truman and his staff, MacArthur appeared to have lost his mind. He even issued his own ultimatum to the Chinese government, as if he were president.

At last, Truman asserted the priority of strategy over tactics, civilian over military command, by firing MacArthur. This was an obvious step, but not an easy one. MacArthur, to ordinary Americans, was still a swash-buckling and valiant war hero, whereas Truman's approval was at an all-time low of 26 percent. *Time* magazine wrote that "Douglas MacArthur was the personification of the big man," whereas "Harry Truman was almost a professional little man."[15] In a public-opinion poll at the time,

69 percent of the country backed MacArthur. There were calls to impeach Truman.

Eventually, minds cleared. Truman settled for a stalemate in Korea that continues to this day, a "defeat" of sorts that has brought lasting peace. Had MacArthur prevailed, America might well have achieved "victory" at the cost of another world war, the nuclear annihilation of millions, and perhaps nuclear counterstrikes on America from the Soviets, who were fast catching up to the Americans in the technology. It would have been the ultimate impostor of a triumph, with nobody left to march in the victory parade across the radioactive planet.

MacArthur had proved throughout his life that he was an excellent tactician, but Hannibal's teacher Sosylus would pointedly have refused ever to call him a *strategos*. By contrast, Truman proved that he was a strategist, able and willing to see the ultimate objective, "the peace," and to keep subordinating battles and entire wars to that end. Like Tiger Woods on the golf course, Truman thought "green-to-tee."

A few years ago, one of those chain-letter e-mails landed in my in-box. It told the story of a fisherman who was lying in the warm afternoon sun on a beautiful beach, with his pole propped up and his line cast out into the water. An energetic businessman walked by.

"You aren't going to catch many fish that way," said the businessman to the fisherman. "You should work harder."

The fisherman looked up and good-naturedly asked, "And what would I get for that?"

The businessman replied that he would catch more fish, sell them for more money, save the surplus, and invest in a boat and nets, which would let him catch even more fish.

Again the fisherman asked, "And what would I get for that?"

Somewhat impatiently, the businessman explained that he could then reinvest the even greater surplus and buy more boats and hire staff, becoming a small business and catching ever more fish.

Again the fisherman asked, "And what would I get for that?"

Now the businessman lost it. "Don't you understand that you can become so rich that you never have to work for a living again? You could spend the rest of your days sitting on this beach, just enjoying this sunset!"

The fisherman's eyes lit up. "And what do you think I'm doing right now?"

I SMILED when I read this story, because I recognized it for a new variant of a much older (and perhaps archetypal) story. The classic version is in the works of the ancient Greek biographer Plutarch, who describes a conversation between King Pyrrhus—the same one who was so much on the mind of Hannibal as he was planning his strategy—and a Greek orator named Cineas.

Pyrrhus was making preparations to invade Italy and attack Rome when Cineas struck up a conversation.[16]

"The Romans, sir, are reported to be great warriors," said Cineas. "If God permits us to overcome them, how should we use our victory?"

"But that's obvious," said Pyrrhus. "We will be 'masters of all Italy' with all its wealth."

"And having subdued Italy, what shall we do next?" asked Cineas.

"Sicily," replied Pyrrhus without missing a beat. "A wealthy and populous island, and easy to be gained."

"But will the possession of Sicily put an end to the war?" asked Cineas.

"God grant us victory and success in that," answered Pyrrhus, "and we will use these as forerunners of greater things; who could forbear from Libya and Carthage then within reach?" Once we have those, will anybody anywhere "dare to make further resistance?"

"None," replied Cineas, which leaves us to "make an absolute conquest of Greece. And when all these are in our power, what shall we do then?"

Pyrrhus smiled and said, "We will live at our ease, my dear friend, and drink all day, and divert ourselves with pleasant conversation."

"And what hinders us," said Cineas, "from doing exactly that right now, without going through all these troubles?"

Pyrrhus suddenly looked "troubled" and had no answer. Then he went ahead and invaded Italy anyway—without success.

WE LOVE THESE STORIES because they gently mock us, reminding us that we are so often playing tee-to-green in life when we should be playing green-to-tee. Like the businessman or Pyrrhus, we are diligent in execution but lazy in conception, when instead we should spend more time trying to figure out *what matters*, as the fisherman and Cineas did. We are eager to start succeeding at something, without pondering what we should try to succeed *at*.

This, to me, is the application of strategy in life: not a coldhearted way of looking at relationships or career or rivals or conflicts but a constant and thoughtful assessment of what the goal is and what is merely a means to reach it.

When I began my working life in an investment bank that I hated working for, I realized that any success I might have at this bank would be merely tactical, not strategic, because it would not advance me toward my ultimate goal, a fulfilling vocation and ultimately a fulfilling family life. So, with the story of Hannibal in mind, I left the bank and became a journalist. That was the easy part.

But since then, I have begun to try—and it is often surprisingly difficult—to think strategically about other things. What happens, for example, when I get into a fight with my parents, my wife, or a friend? Should I try to "win"? Tactically, it might be possible to outmaneuver them, as anybody knows who has ever said "I told you so" in anger. But would a victory in this particular battle advance my overall strategy? Surely, that strategy must be *to have* a loving wife and parents and friends. Perhaps a tactical defeat or stalemate or bilateral surrender would be more "strategic."

For smart, talented, and ambitious people such as Hannibal, Tiger Woods, Cleopatra, and Pyrrhus, *winning* is sometimes so easy that it makes *success* elusive. Victories, easily obtained, end up obscuring the ultimate goals. Most people would do well to imagine, from time to time, a conversation with Sosylus the Greek: "What sort of peace do you want? I am *demanding* that you define success."

SEVEN

DEALING WITH DISASTER

Can you then doubt that inactivity *is the way to defeat an enemy?*

—Quintus Fabius Maximus

Quintus Fabius Maximus came from one of the oldest and noblest families of Rome, the Fabii, who claimed they could trace their ancestry back to Hercules. But Hercules was not exactly the first image that came to mind when looking at Fabius himself. When he was a boy, one of his nicknames was Verrucosus—"Warty"—because he had a big wart on his upper lip. Another nickname in his youth was Ovicula, "Lamb," because he had an unusually mild temper for an aristocratic Roman boy. He did everything slowly. He spoke slowly, walked slowly, learned slowly. He was bad at sports in a society that was all about athletic, virile, and martial games.[1] Young Fabius was in almost every way the exact opposite of young Hannibal.

And yet the Romans gradually changed their minds about the warty, lamblike Fabius. As the boy grew into a man, that same slowness began to look like steadiness and prudence. Underneath that lamblike demeanor the Romans discovered what they called "lionlikeness"—manly and stead-fast valor.

Fabius matured into a plainspoken, archconservative, and revered Roman stalwart, a member of the elite who was regarded as a reliable guardian of Rome's customs and institutions. If others were quicker to take action, they were also quicker to make mistakes, to lose their heads, and to panic. If Fabius was slower, he also avoided being reckless. The Romans liked that in a leader, or at least in Fabius. He was already in his forties when they first elected him consul. As senator or elder statesman, five times as consul and twice as elected "dictator," Fabius remained one of the republic's leaders for the rest of his life.

By the time the young and dashing Hannibal crossed the Alps into Italy, Fabius was already in his sixties. Fabius might have assumed that his career now lay mostly behind him. His greatest ambition, if he was like most fathers, was probably to watch his son rise to eminence to carry on the name and tradition of the Fabii.

And yet, suddenly, this Carthaginian invader came down from the Alps like a demon. Fabius had never encountered such an enemy. What, Fabius reflected in his slow and methodical way, should he, and Rome, make of Hannibal?

THEN THE REPORTS came into Rome of the first disaster. Hannibal, the few survivors recounted, had routed the combined Roman consular armies at the Trebia, where he had laid a trap for the Romans, trampled them with elephants, drowned them in the icy river, or speared them as they tried to wade out of the water. The defeat was total, the shame unbearable.

Sempronius, the consul in command at the Trebia, had clearly fought Hannibal in the wrong way, thought Fabius. Sempronius was as rash as Fabius was slow. Fabius understood that this Carthaginian enemy was skilled, shrewd, and more dangerous than other enemies Rome confronted. Pure Roman aggression would not suffice against Hannibal, Fabius realized. The younger Roman leaders found this hard to admit, but Fabius simply *accepted* that Hannibal was superior on the battlefield.

That premise led Fabius to a simple but shocking conclusion: if going to battle against Hannibal meant losing, it was clearly not a good policy to go to battle against him at all. With each Roman defeat, Hannibal would only persuade more Italians to defect from Rome to Carthage, which is what Hannibal clearly wanted. To avoid being isolated without allies, Fabius reasoned, Rome had to avoid losing. And if the only way to do that was to avoid fighting altogether, so be it.

There was an obvious problem with this point of view. Nobody else in Rome agreed with Fabius. Not fighting was un-Roman. A mortal enemy of Rome had just invaded Italy, and this enemy had to be opposed, stopped, and subdued. It would be shameful and simply unimaginable not to meet an enemy in battle.

Fabius was as Roman as any of his compatriots. But again and again, his unusual thought process reinforced his conviction. If Rome refused to fight more battles, there would be no victories, but there also would be no more defeats. There would be stalemate, which would preserve the status quo. That was all that Rome, as the defender, really needed in order to survive as a state. In these extreme circumstances, Fabius decided, the strategic definition of success was no longer victory but stalemate. In his slow and methodical way, Fabius thus determined that Hannibal's stunning triumphs on the battlefield might yet lead to nothing. They might be *impostors*.

AS FABIUS was pondering this, bloody stragglers limped through the gates of Rome telling of another, greater disaster. This time, Hannibal had slaughtered an entire army and its consul at Lake Trasimene. All over Rome widows and mothers were wailing, their haunting cries echoing through the city, from the narrow alleys of the poor neighborhoods to the patrician villas on the hills. If these disasters were impostors, they were well disguised. The pain and humiliation of the defeats, the loss of the loved ones, seemed unbearable. Like every other Roman, Fabius yearned for revenge.

But as one of Rome's most senior senators, Fabius also felt a special duty to control his emotions. Within the senate, he wanted to project firmness to keep the younger senators from panicking. The Roman people now saw him as a father figure, stern, serious, and unshakable. When everybody else seemed to be losing his head, Fabius alone still appeared calm.

Such was his gravitas at this moment, and so severe was Rome's crisis, that Rome made use of an institution reserved for the most dire circumstances. They appointed Fabius not merely consul but "dictator" for six months. Fabius got to work at once. As Rome's unwritten constitution prescribed, he appointed a deputy, choosing a man named Minucius. He ordered animal sacrifices to the gods as Roman religion required. He then raised another army and marched out of the city.

AS SOON AS Hannibal's spies told him that yet another Roman army was on its way, Hannibal started trying to provoke Fabius into a battle and a new trap. But Hannibal quickly realized that something had changed. On the first day, the two armies camped within sight of each other, near a town called Arpi in Apulia, Hannibal immediately deployed his troops and offered battle but was "disappointed to see no sort of activity or bustle in the Roman camp." Hannibal then tried other ploys to draw Fabius into a battle. He kept his army moving, forcing Fabius to move as well. When he knew that Fabius or his scouts were watching, Hannibal destroyed fields and crops. But Fabius was not provoked. He seemed to have no ego that welled with rage when insulted.

When addressing his officers or soldiers, Hannibal disparaged Fabius. Look, he taunted; the Romans were "cowed" and "beaten men" who had now officially "yielded their claim to valor and glory."[2] It was good propaganda. But privately, Hannibal became increasingly anxious. He could not read Fabius and simultaneously he feared that Fabius was somehow reading him.

For months, Hannibal and Fabius moved around southern Italy in this way, Fabius always keeping his army on the hills above Hannibal's army so that the Romans could not be ambushed, but trailing him closely enough that the Carthaginians could not easily forage for food or relax their battle formation. Hannibal understood what Fabius was doing. Hannibal was now constrained—not beaten but stalemated. He understood that such stalemate could be the undoing of his entire campaign, so Hannibal tried to find some way of breaking out.

He decided to force-march to a place called Casinum, but Hannibal's Latin was so atrocious that the local guide heard the word as "Casilinum," and promptly led the Carthaginians off in a different direction. They realized the mistake only when they arrived and found a valley that led to a cul-de-sac. The guide was crucified, but that didn't help now. Fabius had already arrived on the heights and occupied the passes, so now it was Hannibal who seemed trapped.

But Hannibal had a clever idea. Along the way, he had plundered about two thousand oxen. He told his men to collect lots of twigs and branches and to tie them to the oxen's horns. He then waited for night, knowing that Fabius would have guards posted on all the passes leading out of the valley but would keep his main army inside the Roman camp and out of danger. Once it was pitch-black, Hannibal ordered the twigs lit on fire, and the oxen driven up the mountain toward one of the passes. As the twigs got hot and burned low, the oxen panicked and stampeded up the hillside. To the Roman guards on top, it looked as though the Carthaginians were charging up one side of the hill with torches to make a break for the pass on that side. As the guards ran off to block the ridge, they vacated the pass they were supposed to guard. As the Roman guards discovered they were confronting oxen instead of Carthaginians, Hannibal was marching his entire army through the gap they left open, past the sleeping Roman camp, and escaping.[3]

It was a tactical success and a reminder to Fabius that Hannibal was no ordinary commander. But in the bigger picture, it hardly made a difference, because Fabius at once set off again to keep shadowing Hannibal as he moved. Both Hannibal and Fabius now knew that they were playing a new game, one in which it was not clear who was hunting whom, who had the initiative and who was passive. Theirs might be a long and drawn-out duel of wits and stamina and prudence. It was the kind of contest that a defending army welcomed and an invading army feared.

BUT BOTH HANNIBAL and Fabius also knew that there was a much bigger threat to Fabius than the Carthaginians. It was the Romans. Most Romans did not understand Fabius's strategy of absorbing Hannibal's momentum and mistook it for cowardice, just as the Roman schoolboys had once made the mistake of thinking that Fabius was stupid.

Fabius's own deputy, Minucius, started ridiculing his commander to the officers. Fabius, said Minucius, was Hannibal's "pedagogue," a word the Romans used for the Greek slaves who walked Roman boys to school and back. He called Fabius a coward and a disgrace. "Are we here merely to enjoy the pleasant spectacle of our friends being butchered and their houses burned?" Minucius asked sardonically. "Smoke from burning farms and smoldering crops drifts into our faces, blinds our eyes; the pitiful cries of our friends ring in our ears. . . . In answer, our army goes strolling like cattle through summer pastures in the hills."

With demagogic malice, Minucius roused his audience of officers: "Rome's power grew by action and daring—not by these do-nothing tactics, which the faint-hearted call caution."[4]

When his spies told Hannibal about these tensions in the Roman camp, Hannibal did all he could to stoke them. He marched to the area where Fabius's ancestral estate was located and gave an order to ravage the entire countryside but to spare one property: the one owned by Fabius. Hannibal even placed guards around Fabius's farms. When this became known in Rome, it had the desired propaganda effect. A ridiculous rumor began circulating that Fabius was in fact colluding with Hannibal behind the scenes.[5]

In such a poisonous atmosphere, the Roman senate turned petty and hostile toward Fabius. Fabius and Hannibal did have an informal agreement, in keeping with traditional norms of war and chivalrous ethics, that each side could ransom from the other its own prisoners of war. But the Romans, in their new and paranoid distrust of Fabius, refused to give him money to pay for Roman prisoners. Fabius swallowed his pride, sold his property, and bought the Roman prisoners from Hannibal with his own money. It was his way of showing his soldiers that he cared for them and that he stood above the slanders by his political enemies.

At one point, Fabius had to leave his army and return to Rome to attend to his duties as dictator. He issued strict orders to Minucius to continue his tactics of shadowing and constraining Hannibal without being drawn into a pitched battle. Minucius barely hid his disdain. After Fabius left, Minucius heard that a few Carthaginian and Roman soldiers foraging for food had skirmished. Minucius sent messengers to Rome with a fantastic tale of a great victory. The Romans loved the story. The only man in Rome who refused to believe it was Fabius, who said to a friend that even if the story of Minucius's victory were true, he would be "more afraid of success than of failure"[6] because it would lead a man like Minucius into disaster.

The Romans had no ear for such irony now. The streets were teeming with mobs, whipped up by demagogues who gave grand speeches about the bravery of Minucius and the cowardice of Fabius. Fabius could no longer go out in public for fear that he'd be mobbed. At the urging of a populist politician named Varro, Minucius was officially promoted to become cocommander, equal in power with Fabius. This was nearly a coup d'état.

IF FABIUS FELT INSULTED, he did not show it. He returned to his army and met with Minucius, who was now openly dismissive of him. But Fabius accepted that Minucius was now of equal rank. They split the army in two and each took command of half.

Hannibal was thrilled when his spies told him about this. Expecting Minucius to do something stupid, Hannibal immediately provoked him into a trap. He sent a few troops to take a small hill in sight of the Romans and personally rode out to be spotted by Minucius. Minucius dispatched his whole army to attack the hill. But Hannibal had hidden other soldiers behind the knolls and they encircled Minucius's force, poised to slaughter every single Roman there.

Fabius, with his half of the army, was watching this from a distance. He had seen it coming. "O Hercules," he sighed. "How much sooner than I expected, though later than he seemed to desire, hath Minucius destroyed himself!"[7] Fabius then marched in with his soldiers toward the Carthaginian rear, and Hannibal, seeing that his ambush would not work, withdrew.

As soon as the danger passed, Fabius, without so much as a look of reproach to Minucius, went back to his camp. Minucius, meanwhile, was in shock. At night, once he calmed down, he marched his half of the army over to Fabius's camp, walked up to the old man, and threw his battle standards at his feet. Then Minucius publicly saluted Fabius and called him his "father." From this point on there would be only one commander, said Minucius, and he himself would be Fabius's most loyal and faithful soldier.[8] Tears flowed as the two halves of the army reunited.

BUT THE SIX-MONTH TERM of Fabius's dictatorship was now over, and the Romans, by law, had to elect two new consuls. The mob was still angry and elected the very same Varro who had recently humiliated Fabius by promoting Minucius to equal rank. As a check against Varro's temper, the aristocracy pushed one of its candidates, the patrician Lucius Aemilius Paullus, to be elected as the other consul.

Just before the two new consuls were to depart, Fabius took Paullus aside. Thinking of his own ordeal with Minucius, Fabius advised Paullus, "Hannibal is your enemy, Varro your rival, but I hardly know which will prove the more hostile." Fabius called Varro a madman who would lead Rome to disaster. "The only way of fighting the war with Hannibal is my way," Fabius said. Hannibal might be invincible, but he was nonetheless in a foreign and hostile land, and his troops were at risk of starving in the next winter. "Can you then doubt that inactivity is the way to defeat an enemy who is daily growing more decrepit?"

The Romans still did not understand this, said Fabius, and would criticize Paullus. "You will have two generals against you, but you will stand firm against both if you can steel yourself to ignore the tongues of men who will defame you." Sounding like an older brother, Fabius told Paullus: "Never mind if they call your caution timidity, your wisdom sloth, your generalship weakness. . . . It is better that a wise enemy should fear you than that foolish friends should praise."[9]

FABIUS'S ADVICE was in vain. The Roman army with its two consuls marched off in pursuit of Hannibal and caught up with him at Cannae. Hannibal, reading the new situation accurately, provoked on a day when he knew Varro was in command, and Paullus, as a dutiful patriot, had to follow Varro's orders. By afternoon, almost all the Roman soldiers lay dead on the plain. Paullus himself was still alive, soaked in his own blood. A Roman rider who was making a dash to escape saw the consul and offered to help him. Paullus refused, telling the man to ride to Rome and take a personal message to Fabius: "That while I lived I did not forget his counsel, and that I remember it still in the hour of death."[10] The Roman galloped away. Moments later, Hannibal's horsemen ran their spears through Paullus's body.

Rome took the news of Cannae as a death sentence. Every family was bereft. Fathers, brothers, husbands, sons—all but slaves, the sick, the very old, and the very young—were dead. It would surely be only days or weeks before Hannibal was *ad portas*, "at the gates," to finish the job by killing every last woman, child, and dog.

Once again, only Fabius managed to control his fear. He made a point of walking through the Forum with a confident and serene face. He was no longer dictator, but he still had unequaled *auctoritas*, the clout and credibility of an elder statesman, so he called the senate to meet. The chamber was a pathetic sight, since about a third of its members had fallen at Cannae and their seats were empty. But Fabius was making it clear that there still *was* a government of Rome, even though many of its leading citizens were gone. Fabius then placed guards at the gates of Rome to keep the Romans from fleeing. Nobody would be allowed to abandon Rome, he made clear. He then set a one-month limit on public mourning. Mourn, he said. But then swallow your pain, and in your minds and hearts move on.

At last, the Romans were receptive to his ideas. They had been calling Fabius *cunctator*, the delayer. Originally, they had meant it as an insult, but now they used his latest nickname, so fitting for an artist of slowness, with respect. Guided by Fabian strategy, the Romans would not fight another large, pitched battle against Hannibal for fourteen years, the entire time he remained in Italy. Instead Fabius taught the Romans to turn the war into an endurance test. Hannibal stayed invincible. But Fabian Rome refused to be beaten. Fabius, and all of Rome, had suffered disaster. But Fabius, and all of Rome, had made the decision to accept it and to "do nothing."

There are two aspects to a Fabian character that make it resilient and that you might remember if ever disaster should strike you: The first is the ability to *accept* reality for what it is. The second is the ability to stop resisting reality and instead to *flow* with it until circumstances begin to change.

Here is how most Romans reacted to Hannibal's unfolding invasion. When Hannibal first crossed the Alps, they were paralyzed by *shock*. Shock turned into psychological *denial*, as many Romans tried to pretend that this "cannot be happening" or might somehow "go away." As their losses mounted, denial turned to *anger*. Sempronius at the Trebia, Flaminius at Lake Trasimene, Varro at Cannae, and many of their common legionaries were furious as they rushed into defeat. Many Romans then resorted to psychological *bargaining*: "I promise to sacrifice to the gods, if you spare me and my family." After Cannae, the entire city succumbed to a deep *depression*, as people felt that the end was nigh and they would all be exterminated. Only Fabius and a few others moved one psychological step further, to *acceptance*.

SHOCK, DENIAL, anger, bargaining, depression, and finally acceptance: these are the stages that make up the human "grief cycle" described by Elisabeth Kübler-Ross, a twentieth-century Swiss doctor who spent her time caring for dying people. Originally, Kübler-Ross thought these emotional states arose only when people prepared for their own death or dealt with the death of a loved one. But soon she realized that the same mental journey occurs after bad news of any sort. Losing your job, losing your house to foreclosure, being diagnosed with cancer, getting divorced—any bereavement, failure, or other disaster triggers the psychological responses of the grief cycle.

But people move through the cycle in different ways. Some progress swiftly, others get stuck at one stage, and yet others cycle back and forth through them. For example, Kübler-Ross became close with a middle-aged woman who was wasting away from "a visible, large ulcerative type of cancer of the breast," as Kübler-Ross described it. The woman's face was sinking into her skull. But you would never have known it from talking to the woman, because she was in total denial, claiming that her diagnosis was a silly mistake and refusing treatment. "As she grew weaker, her makeup became more grotesque," Kübler-Ross observed. "Originally rather discreetly applied red lipstick and rouge, the makeup became brighter and redder until she resembled a clown."[11] Soon she died.

By contrast, anger usually begins with the question "Why me?"[12] Lance Armstrong is a good example. When he was twenty-five, his career as a bike racer was "moving along a perfect arc of success,"[13] with sponsorships, a large house on a lake, and his own powerboat and Jet Skis. Then he began to cough up blood. Soon one testicle swelled to the size of an orange. He found out that he had testicular cancer. The doctors gave him at best a 40 percent chance of surviving. He was diagnosed on a Wednesday, had his testicle removed on Thursday, masturbated into a cup on Saturday (because he would soon be sterile), started chemotherapy on Monday, and discovered on the next Thursday that the cancer had already spread to his lungs and brain. Every devastating day was followed by an even more terrible day. And Armstrong became angry. "I was fighting mad, swinging mad, mad in general, mad at being in a bed, mad at having bandages around my head, mad at the tubes that tied me down. So mad I was beside myself, so mad I almost began to cry."[14]

But people eventually get exhausted by anger, just as children wear themselves out from a tantrum. Once that happens, they usually try bargaining. In Kübler-Ross's observations, this internal bargaining—perhaps with God, or one's own conscience, or an ancestor—usually includes a pledge of good behavior for a prize.

I began bargaining around three o'clock one February morning when my daughter was a few days old. My wife, sleep-deprived and still recovering from the birth, and I tried to wake her up for a feeding; she was unresponsive and cold—alive, but something was clearly wrong. She was tiny and fragile, and with the gentlest and most nervous hands, we took her temperature. It was low—frighteningly low. My wife and I called our pediatrician. When I described the situation, the pediatrician immediately said, "Call 911."

When my wife and I heard that command, without any other context, our first thought was that our baby was dying, that we might lose her. I felt a physical shock, as though I had been hit by a car. In a surreal, trance-like state, I called 911, and soon an ambulance arrived in our dark street. I carried my daughter into the ambulance, where she was strapped to a gurney and hooked up to tubes, looking even more vulnerable and small amid the machinery and blinking lights. We rushed to the hospital.

During the bumpy ride, with nothing to do but look at my wife's worried face or my baby daughter half covered by tubes, I tried to suppress the fear of her death that was threatening to overwhelm me. I was aware that my brain was frantically negotiating with itself. Who was haggling with whom, I do not know.

"Please," I remember thinking, "let me keep my daughter. In return, I promise to be a kinder, better, and more patient person." As the ride wore on, I promised more and more. Every fault I had, I vowed to rectify; everything I valued, I vowed to give up. I offered to surrender my career, red wine, even yoga. Every vice and vanity and every passion I pledged away.

When we got to the hospital, the ordeal continued, with more tubes stuck into my daughter. Tests were done and the results did not come back until the next day. All night and morning I continued to bargain. It was pointless, stupid, and futile, as I knew. But I needed to bargain to make it through these hours.

Eventually, it turned out that my daughter was fine. She was badly dehydrated, but with no infection—infection was what the doctor had feared. We were relieved and exhausted. My daughter had to stay in the hospital for another couple of nights for observation, but the hospital allowed only one parent to spend the night with her. I was the one to go home to an empty house, left exactly as it was when we called 911. Finally, at home and alone, the days of worry and tension poured out of me. I broke down sobbing, for the first time as an adult.

My daughter came home from the hospital and life returned to normal. As the months passed, one by one I broke all the pledges I made that night and reverted to my old flawed self. But I will never forget my utter despair and my reaction to it.

Anger and bargaining are active responses to disaster and demand energy, and eventually our energy runs out. So it is far easier to get permanently stuck in the next stage, depression, which is a passive response and can therefore last indefinitely. It comes in two kinds, according to Kübler-Ross. If the disaster or loss has already happened, depression is reactive. If the disaster is yet to happen—when preparing for death, for instance—depression is preparatory.[15] The Romans after Cannae suffered from both types of depression simultaneously. They mourned their fallen sons, husbands, and fathers. And they mourned their own deaths, which they assumed to be imminent. Lance Armstrong also suffered a bout of preparatory depression. "It's all over. I'm sick, I'm never going to race again, and

I'm going to lose everything."[16] His depression felt "as though all my blood started flowing in the wrong direction."[17]

Eventually, however, *some* grief-stricken individuals will arrive at a state of acceptance. As Kübler-Ross puts it, "Acceptance should not be mistaken for a happy stage. It is almost devoid of feelings."[18] But it is the stage where the person is ready to move on. If death is imminent, the individual is now able to die in peace and with dignity. If a defeat or failure has occurred, the person is now ready to pick himself up and go on living. This cannot happen in the other stages of grief; acceptance is the prerequisite. People whose character allows them to accept sooner rather than later are resilient.

Lance Armstrong accepted his cancer relatively quickly. He simply "decided not to be afraid."[19] Then he confronted his cancer. "Each time I was more fully diagnosed, I asked my doctors hard questions. What are my chances?"[20] He also personalized the disease and made it his "enemy,"[21] as though he were facing Hannibal. "It was me versus him or her or it—being the disease—so I absolutely hated him or her or it, and when the blood work came back, or the tumor markers came back [saying] that I was getting better, I felt like I'm winning, the scoreboard says I'm winning."[22]

Like Armstrong, Fabius quickly accepted that a disaster had struck. Unlike Armstrong, Fabius, as a leader, also had to make his fellow Romans accept it. This was the purpose of all his gestures after the defeat at Cannae. When Fabius convened the depleted senate, which had entire rows of seats empty because their occupants were dead, the cruel and stark emptiness of the chamber made it impossible to *deny* what had happened. When he put guards at the city's gates, not to keep Carthaginians out but to keep Romans in, he made it clear that *bargaining* with fate—by escaping the city—was not allowed. When he walked calmly through the streets, he demonstrated that *anger* would not rule. When he fixed the mourning rituals to one single month, he showed that *depression* would have a definite end. And so Fabius, and eventually his fellow Romans, settled in for their long struggle to deal with the disaster of Hannibal.

THEN THERE is the second and more subtle aspect to Fabius's remarkable response. When Minucius was taunting Fabius, he mocked "these *do-nothing* tactics" of fighting Hannibal without actually fighting. Though Minucius did not understand what he was saying, he chose the correct word. As Fabius himself later told Paullus, "Can you then doubt that *inactivity* is the way to defeat an enemy who is daily growing more decrepit?" Another time he said that Hannibal, deprived of battles, "would at last be tired out and consumed, like a wrestler in too high condition, whose very excess of strength makes him the more likely suddenly to give way and lose it."[23]

Fabius was thus sounding rather like Morihei Ueshiba, the founder and master of aikido, who also allowed his opponents to tire themselves out and consume their energies, and who also used his opponents' own excessive strength to topple them. Ironically, Hannibal was using this same approach to inimitable effect as a tactic on the field of battle. But Fabius was now applying the same principle to the *overall* war, the whole Italian peninsula, the entire *strategic* situation. It was as though Fabius, hopelessly outdone by Hannibal at the tactical level of battles, raised his perspective to a strategically higher level. "Attaining one hundred victories in one hundred battles is not the pinnacle of excellence," as Sun Tzu, China's ancient philosopher of war, observed. "Subjugating the enemy's army without fighting is the true pinnacle of excellence."

One translation of Minucius's taunt about Fabius's *do-nothing* tactics into Chinese is *wu wei*, which means "nondoing" or "doing by not doing." *Wu wei* happens to be a central concept of "the way," the Tao, in Chinese philosophy. This Taoist notion of *wu wei*, nondoing, is often mistaken for passivity, which it is not. Instead, nondoing is really a very active way of letting inevitable things happen without wasting energy resisting them, instead bringing one's own position into harmony with this flow of nature. The principle of *wu wei* might say, for instance, that it is better to use a rushing stream to spin a wheel and transfer its energy than to block the stream and try to make it stop flowing. Or it might say that a skipper is better off tacking through the wind than trying to go against it, which would be futile. Indeed, the best skippers often look, as Fabius did, as though they were "doing nothing."

Eleanor Roosevelt is a good example of the first part of a Fabian response, of moving through the stages of the grief cycle and arriving at acceptance. Roosevelt's disaster struck in 1918, when she was thirty-three. For thirteen years, she had been a traditional wife and mother, bearing six children and losing one to influenza, working ceaselessly to preserve harmony in a household dominated by a harridan of a mother-in-law, and above all supporting the career of her husband, Franklin Delano Roosevelt. One day, Roosevelt picked up her husband, who was returning from a trip by ship, brought him home, and unpacked his luggage. And there she found a thick packet of Franklin's letters. As she opened the bundle and began reading, "the bottom dropped out" of her world, as she later said.

The letters were from Lucy Mercer, her own friend and social secretary. Eleanor herself had hired her two years earlier. Mercer was young and attractive, warm and efficient and great with the children. But as Roosevelt now saw in Mercer's own ink, she had been sleeping with Franklin. More than that, Mercer and Franklin were passionately in love. Eleanor could barely breathe.

She confronted her husband with this information. She wanted a divorce. But her mother-in-law was dead set against it. All of the Roosevelts' advisers insisted that divorce would mean the end of FDR's political career—he was assistant secretary of the navy at this time. Eleanor, still shocked by her discovery, gave in to the pressure and stayed in her marriage. But things would never be the same again. She descended into a deep valley of grief.

Her pain was such that her body seemed to shut down. For about a year, she lost her appetite. Whenever she did eat, she threw it up again. "I might as well not have eaten it for I promptly parted with it all!" she wrote in one letter.[24] She lost weight, and her teeth loosened in her gums, making her mouth appear even bigger than before. In pictures taken at the time, she never looked into the camera.

TO FIND SOLACE, Roosevelt began going to a particular holly grove in Rock Creek Cemetery in Washington, D.C. In it there is the so-called Adams Memorial, where a shrouded woman in bronze is seated against a block of granite in eternal contemplation. The statue was commissioned by the writer Henry Adams to commemorate his wife, Clover, who had committed suicide in 1885 by drinking photographic acid after finding out about her husband's infidelity.

Several days a week for several months, Roosevelt drove to Rock Creek Cemetery to sit alone on a curved stone bench at this memorial, sometimes gazing quietly at the statue but often crying and raging.[25] There, gazing at the endurance on that robed bronze figure, Roosevelt went through the stages of her grief.

Eventually, she began to accept, and even to forgive. As she did so, she began to see the world in a new way—the way it really was.

The statue's sculptor, Augustus Saint-Gaudens, had called it *The Mystery of the Hereafter and the Peace of God That Passeth Understanding*, a peace that he described as "beyond pain and beyond joy." That is how Elisabeth Kübler-Ross described acceptance. But most people, including Eleanor Roosevelt, never called the statue by its full title. Instead, its most common name is simply *Grief.*

The explorer Ernest Shackleton, a brooding Anglo-Irish man with a wide face and a deep brogue, is a good example of the second aspect of a Fabian response to disaster, of seeing the wisdom of nondoing.

Shackleton in his youth had the audacious dream of crossing the Antarctic continent. In this he resembled Meriwether Lewis, who had had the American equivalent of that dream—crossing the North American continent to explore the Louisiana Purchase—a century earlier. Shackleton had already been to the Antarctic twice, in 1901 and 1907, but had never reached the South Pole. Then, in 1912, a Norwegian, Roald Amundsen, beat him to it, followed by another Briton, Robert Scott, who died while trying to get back to his base. So Shackleton chose a new and even bigger quest: he decided to cross the entire Antarctic continent on foot. It was as daring in 1914 as it had been in 218 BCE for Hannibal to cross the Alps, or from 1803 to 1806 for Meriwether Lewis to cross North America to the Pacific.

Like Hannibal and Lewis, Shackleton prepared meticulously. His plan was to take a ship into the Weddell Sea on the side of the continent facing South America, where six men and seventy dogs would disembark and set off for the pole on sleds. Simultaneously, a second ship would sail into the Ross Sea on the side of Antarctica facing New Zealand and Australia. Its crew would deposit rations at various caches that the group on sleds could later use on the second half of its journey.

Shackleton chose a Norwegian ship with three masts and a coal-fired steam engine, made from specially treated oaks and firs. The ship had an extra-thick keel and sides and a sheathing of steel-hard greenheart wood that he hoped would be tough enough to withstand the chafing of the ice. It was the strongest wooden ship ever built in Norway and probably the world. Shackleton's family motto was *Fortitudine vincimus*, "By endurance we conquer."[26] So he christened his ship the *Endurance*.

Out of many volunteers, Shackleton chose twenty-seven men and sailed from London in August 1914, just as war was breaking out in Europe. By November, the *Endurance* pulled into her last port on the desolate island of South Georgia between South America and the Antarctic. Then, in early December, at the height of the southern hemisphere's summer, she was off to the Weddell Sea. Another seaman had smuggled himself on board, so the *Endurance* now carried twenty-eight. There were also sixty-nine huskies on board.

The Weddell Sea is a roughly circular sea between three landmasses, the Antarctic mainland, Antarctica's long and thin Palmer Peninsula, and the South Sandwich Islands. Much of the sea is covered with ice, some loose, some dense. The ice mostly stays in the Weddell Sea and moves in a slow clockwise semicircle, away from the eastern side and toward the Palmer Peninsula on the western side. Shackleton was aiming for that eastern side, hoping that the ice was loose enough for the *Endurance* to sail through.

On December 7, the *Endurance* first skirmished with the enemy. It was a small patch of ice, easily evaded. Soon the ice was heavier and denser. The *Endurance* smashed into a few floes, but her greenheart wood held firm. As she traveled south, she began passing icebergs. For two weeks, Shackleton squirmed through the thickening pack of ice. In January, the *Endurance* seemed to have broken through the pack and for a while it was smooth sailing. Then, ice again. The floes were now thick but soft and snowy. Suddenly, the *Endurance* was stuck. As one crew member put it: "frozen, like an almond in the middle of a chocolate bar."[27]

SHACKLETON'S FIRST REACTION was to order his crew to do what heroes normally do: fight. The men climbed onto the ice and hacked away at it with picks, trying to open a sea-lane. But it was useless. They tried to use the radio, a new technology at the time, to call for assistance, but they heard only static. Slowly, the realization sank in that their situation was grave. Shackleton knew at once that his expedition had failed.

If he was devastated, he tried not to show it, because he had twenty-seven other men looking at him. And they knew that the Antarctic summer was ending in late February and that they could well be stuck in the ice for the entire winter. Lest anybody think about the implications too much, Shackleton kept the men busy transferring the dogs to the floes and building igloos for them, issuing winter clothing, and preparing the ship for its new purpose: as a fortress against the Antarctic weather. Then there was nothing to do but wait.

In May, the sun appeared for the last time. For a while there was only twilight, a dull gray that grew dimmer and dimmer. Then total darkness. The long Antarctic night had begun.

Shackleton knew that the men on another ship caught in the Antarctic night had gone mad. That crew had become melancholy, then depressed, then insane. They walked around their ship in a circle, the so-called madhouse promenade.[28] One man died from fear of the darkness, another from paranoia that the others were trying to kill him. Yet another went deaf and dumb.

Shackleton decided that this would not happen on the *Endurance*. They would stay busy and active. In the eternal dark, the men played cards and threw dice, pulled pranks on each other, shaved their heads for fun, dressed up as women, and made music from a hand-cranked phonograph until its needles wore out. They were determined to stay human and civilized. Shackleton would not allow depression or anger.

Nor would he allow denial. When the winds picked up, the men watched floes bash into each other with the force of artillery and form ice ridges as high as church steeples. The floes also started ramming into the *Endurance*. One day, Shackleton overheard some of his men protesting rather too much that the *Endurance* was invincible. Shackleton sat down at the table with them and told the tale of the "mouse who lived in a tavern. One night the mouse found a leaky barrel of beer, and he drank all he could hold. When the mouse had finished, he sat up, twirled his whiskers, and looked around arrogantly. 'Now then,' he said, 'where's that damned cat?'"[29] The men understood that there would be no more boasting.

After a while, the winds and ice pressure picked up. The *Endurance* was being crushed as though a giant vise were being applied to her. She made sounds as though she were crying in agony, her timbers creaking, then cracking like gunfire. The men had already built tents on the ice, in the freezing cold. They had been stuck on their ship for nine months when Shackleton gave the order to abandon the *Endurance*. Within two hours all essential gear had been brought onto the ice. When their floe cracked, the camp was moved to another one. Soon after the last men were off the

Endurance, the ice broke through her sides. Slowly, she sank. Suddenly, the men were all alone, floating on ice somewhere near the South Pole.

SHACKLETON WALKED across the ice, away from where the *Endurance* had been and toward their new campsite. He found his men trying to figure out how to stay warm. Some tried lying on pieces of lumber to sleep off the snow, but there were not enough planks for everyone. They hugged their tent mates for the illusion of warmth, until one A.M., when a jolt woke them. A crack was sneaking across the floe between the tents. Shackleton hurried from tent to tent to get everybody up. Working frenziedly for an hour, they transferred the camp to the larger part of the cleaving floe.

Shackleton soon announced his plan of attack. It was daring, even heroic. They would march across the ice toward Paulet Island—346 miles to the northwest, almost the distance from San Francisco to Los Angeles—where another expedition years ago had apparently left caches of rations. To be ready for an open-sea crossing, they would drag two of their three lifeboats with them, each weighing more than a ton, as well as their sleds.

Shackleton explained that in order to survive they would have to shed all unnecessary weight. Each man was to keep the clothes he was wearing, two pairs of mittens, six pairs of socks, two pairs of boots, a sleeping bag, a pound of tobacco, and two pounds of personal gear. Nothing else, said Shackleton, had any value anymore. To make his point, he held up his gold coins and threw them into the snow.

The next morning, Shackleton ordered the puppies that could not yet pull a harness and the cat killed. Then one party went ahead with axes and shovels to try to hew a flattish path for the sleds and boats to be pulled through. They also checked for cracks in the floes. After three hours of hard toil, they had moved one mile. It began to snow. The next day they tried again, but the snow was like glue. They were soaked inside their tents and sleeping bags. The next morning they tried again. Shackleton went ahead and scanned the ice. He saw pressure ridges where colliding ice floes had formed mountains that looked as forbidding as the Alps.

SHACKLETON TURNED around and walked back to the group. He took
deep breaths of the icy air and prepared to announce his decision, which he
knew was probably the weightiest of his entire life. At first, he had thought
that attacking the enemy was the best thing to do, both for morale and for
their chances of survival. But he now thought that he might have been in
denial. During the night, he had accepted reality, and seeing the endless
ice mountains around them had confirmed it. Instead of attacking and
wasting caloric energy to make at most a mile a day toward who knew
where, they would instead . . . *do nothing.*

By doing nothing, he explained, they would in fact be doing the most
they could do. For they had noticed that the entire ice pack around them
was moving as one huge unit, at an average of about two miles a day in a
clockwise circle. By staying in place, they would conserve their energy and,
though it might not seem that way, ride the slow and invisible rotation
of the ice pack. The enemy itself, the ice, would deliver them into the direction they needed to go, Shackleton told his men. With luck, they would
eventually find themselves, without having moved, at a location where a
new, decisive, and properly timed attack would let them launch the boats
into open water and make for land.

There were to be absolutely no regrets, he said. He sent small teams
with dogs back to the original camp to bring up as much food as possible
and to salvage the third boat, which would, he hoped, become crucial one
day. The men were still hunting seals and penguins, but their food would
migrate away with the next Antarctic winter. So Shackleton ordered the
cook to start mixing seal blubber into the men's meat rations so that they
might get used to the all-blubber diet that lay ahead. It was rubbery and
tasted worse than cod-liver oil. Learn to savor it, said Shackleton.

That Shackleton was able to get not just himself but his men to accept
their situation was perhaps his greatest achievement as a leader, for the
men were entering a frozen hell. They had only sleeping bags of reindeer
skin or wool to protect them against the wind. In the summer, when the

sun briefly melted layers of snow into thin lakes, the bags and boots and gear were always wet. To drink, the men gathered snow into tobacco tins and pressed them against their bodies to melt, which yielded about one tablespoon at a time. To eat, there was the blubber, which left nothing to move through their bowels. Defecation was rare and painful. A man would go behind an ice ridge, for shelter from the wind rather than privacy, then wipe himself with snow, which chafed and led to bleeding. The wind caused tears to run down their cheeks, which froze into icicles that tore off skin when removed and caused sores. All the while, the floe moved underneath their feet, threatening to crack at any moment.

There was a lot of time to think, and the big controversy was the wisdom of doing nothing. If the ice pack kept moving northwest, it would carry them toward the peninsula. But if it turned east, they would be stuck on the ice for the next polar night, lasting months.

Shackleton knew that his challenge now was twofold. First, he had to preserve morale, cohesion, and discipline among the men. He constantly observed them to see who might make trouble, then gave these men special attention. Like Hannibal, he mingled with his men, who simply called him "boss," but he also kept a psychological distance.

Second, he had to get the timing of their final attack just right. Once, he thought they had a chance to get off the ice and paddle for land. So he gave the order, and again they left their camp and set out. But again they failed. Shackleton was devastated, but he did not show it. He wrote in his diary that night: "Turned in but could not sleep. Thought the whole matter over & decided to retreat to more secure ice: it is the only safe thing to do. . . . Am anxious: For so big a party & 2 boats in bad conditions we could do nothing: I do not like retreating but prudence demands this course."[30] He was still learning the art of nondoing. "I am rather tired. I suppose it is the strain," he wrote another time. "I long for some rest, free from thought."[31]

Onward they drifted on the ice until Shackleton realized with alarm that they were now moving *past* their targets, the island and peninsula that seemed to be their best hope. They also seemed to be getting close to the open ocean, as the swell under their floe suggested. This heightened the danger because it might break their floe, but it also meant that the big moment, the launching of the boats, was approaching. The Antarctic winter was near again, temperatures were dropping, and food was running out. They shot the remaining dogs, whom they had loved, and ate them.

Then they heard cracks. One ran right through the tents and sent the men scurrying to move everything to one side, jumping over the crack in the process. Then another crack opened right under the boats. With each crack they found themselves on a smaller floe until all of the men stood on a triangle the size of a tennis court. Shackleton knew that the time had come. "Strike the tents and clear the boats," he ordered.[32] Minutes later a crack opened up right where Shackleton had stood. The oars came out, and every man in the three boats pulled for his life.

AFTER FIVE DAYS in their lifeboats, sleep deprived and frostbitten, they reached a desolate shore of black rocks called Elephant Island. It had been fourteen months since the *Endurance* got stuck in the ice and five months since they abandoned her. By doing nothing, they had survived their most formidable enemy, the ice. They were not safe yet, but they were alive.

They made a camp. But Elephant Island was far away from shipping routes and the nearest inhabited island, British-controlled South Georgia, was more than seven hundred miles away. Nonetheless, somebody had to attempt to reach South Georgia to get help.

Shackleton chose five men to join him in a daring attempt to cross the open ocean in a lifeboat. For seventeen days, the six men rode the ocean in their open vessel, their tongues swollen from dehydration and lack of sleep, until they straggled ashore on an uncharted part of South Georgia. Exhausted and weak, Shackleton again chose the two strongest to cross the island with him to the whaling station. Without backpacks or proper shoes, and with only forty-eight remaining matches,[33] the three men trudged for thirty-six hours through glaciers and around crevasses, in the moonlight and through fog, until, on May 20, 1916, they saw a whaling station beneath them, their first glimpse of human civilization in a year and a half.

Like the Carthaginians when they came out of the Alps, Shackleton and his men looked barely human, and two boys who saw them ran away in fear.[34] But some Norwegian whalers took them in and celebrated them as heroes. Shackleton at once set about rescuing the rest of his men, marooned on Elephant Island.

He borrowed a ship but had to turn back in bad weather and ice. He tried again with a second and a third ship, and failed both times. Anguished over the fate of his men, who were probably starving or freezing to death by now, Shackleton found a fourth ship and broke through to Elephant Island. A boat was lowered from the ship and rowed toward the camp. Shackleton stood in the bow and, screaming over the surf, asked whether all were well. Yes, all were well, came the reply, and Shackleton probably felt the greatest relief of his life.

SHACKLETON HAD SET OUT to be a Hannibal or a Meriwether Lewis and had failed in every respect. In the ice, he met his disaster. But he found it in himself to accept this, and then found the courage to fight the ice by *not* fighting it, by *flowing* with it. It might have dawned on him, as on Fabius, that he had achieved a much greater success than any he could have hoped for, that to confront, accept, and survive disaster can *be* the greatest triumph.

EIGHT

THE PRISON
OF SUCCESS

*He could no longer take in certain new ideas in phys-
ics which contradicted his own firmly held philosophical convictions. . . . Many of us regard this as a tragedy.*
—Physicist Max Born, speaking of Albert Einstein

Hannibal and his soldiers spent the winter after their great victory at
Cannae in Capua, the languid and seductive metropolis in southern Italy, richer and more beautiful at the time than Rome. The Capuans
had never really liked Rome and were thrilled to host a new conqueror.
To show their enthusiasm, the Capuans herded the Romans still remaining
in the city into a bathhouse and suffocated them in its furnace. Just as
Hannibal had expected, they cast their lot unequivocally with Carthage.

Hannibal's soldiers, meanwhile, were having a great time. For the first
time in three years of danger, discomfort, and toil, they slept in beds again.
And not only that, but in beds with women. With girlfriends and prostitutes, baths and wine, they whiled away the winter months. And why not?
Hannibal could hardly begrudge them these joys of living after asking
them to be ready to die for him.

But Hannibal also noticed that his officers were getting fat and lazy.

Often they were drunk. They fought over women. Several of his fearsome Carthaginian killers began looking disturbingly docile. The Romans would later joke, "Capua was Hannibal's Cannae."[1]

And thus began a new and very strange phase of the Second Punic War. After three years of high drama and adrenaline—of Alpine peaks, Etruscan swamps, and three of the bloodiest battles in human history—there now followed thirteen excruciatingly long years of *limbo*. In the first of these thirteen years, Hannibal, aged thirty-one, was still a youthful hero. In his last year in Italy, Hannibal, aged forty-four, still had an unbroken record of victories but he looked like the middle-aged man he had become, with gray in his hair. His enemy Fabius, a generation older than Hannibal, had died, and a new generation of young Romans was taking over. Hannibal felt old.

HANNIBAL MUST HAVE FELT, throughout these thirteen years, a painful sense of anticlimax. Time and again, he thought back to his greatest moments—his first sighting of Italy from the Alpine pass, his view of the bloody field of Roman corpses at Cannae.

In particular, he remembered one moment in the dusk of that day at Cannae, when he surveyed the carnage and his officers were rushing back from the battlefield to congratulate him. One of his favorites, a fierce cavalry general named Maharbal, galloped up to the group, leaped off his horse, and shouted his congratulations. Then he took Hannibal's arm and pulled him close.

Let's not even pause, let's set off for Rome tonight to finish the job, said Maharbal. "Within five days you will take your dinner, in triumph, on the Capitol."

But Hannibal only smiled. "I commend your zeal," he said to Maharbal, "but I need time to weigh the plan."

Maharbal let his arm drop. With a whisper the other officers could not hear, he said, "You know, Hannibal, how to win a fight; you do not know how to use your victory."[2]

———

NEITHER HANNIBAL nor Maharbal ever brought it up again. On the one hand, Hannibal knew that Maharbal might be right. On the other hand, Hannibal also knew that his army, though flush with its greatest victory ever, was tired and hungry after Cannae and needed rest. And he knew that a triumphal march to Rome would have come to a hard stop at the city walls. If Rome was ready to surrender, it would do so whether he was at its gates or not. If Rome was not ready to surrender, showing up at its walls could not force it. Hannibal could not risk his reputation as a new Hercules, an invincible demigod of war, by showing up at the walls of Rome only for the world to discover that even he could not leap over them.

Instead, Hannibal tried to make it easier for Rome to surrender. He sent a Carthaginian envoy to explain his terms of peace to the Roman senate. Hannibal was prepared to allow the Romans to end the war with dignity, just as good strategy dictated.

But Fabius would have none of it. Under his counsel, the Roman senate did not even let the Carthaginian envoy enter the chamber to speak. Nor did the Romans consider ransoming their own prisoners or negotiating with Hannibal about anything at all. Yes, the Romans were wailing after Cannae. But Fabius picked them up out of their depression. The standards and protocols for becoming a senator were eased, and the empty seats in the senate chamber filled. Slaves and criminals were freed and drafted, along with teenage boys, to form new legions. Fabius was making his own gesture to Hannibal: this war was *not* over.

SO WHAT ON EARTH were these two men, Hannibal and Fabius, doing for thirteen years in the Italian countryside? Throughout these years, there were skirmishes, tricks, and ploys, with both sides scoring points. There were even a few small battles. But these were not big events anymore, because Fabius had instructed all Roman commanders to avoid decisive encounters. So the Romans attacked wherever Hannibal was not; Hannibal reconquered wherever he happened to be. But he could not be everywhere at once.

Because sieges at this time were so difficult for the attacker, cities were won or lost through betrayals and ruses. One city that had its share of back-and-forth was Tarentum, a Greek city on the southern coast of Italy. Like other Greek cities at the time, Tarentum was rich and cultured, with artists and philosophers, poets and playwrights. From the Tarentines' point of view, the Romans were brutes.

Sixty years earlier, it was the Tarentines who had invited the swashbuck-ling Greek warrior-king Pyrrhus of Epirus (in today's Albania) to invade Italy and kick out the Romans on their behalf. But the Romans had won that war, and both sides still held a grudge. The Romans kept Tarentine hostages in Rome, and when these were caught trying to escape, the Ro-mans flogged them and hurled them from a cliff to their deaths. The Tarentines were outraged and conspired secretly to evict the Roman gar-rison from the city.

Two Tarentine aristocrats, Philemenus and Nico, sneaked out of town at night and went to see Hannibal, who was encamped in the area. They offered him Tarentum, and Hannibal thanked them and began negotia-tions. To give them cover, Hannibal told them to take some Carthaginian cattle, so that they could claim they had gone out to raid. This became a little ritual. Several more times, Nico and Philemenus met with Hannibal, and each time they brought back cattle or game and made themselves quite a reputation in the city as hunters.

They prepared carefully. Philemenus now went in and out almost every night, always by one particular gate, and he always brought home some game, which he shared with the guards. Soon, the sentries knew him so well that they opened the gate as soon as they heard his familiar whistle. On the agreed-upon night, Philemenus approached the gate, carrying a boar so huge that he needed help from a few friends who happened to be Carthaginians. He whistled, and when the sentry opened a small side door and bent over to admire this juicy catch, Philemenus ran his hunting spear through him. The others killed the remaining guards, who were sleeping, and opened the gate to let in a bigger cohort of crack troops who had been hiding nearby.

At the same moment, Hannibal was leading another group to the main gate of Tarentum on the other side of town and lit a torch as a signal. Nico, who was waiting for them inside the city, answered with his own torch. He then took a group of conspirators down to the gate, murdered the sentries in their beds, and opened that gate for Hannibal and his column. Before anybody in Tarentum was awake, both Hannibal and Philemenus were marching their troops toward the marketplace. Hannibal ordered all the roads and intersections occupied and gave orders that all Romans were to be killed but all Tarentines were to be treated well. By the time the Roman garrison grasped what was happening, it was too late. The Roman commander jumped into a small boat and rowed with a few men to a narrow promontory where the city's fortress stood, and hunkered down. Tarentum was Hannibal's.[3]

It stayed Hannibal's for a couple of years, and then it was Fabius's turn. He used sex as his weapon. There was a soldier in his own army who was originally Tarentine and had a sister who was still inside the town. That woman doted on her brother but was also having a passionate affair with the commander of the Carthaginian garrison that now protected her city. So Fabius encouraged his soldier to pretend to defect from the Romans to his hometown. The man did so, entered Tarentum, and used his sister to become close friends with her lover, the Carthaginian commander. Over time he confided in his sister, whose loyalty to her brother was complete. Together, they worked on corrupting the Carthaginian commander. Over a period of time, the sister gave and withheld her sexual favors and played with the Carthaginian's mind until he was a nervous wreck. At the right moment, the brother moved in and promised the Carthaginian commander vast rewards from Fabius if he delivered the town into Roman hands. The commander agreed. The hard psychological work done, Fabius eventually ordered an assault on one side of Tarentum to draw the defenders away, then sent a smaller group to the walls on the other side, where the woman's brother and besotted Carthaginian lover were waiting with ladders.[4]

"As we won Tarentum, so have we lost it," reflected Hannibal when he heard about this treachery. In private he admitted to his closest advisers for the first time that it was now probably "impossible, with the forces he then had, to master Italy."[5]

As Fabius returned to Rome to celebrate a triumph—the second victory procession for Fabius in his life, and Rome's first since Hannibal had crossed the Alps—Hannibal pondered the bigger picture. He was still undefeated. But time was now on the Roman side. His crack Carthaginian, Libyan, Iberian, and Gallic force was slowly shrinking from casualties, illness, occasional defections, and even old age. During this entire thirteen-year limbo, Hannibal received only one reinforcement of troops, elephants, and weapons from Carthage.[6] Rome, on the other hand, armed and trained another batch of seventeen-year-olds every year.

BOTH HANNIBAL and Fabius understood that the invincible invader of Italy was now, paradoxically, *captive* in Italy, as though it were a shrinking *prison of success.* The fact that Hannibal was still officially successful made it impossible for him to escape this captivity. If he had suffered a military disaster of some sort, Hannibal would have had to evacuate Italy. It would have been humiliating, but he would have started over, with a different strategy, and the overall war might have gone in a new direction. But Hannibal was still victorious, and victors don't flee. So while he stayed put, he was probably aware of, and frustrated by, the irony of his dilemma.

At times during these years of strategic stalemate, it seemed as though Hannibal and Fabius were playing a game. Once Hannibal forged a letter to Fabius from the leaders of Metapontum, a city he held at the time, in which the elders appeared to offer to defect to Fabius and invited him to present himself at a specific time in a specific place to execute the handover. Two Metapontine messengers delivered the letter to Fabius, and Fabius fell for it, sending his own letter back to Metapontum, where it got into the hands of Hannibal, who made preparations to capture Fabius. Fabius started marching, but along the way he began to smell a rat—or rather the entrails of the animals he was sacrificing to divine the omens.[7] The two enemies had, over the course of their time as adversaries, become as intimate as aging spouses. They were onto each other.

THEIR LIVES WENT ON in other ways during these thirteen years. Hannibal, who usually lived the disciplined life of an ascetic, had a passionate affair with a prostitute in the town of Salapia, which gave the city a lurid notoriety that it merrily used to grow its tourism industry.[8] Fabius, meanwhile, was elected consul three more times, and the Romans, as a gesture of gratitude to him, also once gave the consulship to his son, also named Quintus Fabius Maximus. This probably pleased the elder Fabius more than anything else.

Fabius Senior proudly joined his son's army as second-in-command and mischievously tested Fabius Junior. It was the Roman custom that twelve lictors, or guards, accompany a consul, each carrying a bundle of sticks and an ax, the fasces, as signs of the consul's power to flog and behead. Anybody seeing the lictors had to dismount. But as Fabius Senior approached his son, he rode past eleven of his son's lictors, who had no idea how to handle this situation, until Fabius Junior understood the joke and gave a military order for his father to dismount and pay his respects. "My son, I wished to find out if you really knew that you were a consul," said his father, beaming with glee.[9]

But such moments of happiness did not last long in this era of war, and Fabius Junior was one of those who died, probably in battle. Fabius, the father, was the one to give his son's funeral oration. What was the purpose of absorbing the disaster of Hannibal, Fabius may have wondered, if his son wouldn't be alive to see the final triumph? Soon after his son's death, Fabius himself died.

Hannibal also suffered the deaths of loved ones. His brother Hasdrubal, who had been defending the Barcid home base in Iberia, marched with his army across the Alps, taking an easier route than Hannibal had, with the intention of joining Hannibal. He succeeded in crossing and arrived in Italy. But the Romans intercepted his messages to Hannibal and, without Hannibal's even knowing that his brother had arrived in Italy, massed their armies against Hasdrubal and surrounded him. Hasdrubal saw that all was lost and "setting spurs to his horse, galloped straight into the midst of a Roman cohort. There, still fighting, he found a death worthy of his father Hamilcar and his brother Hannibal,"[10] as a Roman historian put it.

One of the Roman generals cut off Hasdrubal's head and meticulously preserved it. He then marched his army back to where Hannibal was encamped. The Romans catapulted Hasdrubal's head over the lines and at Hannibal's feet to let him know what had transpired. Hannibal, seeing his little brother's head, broke down and cried, "Now, at last, I see the destiny of Carthage plain!"[11]

A few years later, Hannibal's other brother, Mago, the youngest of Hamilcar's three lion cubs, was commanding an army in northern Italy against the Romans. He was fighting in the front lines when a spear pierced his thigh. He fell and was carried "half dead" off the field. His army, seeing their commander down, gave up and was routed. Mago escaped to the nearby coast, where he received orders to sail back to Carthage. He boarded a ship, but just as he was passing Sardinia, that island that had once been Carthaginian but was now Roman, he died.[12] Hannibal had now lost both of his brothers.

THE MOMENT that perhaps captured the whole crushing sense of anticlimax that pervaded these thirteen years occurred just outside Rome itself. Hannibal had never actually seen this city that he had vowed as a nine-year-old to defeat. But an opportunity arose. A Roman army was besieging Capua again, the city that had been Hannibal's greatest prize. For purely pragmatic reasons, Hannibal decided to march on Rome, hoping that the Romans would withdraw from Capua and follow him to save their own city. At first this seemed to work. But once again, Fabius understood that Hannibal was bluffing and was intending only to relieve Capua, not to attack Rome. So, with steely nerve, Fabius sent word from Rome to the Roman army at Capua to stay there and continue its siege.[13]

And thus it was that Hannibal, for his first and only time, saw Rome. He arrived and pitched his camp three miles away. He then took two thousand horsemen and rode all the way up to the walls to take a closer look.[14]

Even though he was outside the walls and accompanied by a small force, the mere sight of him caused panic all over Rome. There must have been enormous turmoil inside Hannibal's mind as well. Here he was, close enough to Rome to see the individual stones of its walls and to hear the cries of its citizens, and yet so far from taking it.

The next morning, Hannibal deployed his army for battle. The Romans came out to engage. But the skies suddenly dumped torrential hail on both armies, forcing them to return to their camps. The next day, the armies deployed again, and again the hail came down.

Hannibal decided to see this as an omen. He told himself that he was here only to relieve Capua anyway and withdrew.

But two details rankled. One was that the Romans decided to send an army to Iberia as planned; these soldiers marched out of one Roman gate even as Hannibal was encamped in front of another. The other was that a land auction took place as scheduled inside Rome. One of the plots for sale was the land that Hannibal at that very moment happened to be camped on. As Hannibal heard later, the land sold for the normal price.[15] Clearly, nobody in Rome still thought that Hannibal, invincible or not, was winning. It is possible that Hannibal himself no longer did.

What Hannibal suffered in his thirties and early forties was "the catastrophe of success," as Tennessee Williams, the great American playwright, called it when the same affliction struck him with full force in

1944, at the age of thirty-three. What the great victory at Cannae was to Hannibal, *The Glass Menagerie* was to Williams. It was a soaring triumph. Overnight, Williams's play of tension and anguish in the American South, told with all the pain of his own upbringing and family life, catapulted him into the American cultural pantheon.

And what happened next? Williams was "thrust into sudden prominence, and from the precarious tenancy of furnished rooms about the country I was removed to a suite in a first-class Manhattan hotel."[16] The life that he had led and that had made him what he was, "a life of clawing and scratching along a sheer surface and holding on tight with raw fingers to every inch of rock higher than the one caught hold of before," was gone. Instead, all sorts of people were smothering him with praise. Luxury, leisure, flattery, wealth, and fame—all the trappings of success—arrived to dazzle and seduce him.

"I looked about me and was suddenly very depressed," Williams wrote. "I was already getting too fat for the suit which a fashionable acquaintance had selected for me." He felt "a spiritual dislocation." Success, Williams wrote, is "a kind of death, I think, and it can come to you in a storm of royalty checks beside a kidney-shaped pool in Beverly Hills or anywhere at all that is removed from the conditions that made you an artist." He was feeling just about as Hannibal did in the decadent comfort of his winter quarters at Capua.

Or as Amy Tan felt when *The Joy Luck Club* suddenly made her a success among novelists. "I expected failure," she recalls.[17] "So, I was more prepared for failure and for rejection than success. The success took me by surprise and it frightened me. On the day that there was a publication party for my book, I spent the whole day crying. I was scared out of my mind that my life was changing and it was out of my control and I didn't know why it was happening." She now realized that all the time prior to this new success she had actually been happy. She had been in a good marriage, with good friends and a comfortable life. Now, however, she had a vague idea that "things are going to get messed up here and I have no control over this."

"By the time it came to the second book, I was so freaked out, I broke out in hives," recalls Tan. "I couldn't sleep at night. I broke three teeth grinding my teeth. I had backaches. I had to go to physical therapy. I was a wreck!" Successful people in other areas of life feel a similar anxiety.[18] Athletes talk of the "*Sports Illustrated* jinx," the phenomenon of an athlete's appearing on the cover of *Sports Illustrated* and then fading into mediocrity. Show business has the "sophomore jinx," which sets in after a spectacular stage debut and makes performers flop when they try to repeat that initial success.

Then there is the paradox of the Nobel Prize, which Paul Samuelson, an economist and winner of the prize in 1970, has reflected on.[19] Alfred Nobel established the prize in 1895 to subsidize continued success by its winners. Instead, "the reverse of Nobel's wish is what actually happens," observed Samuelson. "After winners receive the award and adulation, they wither away into vainglorious sterility. More than that, they become pontificating windbags, preaching to the world on ethics and futurology, politics and philosophy. At circular tables, where they sit they believe to be the head of the table."

As you may have found if you have achieved a great success, triumph is a shock just as destabilizing as disaster. When disaster strikes, as Elisabeth Kübler-Ross observed, people go through a painful grief cycle, from denial to anger, bargaining and depression, before finally, if their character allows it, arriving at acceptance. Triumphant people also go through a cycle of largely unhelpful mental states. You might call it the "exultation cycle." And just as different people respond in different ways to disaster—some going into denial but not bargaining, others becoming angry but not depressed—people also react in their own individual ways to success.

HUBRIS, the arrogant overconfidence that comes with success or power, is by far the most notorious psychological response to triumph. We use the Greek word because the Greeks were obsessed with it. Their greatest playwrights—Aeschylus, Sophocles, and Euripides—told timeless stories about people who met ruin because of their hubris. Hubris is real: researchers have found that the feeling of power that comes with success makes people start believing, for example, that they can evade a venomous snake or survive a tornado, an airplane crash, or lung cancer.[20] Hubris may have been the reason Tiger Woods risked his marriage and career by having affairs with other women.

Hubris is also what brought down Eliot Spitzer, once a promising attorney general and governor of New York who fell from grace because of a sordid sex scandal. The son of a demanding and wealthy Manhattan real-estate tycoon, Spitzer soared through his education and early career, going from one success to the next. He went to Princeton and Harvard Law School, then became a prosecutor in Manhattan and in 1998 was elected New York's attorney general.

With a relentless and vengeful zeal he went after Wall Street's biggest tycoons. Banks, insurance companies, brokerages—everywhere, Spitzer spotted "betrayals of the public trust" that were "shocking" and "criminal."[21] He was on a mission to make New York ethical. In 2002, *Time* magazine called him "Crusader of the Year." His fans mused that he might one day become America's first Jewish president. When he ran for governor in 2006, *The New York Times* endorsed the "nationally known Sheriff of Wall Street" for his "formidable talents" and hoped that his victory might be "big enough to use as a cudgel in the State Capitol."[22] He won in a landslide.

Then, one Thursday in March 2008, less than two years into his term as governor, a routine press release by the United States Attorney for the Southern District of New York announced that a man and three women had been arrested on charges of running a high-class prostitution ring known as Emperors Club VIP. Oddly, the lead prosecutor was also the boss of the unit investigating corruption by elected officials. The next day, the government told Spitzer that he had been identified as "Client 9" of the Emperors Club. Spitzer took a long run in Central Park and walked his dogs with his wife, Silda Wall Spitzer.[23] The following day, he attended a white-tie dinner in Washington. The day after, Sunday, he told his wife.

On Monday, the political tornado began. On Wednesday, Spitzer held a three-minute press conference at his Manhattan office. His own sharp and severe features were under tight control. But his wife, Silda, standing by his side, looked at oblique angles into the room, with eyes red from crying. Spitzer confessed that he had slept with a prostitute and was resigning as governor. His political career appeared to be over.

Why had Spitzer thrown it all away? "I think he felt he was totally invulnerable and could do whatever he wanted and there would be no consequences," said Ed Koch, a former New York City mayor and a friend of Spitzer's.[24] This is the definition of hubris.

Perhaps Spitzer was even tempting his fate on purpose. He risked his career and family to have sex—for $1,000 an hour, roughly in the middle of the seven-diamond scale by which the club's prostitutes charged[25]— with "Angelina," his regular, or with "Kristen," described in the affidavit as "an American, petite, very pretty brunette, five feet five inches, and 105 pounds." In fact, Kristen was a twenty-two-year-old who, according to her MySpace page, had been abused as a child, changed her name several times, and dreamed of becoming a singer. Spitzer made almost a mockery of covering up his clandestine meetings. He used the name of a friend— without that friend's knowledge—to check into hotels. And he tried to disguise his payments with the sort of money transfers through sham companies that he knew the government would monitor, since he himself had once overseen this monitoring as attorney general. He also confirmed the details of his assignations by phone and was recorded on just the sort of wiretap that he had been a master of when rooting out white-collar crime. And he did all this one year after he himself had signed a law that lengthened jail time for johns from three months to a year.[26]

With several lives, including his own, shattered, Spitzer took his wife and three daughters on an extended trip to Southeast Asia. When he returned, he went back to work in his ailing father's firm. A politician who ran into him recalled Spitzer lamenting, "It's been horrible living a Greek tragedy."[27] And yet, many successful people have fallen prey to hubris in every generation since Sophocles, and will continue to do so in every future generation.

DISTRACTION MAY BE less spectacular than hubris in bringing success-ful people down, but simultaneously more common and harder to resist. As Amy Tan found, success leads to unforeseen opportunities. Somebody suggests that the book could become a movie. Somebody else suggests a television series. The mail starts bringing invitations to give speeches, to review other people's books, to do any number of things other than what had made her successful in the first place, which was to write. "You can get sucked into the idea that, 'Gosh, this is impressive. Maybe I should do this. It will look good,'" Tan says. But then she would no longer be doing what had made her successful, or at least not doing it *well*.

So the distractions of success seduce in the original sense of the word, which is "to lead astray." One academic study examined corporate bosses who became successful and famous, and found that they subsequently spent disproportionate amounts of time writing their memoirs, giving speeches, and joining boards of other companies. Perhaps most tellingly, their average handicap on the golf course fell from 15 to 13 after they became famous.[28] Meanwhile, their companies often began failing.

PARANOIA BEGINS when a successful person suspects the motivations of the people around him. After *The Glass Menagerie*, Tennessee Williams noticed that his human relationships were deteriorating. "Sincerity and kindliness seemed to have gone out of my friends' voices. I suspected them of hypocrisy. I stopped calling them, stopped seeing them. I was impatient of what I took to be inane flattery. I got so sick of hearing people say, 'I loved your play!' that I could not say thank you any more." Over time,

"I no longer felt any pride in the play itself but began to dislike it, probably because I felt too lifeless inside ever to create another."

Amy Tan had a similar experience. "I could already see how people were treating me differently," she recalls. "That's the scary thing. You know, when people say, 'How has success changed you?' you have to say, 'No. How have people changed toward you as the result of success?' And 'How have you dealt with that change in how people have changed toward you?' That's the most difficult thing."

BUT ARGUABLY the subtlest and thus most insidious of all of the effects of success may be the strange sense of *captivity* that Hannibal experienced. Success appears to imprison the *imagination* of many people who achieved it.

How *did* a Pablo Picasso, for instance, have the idea to draw a group of prostitutes in a brothel as though their faces were primitive African masks and their limbs disembodied "cubes"? Nothing of the sort had ever been done before. It was a leap of the imagination, a wild and shocking idea, an idea that required his imagination to roam *free* and unrestrained. His triumph came out of that freedom.

And how did an aikido master such as Morihei Ueshiba manage, time after time, to achieve the inner peace and balance that allowed him, as he put it, to merge with the energy of his opponent and throw him? It was a state of hyperalertness but not tension; a mixture of *confidence* and *relaxation*. Ueshiba's mental state was that proverbial "zone" that all athletes know when they function at peak performance, a state I have slipped into a few times while skiing and that feels like freedom.

Fighters, artists, writers, thinkers, speakers, and lovers all know this "zone." They may call it "flow," as when their confidence and relaxation allow them to harmonize with a situation and excel in it. During relaxation, the brain is bathed in chemicals that allow its neurons to fire at frequencies where *new* connections are established. This is "lateral thinking," and ideas are born. This is the state of mental freedom that leads to success.

But once success arrives, it subverts that relaxed and confident feeling and replaces it with anxiety, a sense of vertigo. People who are climbing are looking up, not down, and are totally focused on the ascent, as the young and aspiring Tennessee Williams was while "clawing and scratching along a sheer surface and holding on tight with raw fingers to every inch of rock higher than the one caught hold of before." But once they get to the top, they pause to look down to see where they are, and although the view may be great, this is when a paralyzing vertigo sets in. Adrenaline pours into the brain and the relaxed, free, lateral thinking stops. It is re-placed by anxious, defensive, and linear thinking. The "zone" is locked, the "flow" is interrupted, the ideas stop.

Thus Amy Tan perceived the height of her success as a "plateau," a lofty, windy, and exposed place that now had to be defended. And being on this plateau felt like entrapment, with her imagination as the prisoner. She had writer's block. "I started a second novel seven times and I had to throw them away," Tan remembers. "You know, a hundred pages here, two hundred pages there and I'd say, 'Is this what they liked in *The Joy Luck Club*? Is this the style, is this the story? No, I must write something com-pletely different. I must write no Chinese characters to prove that I'm multi-talented.' Or 'No, I must write this way in a very erudite way to show I have a way to use big words.' It's both rebellion and conformity that attack you with success." It feels like prison.

Albert Einstein entered just such a prison in about 1925, when he was in his forties and at the height of his success. He had spent three decades changing forever the way we think about space, time, light, matter, and energy. From then on, however, he would spend another three decades in a frustrating mental prison, unable to accept the changes he himself had brought about, unwilling to break out of the straitjacket of his own mind, utterly stuck in his search for the answers to questions of physics that he himself had raised.

Born into a middle-class Jewish family in southwestern Germany, Einstein as a child had more in common with Fabius than with Hannibal. He was slow to start speaking and slow to learn. His family called him *"der Depperte,"* the dummy. One of his teachers said that he would never amount to much. Instead, Einstein would later say that his slow development was a boon to his imagination, rather as it was for my great-uncle Ludwig Erhard, who was also mediocre in school but who in later years grasped big concepts of economics with greater ease than others. Usually, only toddlers wonder about things such as space and time and then forget to be amazed by them once they grow up. But Einstein, having started thinking about these phenomena relatively late, never ceased to be amazed by the mysteries of the world.

He was incapable of the rote learning required in school and, like Uncle Lulu and Pablo Picasso, had very little respect for authority. At least one of his teachers wanted Einstein ejected from class because of his insolence. When Einstein pointed out that he had not actually done anything wrong, the teacher replied, "Yes, that is true, but you sit there in the back row and smile, and your mere presence here spoils the respect of the class for me." Later he would write to a friend that "a foolish faith in authority is the worst enemy of truth."[29] "Imagination is more important than knowledge," he said another time. "Long live impudence!" he exulted.[30]

Impudent and irreverent but astonished by the universe around him, Einstein thus let his imagination roam freely. And what sorts of things did he imagine? All sorts of things, including, when he was sixteen, what it would be like to ride alongside a beam of light at the speed of light. His musings on that imponderable would lead to great things. Other thought experiments over the years included visualizing bolts of lightning, moving trains, elevators accelerating through space and painters falling downward through them, two-dimensional blind beetles crawling on curved branches, and much, much else.[31]

He felt *free*, not only intellectually but also socially, which made him disarmingly spontaneous. Once, while he was at college in Zurich, he was at home with his landlady and heard somebody playing a Mozart piano sonata. He asked who it was and his landlady told him that it was an old woman in the attic next door. Einstein grabbed his violin and dashed out without putting on a tie. "You can't go like that, Herr Einstein," the land-lady cried. But he was already running into the neighboring house, where the old woman looked up in shock. "Go on playing," Einstein pleaded. A few moments later, the air was filled with the sounds of a violin accom-panying the Mozart sonata.[32]

FOR MANY YEARS, his free spirit did not earn Einstein conventional suc-cess. He was the only person graduating in his year and course at his university who was not offered a job in academia.[33] He wrote postcards with postage-paid reply attachments to professors all over Europe, but in most cases he received no answer at all, never mind a positive one. "I leave no stone unturned and do not give up my sense of humor," he wrote to a friend.[34] To make a living, he worked as a clerk in the Swiss patent office in Bern. Then, in 1905, his life and, literally, the world changed abruptly.

In the space of just a few months during that year, Einstein wrote five consecutive and surprisingly short papers that upended human under-standing of the universe.[35] In the first, Einstein argued that light is not only a wave, as conventional wisdom had it, but also a stream of particles called quanta. In the second, Einstein determined the size of atoms. In the third, he explained the weird jittery motions of tiny particles, in the process proving that atoms and molecules actually exist. In the fourth, which he regarded as "only a draft at this point," he proposed a "modification of space and time" that would become known as the special theory of relativ-ity and replace classical, Newtonian physics. Soon after, he elaborated with a fifth paper, which explained the relationship between energy and mass and contained the most famous formula in science, $E = mc^2$. The year 1905 would be called a "miracle year."

With his willingness to think outside the proverbial box, the freedom of his spirit, and his utter disregard for what others considered reasonable, Einstein began a revolution in physics that spilled over into the way humans think about their world. His first paper in the series spawned quantum mechanics, which dominated the rest of twentieth-century physics. His special theory of relativity, though fiendishly hard to understand, shocked laypeople, who had always assumed that space and time were absolute. It took another decade for Einstein to expand his special theory to a general theory of relativity. Space-time was warped and infinitely weird, he explained to a spellbound world. All of this seemed too fantastic to be believable.

His ultimate triumph came on May 29, 1919, soon after he turned forty. Since 1905, Einstein had become well known among scientists and had moved to ever better academic positions, from Zurich to Prague, back to Zurich, then to Berlin, the world capital of theoretical physics at the time. But he had not had an opportunity to *prove* that his otherworldly theories were correct. This would change, however, with the next eclipse of the sun, which was due to occur on that day in 1919.

Einstein's theory of relativity predicted that light bends with the space through which it travels, and that space itself curves around massive objects. During the solar eclipse, the light of a star whose position was known would briefly be visible behind the darkened sun. Since its light had to travel past the sun, it should bend, making the star appear slightly out of place. And this it did, exactly as Einstein had predicted. Relativity, and Einstein, were right. He himself was now the star.

Einstein became a celebrity. He looked the part, with a humorous glint in his eyes, a mustache, and a shock of hair that was already whitening into the chaotic hirsute halo that would become the indelible image of the mad professor. He flirted with the world's press and dropped witty aphorisms. In 1921, he even went on a tour of America, not unlike a modern rock star's, with reporters hanging on him at every stop. He visited President Warren Harding, who confessed that he did not understand relativity at all, which hardly mattered. Einstein's fame and popularity only grew.[36] Einstein was the guest of honor at movie premieres and hung out with Hollywood stars such as Charlie Chaplin. In 1933 he moved to Princeton, New Jersey, where he stayed for the rest of his life, during which the public would remain in love with its idea of Albert Einstein.

BUT THERE WERE subtle hints that Einstein's success was, right from the start of his fame, turning into what Tennessee Williams would have described as a catastrophe. Einstein had a love-hate relationship with publicity and would complain to friends that he felt "hounded by the press and other riff-raff" and that "it's so dreadful that I can barely breathe anymore, not to mention getting around to any sensible work." His success was *distracting* him. "I dream I'm burning in Hell and the postman is the Devil eternally roaring at me, hurling new bundles of letters at my head because I have not yet answered the old ones," he complained.[37] He told another friend that "with fame I become more and more stupid, which of course is a very common phenomenon."[38]

For a few more years after the solar eclipse Einstein continued to make contributions to physics, but his genius gradually dried up. It did so in an ironic way. His own first paper in 1905 on light as quanta, along with the work of another physicist, Max Planck, had launched the quantum revolution in physics, and a new generation of up-and-coming young scientists was building on it and pursuing it in all directions. They were freethinking, irreverent, imaginative, iconoclastic, and in every other way exactly as Einstein had been a few decades earlier. And Einstein could not handle it. As he grew older, he became conservative and his mind closed. He resisted the ideas of these cutting-edge physicists about quantum mechanics until he died.

What bothered him so profoundly about these ideas was that they pointed toward fundamental uncertainties in the universe. At the smallest scales, deep inside atoms, particles were no longer definitely here or definitely there, definitely moving this way or that, but rather *probably* here and *probably* moving there, possibly even interacting with other particles far away. Einstein could not accept these concepts. "God does not play dice with the universe," he said again and again, and closed his mind to an entire line of thinking. He found the new ideas "quite intolerable," as he told his friend Max Born, one of the physicists of the younger generation. "In that case, I would rather be a cobbler, or even an employee of a gaming house, than a physicist."[39]

Such was his personality that Einstein never directed his frustration at people but only at their ideas. The ringleader of the new generation of physicists was Niels Bohr, a shy and gangly Dane. Bohr met Einstein for the first time in 1920, when he visited Berlin and showed up at Einstein's door with Danish cheese and butter. They instantly started discussing physics and hit it off. The next year, on the way back from receiving the Nobel Prize in Physics in Stockholm, Einstein stopped in Copenhagen to see Bohr. Bohr picked him up at the train station and they boarded a streetcar and immediately began discussing physics. "We took the streetcar and talked so animatedly that we went much too far," Bohr later recalled. And thus "we rode to and fro," engrossed in conversation, according to Bohr. "I can well imagine what the people thought about us."[40]

But despite their shared enthusiasm for physics, they disagreed on everything, which exasperated both of them. "Einstein, Einstein, Einstein," Bohr muttered to himself after each frustrating debate.

THE ROLES HAD, in an ironic way, reversed, with the quantum physicists becoming the freethinkers and Einstein the inflexible curmudgeon. Once Einstein was debating with Werner Heisenberg, a student of Bohr's who was in his twenties and became famous for his "Heisenberg uncertainty principle," which said that the properties of physics inside atoms were uncertain, subject to probability. Heisenberg was making his points with the sort of thought experiments that Einstein had once used.

"But," Einstein protested, "you don't seriously believe" your thought experiments?

"Isn't that precisely what you have done with relativity?" Heisenberg asked with some surprise.

"Possibly I did use this kind of reasoning," Einstein admitted, "but it is nonsense all the same."[41]

Where once Einstein had defied and ignored the scientific establishment and broken new ground with his original and shocking ideas, he himself was now the establishment. "He could no longer take in certain new ideas in physics which contradicted his own firmly held philosophical convictions,"[42] said Max Born. "Many of us regard this as a tragedy."[43]

Einstein himself was well aware of what the new young heroes of physics thought of him. "The current generation sees in me both a heretic and a reactionary who has, so to speak, outlived himself."[44] One time he admitted to Louis de Broglie, another of his colleagues, "I must seem like an ostrich who forever buries its head in the relativistic sand in order not to face the evil quanta."[45]

Contemplating the paradox of his continued fame in mainstream culture and his intellectual stagnation, he told a friend that "the intellect gets crippled, but glittering renown is still draped around the calcified shell."[46] He lamented "the age of stagnation and sterility when one laments the revolutionary spirit of the young." Einstein compared his intellectual limbo to "being in an airship in which one can cruise around in the clouds but cannot see clearly how one can return to reality, i.e., earth."[47]

But he remained stubborn. He had fixated not only on the idea that quantum mechanics was wrong but also that there had to be one single formula that would explain everything, a "unified" theory. Though Einstein loved simplicity and elegance, his math got more and more complex. There were false hopes of success along the way, which turned out to be dead ends and only led to more frustration. But he persevered. "I feel like a kid who cannot get the hang of the ABCs, even though, strangely enough, I do not abandon hope. After all, one is dealing here with a sphinx, not with a willing streetwalker."[48]

When Einstein died in Princeton at the age of seventy-six, twelve dog-eared pages of corrected and crossed-out equations were strewn around his bed. His success had hardened a mind that once was supple. It had imprisoned an imagination that once was free. He never found what he was looking for. "To punish me for my contempt for authority," Einstein once said, success "made me an authority myself."[49]

NINE

THE LIBERATION
OF FAILURE

I didn't see it then, but it turned out that getting fired from Apple was the best thing that could have ever happened to me. The heaviness of being successful was replaced by the lightness of being a beginner again, less sure about everything. It freed me to enter one of the most creative periods of my life.

—Steve Jobs

Publius Cornelius Scipio was just a teenager[1] when he first encountered the disastrous force of Hannibal at the skirmish of the Ticinus River, the first clash of the Carthaginians and Romans in Italy. Scipio was serving in the Roman army under the command of his father, also named Publius Cornelius Scipio, who was consul at the time. His father had put him in a group of horsemen and kept him at a safe distance from the fighting. But as the young Scipio watched from a hill overlooking the battle, the Carthaginian cavalry routed the Romans, wounded his father, and prepared to kill him. With the unthinking abandon of a teenager, Scipio galloped down the hill to attack the Carthaginians. The Roman riders charged with protecting him had no choice but to race after him. This sudden and unexpected charge momentarily stunned the Carthaginians, and in the chaos Scipio was able to rescue his father and retreat. Young Scipio gained a reputation for precocious bravery.[2]

As a Roman nobleman, Scipio continued to serve in the Roman army, and so became a witness to the three great massacres at the hands of Hannibal—at the Trebia River, at Lake Trasimene, and at Cannae.[3] Somehow, he was among the few survivors in each case and yet preserved his reputation for valor. During the night after Cannae, for example, he was escaping with a few other legionaries. There was talk of abandoning Italy by ship and seeking refuge at some foreign court. When Scipio, eighteen or nineteen at the time, heard the others say this, he drew his sword and swore to cut down any Roman who tried to desert. He then made every man in the group renew his oath of loyalty to Rome.[4]

SCIPIO EXPERIENCED these disasters differently from how the much older Fabius did. Scipio was too young to have known adult life *without* the specter of Hannibal. To Scipio, Hannibal was simply a force of nature, a part of the world, like lightning, storms, or floods. Being angry at Hannibal would have struck Scipio as pointless—like being angry at the weather or earthquakes. In fact, as Scipio thought about Hannibal, he probably not only failed to hate him but admired him.

The truth was that Hannibal and Scipio were remarkably similar. Both came from noble families, both had illustrious fathers who were great commanders, both had brothers who were brave soldiers in their own right but less gifted than they themselves were. Both felt a special calling to achieve great things, and both were keenly aware of their own charisma. Both spoke and appreciated Greek culture and literature; Scipio later even grew his hair as the Greeks did in those days, to the chagrin of conservative Romans. Hannibal and Scipio, about a decade apart in age, also shared a subtle code of chivalry.

Scipio, as the younger man, also understood that Hannibal was the best general of his time, and thus the example to emulate. Scipio revered his father and uncle, both Roman commanders, but he didn't believe for a minute that they were his best teachers. Instead, Scipio looked to his enemy Hannibal for lessons. From his perspective as a soldier in the losing army, he observed Hannibal's every move and every tactic, never letting his emotions—anger, grief—get in the way of gaining valuable insights.

Thus he took note of the way Hannibal used his surroundings—lakes, rivers, hills, forests, fog—as if they were soldiers under his command. He analyzed the feints and gestures Hannibal used to provoke the Romans into his traps, and the way he instilled passion in soldiers from foreign lands who spoke alien tongues and felt no inherent loyalty to Carthage. He observed how Hannibal combined great generosity and mercy toward the local populations of Italy with brutal retribution when it was necessary to crush resistance. Scipio, from a distance, became more than Hannibal's enemy: he became his disciple.

Scipio also observed his own leaders, and not only his father and uncle, who went to Iberia as commanders to attack Hannibal's brothers. He watched the great Fabius and how he absorbed the disaster of Hannibal and kept Rome alive when extermination seemed imminent. As he grew up, Scipio must have had deep respect for Fabius, and even for his son, with whom he served at Cannae.

But Scipio always felt that Fabius could offer only *part* of the answer to Hannibal. Yes, somebody had to absorb these great blows. But ultimately, a Fabius could only prevent disaster from becoming extinction; he could not turn it upside down, into victory. That, Scipio decided with the self-assurance of youth, would be *his* job. It had to be a younger man, one willing to take a fresh look at Hannibal, somebody willing radically to reinvent Roman strategy. Like Hannibal when he planned his invasion of Italy, Scipio believed that the answer was to do something so bold and so unexpected that his enemy would hardly be able to imagine it.

SCIPIO'S OPPORTUNITY came wrapped in personal disaster, the worst one to strike yet. When he was about twenty-three, the news arrived from

Iberia that his father and his uncle had been killed in two separate defeats against Hasdrubal and Mago, the younger brothers of Hannibal. The Barcas had thus wiped out the patriarchs of the Scipiones.

Scipio was devastated. He had an older brother, Lucius, who became the official head of the clan under Roman custom. But Lucius, although well-meaning, was no leader—and everybody knew it. Scipio decided that his time had come to step forward. This was itself iconoclastic. Roman custom required a minimum age of thirty for even the most junior public office—that of quaestor, or treasurer—and forty-two for consul. Scipio, however, was only twenty-four.

It was now 211 BCE, and with Hannibal and his army encamped south of Rome, Italy was naturally the main theater of the war. Distant Iberia seemed to be well defended by the Carthaginians and for most ambitious Roman commanders a mere distraction from the real threat at home. So nobody wanted to take the place of Scipio's father and uncle and go to command the remnants of their armies.

Scipio suddenly stepped forward before the assembly, stood on a little mound where everybody could see him, and declared his candidacy. The crowd was immediately enthralled by the romantic symbolism of sending the son and nephew of the fallen generals to lead the Roman army in Iberia, and by Scipio's confident and commanding presence. But there were objections. Some speakers pointed out that it was technically illegal to make Scipio commander, since he was both too young and a private citizen who had never held a senior magistracy. Others argued that it was morbid to send Scipio to fight atop the graves of his father and uncle.

Despite these reasonable objections, Scipio managed to charm his way into the command. He arrived in Iberia the following year.[5]

WHY IBERIA? Avenging his father and uncle was part of it. But the real reason was that Scipio, alone among the Romans, already had an idea that Iberia was not a strategic sideshow in the war against Hannibal. In fact, Scipio believed Iberia could become the stepping-stone to Roman victory.

Scipio knew it was the power base of Hannibal's family, the land of silver mines and Carthage's bravest mercenaries. Scipio wanted to take all this away from Hannibal, to make Hannibal feel weak in his back and to distract him from Italy.

But Scipio was seeing even farther ahead than that. Once he captured Iberia, he wanted to invade Africa itself and attack Carthage. Scipio was thus planning exactly the opposite sweep that Hannibal had made seven years earlier. Hannibal had used Iberia to invade Italy, keeping Carthage safe in Africa. Scipio wanted to use Iberia as a prelude to invading Africa, in order to force Hannibal to leave Italy and meet him in Africa, so that Rome would be safe again. As a plan it was so bold that Scipio dared not talk about it yet with anybody except his trusted deputy, Laelius.

FIRST, OF COURSE, Scipio had to conquer Iberia. He started as Hannibal had once started: by winning the respect of his father's and his uncle's armies. Scipio looked like his father, as Hannibal resembled Hamilcar. He also had charm and a natural confidence. Rather than demote or push aside the older officers who had led the army in the absence of a commander, he praised and promoted them.

Then he sized up the situation. The Carthaginians had three big armies in Iberia, one led by Hannibal's younger brother, Hasdrubal, the other by the youngest brother, Mago, and the third by an unrelated commander named Hasdrubal Gisco. The Iberian tribes were still loyal to the Carthaginians, whom they regarded as the winners since the deaths of the elder Scipiones.

While observing Hannibal in Italy, Scipio had long pondered the paradox that Hannibal had not been more successful in conquering the whole country even though he kept defeating Rome's armies. What eluded Hannibal for victory, Scipio understood, was Rome itself. Here in Spain, Scipio therefore decided, he would not attack any of the Carthaginian armies, at least not yet. This idea was counterintuitive: armies were meant to confront armies.

Instead, Scipio fixed his attention on Cartagena, "New Carthage," the Carthaginian capital in Spain. It was the Carthaginians' treasury, their granary, and their arsenal in Spain. And it was the city where the Carthaginians kept hundreds of hostages from the royal families of the Iberian tribes, as collateral to keep the tribes loyal. "In that one town you will have taken the whole of Spain," Scipio told his troops when they arrived at Cartagena. "In it are the hostages of all the great princes and peoples."[6] There was only one problem. Sieges, as everybody knew, didn't succeed.

It was characteristic of Scipio, as it is of other visionaries in history, that he simply ignored this conventional wisdom. No matter that Hannibal himself had taken eight months to take the small city of Saguntum at the start of the war. No matter that the Greeks had taken ten years to sack Troy, and even then only by hiding in a wooden horse. Scipio would simply have to create the equivalent of a Trojan horse on the first day of his siege.

SCIPIO'S TROJAN HORSE turned out to be the tides. Like Hannibal, Scipio had been meticulous in his reconnaissance of the local land and people. While interviewing fishermen, he learned that Cartagena, which was on a promontory jutting out into a bay, was protected on one side by the open sea and on the other by a shallow lagoon.[7] At high tide, that lagoon provided as much safety from a siege army as the sea. But during the ebb, the water briefly became so shallow that men could wade across the lagoon.

Once he knew the precise timing of the tides, Scipio planned for the crucial moment. When the time came, Scipio first attacked Cartagena from the narrow isthmus of land, walking among his soldiers to motivate them, protected only by three men holding shields.[8] Again and again, the Romans scaled ladders to mount Cartagena's walls, but the ladders broke and were toppled by the defenders.

With the attention of the Carthaginians thus fixed on these walls, Scipio personally led a group of five hundred soldiers with more ladders to the lagoon. There he told his men that Neptune, the god of the sea, had appeared to him in a dream.[9] As if on cue, the tide began to recede, sucking the water out of the lagoon. The Roman soldiers gaped in awe. Then they waded across the lagoon and placed their ladders against an undefended stretch of Cartagena's wall. They scaled the wall, then fought their way on the inside to the main gate, opened it, and let in the main Roman force.

What followed was horrible—a bloodbath. It was a Roman custom to massacre conquered populations to break the will of the defenders and others elsewhere who would hear about it. The Romans poured into Cartagena and killed every man, woman, and child they saw. But as soon as Scipio believed that there was no more opposition, he ordered the trumpets to give the signal, and the entire Roman army throughout Cartagena stopped the slaughter. It was a remarkable display of discipline. The Romans then set about plundering the conquered city in an orderly, almost bureaucratic, way.[10]

With Cartagena's wealth, weapons, and manpower, Scipio replenished and strengthened his own army for the struggles to come. But he was most interested in the Iberian hostages the Carthaginians kept in Cartagena. Scipio freed them. To an old woman who hinted that the Carthaginians had raped the younger women and pleaded with Scipio for better treatment, he promised that the Romans under his command would treat the female hostages as if they were his own sisters and daughters.[11]

When his soldiers brought him the most beautiful woman of them all—as spoils of war, they thought—Scipio discovered that she was betrothed to a young Iberian chieftain named Allucius. He sent for this man. "I address you as one young man talking to another, so that what I have to say may cause neither of us embarrassment," Scipio said to Allucius. "Your bride has been treated under my protection with all the delicacy she would have found in the house of her own parents, your own parents-to-be; she has been kept for you, an inviolate gift, worthy of myself and of you. The only payment I would ask in return is that you should be a friend of the Roman people."[12]

Allucius was beside himself with relief. So was his bride, presumably. When the girl's parents came with gold to ransom her, Scipio told them that no ransom was necessary. The parents put the gold at his feet as a gift. Scipio promptly passed it on to Allucius to top off the dowry. Allucius and his bride then went home for a brief honeymoon. But a few days later, Allucius returned with fourteen hundred crack horsemen from his tribe, pledging his service to Scipio.

SCIPIO'S FIRST GREAT TRIUMPH already showed what would make him special in the years to come. He had drawn all the best lessons from Hannibal. As Hannibal had used a river, the Trebia, or a lake, Trasimene, to his advantage, Scipio had used a lagoon. As Hannibal had fixed the attention of the Romans on a point of his choosing in order to attack them at another point they neglected, Scipio had drawn Cartagena's defenders to one side of the city's wall in order to scale it on the other side. As Hannibal had shown mercy and generosity to the Gauls in northern Italy to woo them away from the Romans, Scipio had charmed the Iberian tribes into defecting from Carthage and joining Rome.

But Scipio had done more than merely copy Hannibal. He had improved upon him. Whereas Hannibal, like most generals of the time, feared and avoided sieges, Scipio began his first campaign with a siege and won it in a single day. And while Hannibal had missed or played down the strategic importance of Rome, Scipio built his entire strategy on taking the Iberian capital. It was becoming clear that in Scipio the Romans had found a very un-Roman leader. They had found an innovator.

But the three Carthaginian armies were still in Spain. Scipio first encountered Hannibal's brother Hasdrubal. Showing how well he had studied Hannibal's tactics, Scipio outmaneuvered Hasdrubal and threatened to encircle his army. Hasdrubal, who was already planning to reinforce his brother in Italy and win the war there, retreated from Scipio, left Iberia, and marched toward Italy.

When news of this Roman victory spread in Iberia, several tribes offered to celebrate Scipio as a new king. But this made Scipio uncomfortable. He was a Roman, and at the time, the Romans were proud republicans who hated the memory of their own kings. If word got back to Rome that Scipio had allowed himself to be crowned, it would be political death. Besides, Scipio did not care much for official titles. So he declined the Iberian offer.[13]

There was another little glimpse into his character—of his generosity, his humanity, even his sense of humor, and his talent for spotting opportunities. Among the prisoners was a handsome African boy, a Numidian, who claimed he was of royal blood. Scipio was intrigued and sent for him. The boy was named Massiva and had come from Africa with his uncle Masinissa, who was a Numidian king fighting with the Carthaginians. Masinissa didn't allow his nephew to fight, but Massiva had stolen a horse and armor and fought anyway—Scipio probably chuckled as he remembered himself doing something similar—but Massiva's horse fell and the Romans captured the young man.

Scipio liked the boy and also grasped intuitively that Masinissa, the boy's uncle, was a man who might become useful. He gave Massiva a gold ring and brooch, a tunic, a cloak, and a horse, and sent him off to his uncle with a cavalry escort for his safety.[14] Before long, Masinissa became Rome's most loyal ally in Africa. Scipio, like many successful people, had an eye for opportunities where others saw none, as well as a capacity for well-timed generosity.

AFTER THESE SUCCESSES, the fighting paused for more than a year, as both Scipio and the two remaining Carthaginian commanders consolidated their areas of Iberia. But in 206 BCE, Mago and Hasdrubal Gisco joined forces and went on the attack. They met at a place called Ilipa, near modern Seville.

For several days the Carthaginians and the Romans marched out of their camps, deployed their entire armies in battle formation, stared at each other menacingly, then retired for the night, without a single javelin thrown. Scipio probably thought about what Hannibal might do in this situation. Day after day, he deployed his army in exactly the same order:

the Roman legions in the center, the Iberian allies on the wings. The Carthaginians had their own order, which they also did not change. Scipio realized that a habit had formed on both sides. And whenever a habit is formed, there's an opportunity for surprise.

The next day Scipio changed tactics. Instead of marching out late in the morning as before, he got his army up early, made them eat in the dark, then deployed them at dawn. This was the first surprise for the Carthaginians, who suddenly had to deploy in great haste, before eating. Hannibal had done exactly this to the Romans at the Trebia, and Scipio remembered vividly what effect this had had on the Romans throughout the long day of fighting.

The next surprise, which the Carthaginians noticed only when they were already in their usual formation, was that Scipio had reversed the order of his legions.[15] The Roman elite was now on the wings and the Iberian allies were in the middle. Once a big army was lined up, it was difficult to change its formation, so the Carthaginians merely stood there and wondered what Scipio's shuffle might mean. Scipio then waited. As the hours passed, the Carthaginians got hungrier and more nervous. It was clear that something was about to happen, but they did not know what.

It was afternoon when Scipio gave the order to advance in a simple but strange pattern. His middle, made up of his Iberian allies, was to march forward very slowly. His two Roman wings were to jog, rather than march, diagonally to the left and right, running right past the Carthaginian lines. The Carthaginians saw this, but could not divide in two to face these flanking maneuvers, because of Scipio's Iberian allies coming toward their center. Transfixed, they stood in place as the Romans surrounded them.

Then it was butchery. The Carthaginians tried to flee, but Scipio had posted outposts along the escape routes, and during the night and following day, his cavalry pursued the Carthaginians and cornered them until the Roman infantry caught up and finished the job.

Once again, Scipio had paid homage to his master by surpassing him. This victory in some ways combined all of Hannibal's tactics. Scipio starved the enemy as Hannibal had done at the Trebia. Then he transfixed the enemy's center and encircled him as Hannibal had done at Cannae. But while Hannibal had not followed up his victory at Cannae by sweeping up the routed and fleeing army—as Scipio recalled from his own escape—Scipio had also ensured that the deadliest and most decisive part of his victory would occur after the actual battle, as the retreating enemy was completely annihilated. Only the commanders and their personal bodyguards escaped. The Carthaginian armies had been crushed. In four years, Scipio had conquered Iberia.

SCIPIO VIEWED this stunning achievement as just the first phase in his bigger plan, which was the invasion of Africa so that Hannibal would have to leave Italy. Even before discussing this plan with the Roman senate, he began preparations. Masinissa, the Numidian king and Carthaginian ally whose nephew Scipio had saved, came to his side, which was an important diplomatic gain, since a large part of what is today Algeria would now support Scipio in his African campaign.

Another Numidian king and Carthaginian ally, Syphax, seemed to have an open mind, so Scipio took a great risk and sailed with only two ships across the hostile sea from Iberia to Africa to negotiate with him. A fleet led by Hasdrubal Gisco, the Carthaginian commander whose army Scipio had just annihilated in Spain, spotted Scipio's ships and set off in pursuit. Gisco and Scipio arrived in Syphax's harbor at the same time.

This led to a bizarre situation. The two mortal enemies stepped off their ships and simultaneously paid their respects to Syphax. Syphax, flattered and amused, invited both to dinner. Indeed, he made Scipio and Hasdrubal Gisco sit together. This was awkward for a moment, but Scipio, with his sophistication, humor, and charm, entertained both Syphax and his enemy so magnanimously that both men were impressed. When Scipio sailed back to Iberia, he, rather than Hasdrubal Gisco, had a treaty of alliance with Syphax, at least for the time being.[16]

Scipio then returned to Rome to declare Iberia conquered just in time for the next consular election. Because he was too young, the senate did not grant him the right to enter Rome in a triumph. But he was now the hero of the people, and they swept him into office as one of the two consuls for the year 205 BCE.

Yet Scipio noticed, somewhat to his surprise, a new resistance. His rise had been sudden, fast, and steep. Some of the senators and aristocrats distrusted or, worse, envied him. The most severe critic, as it turned out, was old Fabius.

JUST AS, eleven years earlier, Fabius had faced bitter opposition from his Roman political rivals when he proposed a new strategy to cope with Hannibal, Fabius himself now became that bitter opposition to Scipio. Old but revered, Fabius got up in the senate, with the young and virile Scipio sitting in front of him.

"I shall be blamed for my natural tendency to avoid precipitate action, which the young are at liberty to call fear or indolence," Fabius said with self-deprecating humor. But don't think that I am jealous or envious, Fabius continued, "for how can I compete with a man who is younger even than my own son?" Some senators nodded, since Fabius, a former dictator of Rome and five-time consul, clearly had nothing to prove. Others probably glanced at Fabius Junior, his son, wondering whether the elder Fabius might not in fact begrudge Scipio his success precisely because it eclipsed that of his own heir.

"I prevented Hannibal from defeating us, and thus enabled you who are young and strong to bring him finally to his knees," Fabius continued, looking at the younger men in his audience.[17] Then Fabius opened a direct attack on Scipio. "Tell us no more that when you have crossed to Africa Hannibal will surely follow you; cut short those devious ways; march direct to where Hannibal at this moment is, and fight him there." Fabius had walked to Scipio's seat and was looking straight at him. "Beat Hannibal here first, then cross the sea and capture Carthage." Some senators must have squirmed at this hostile tone. "Just suppose, I say, that Hannibal is victorious and marches on Rome. Are we then, and not before, to recall you from Africa?" Fabius asked mockingly. "Remember, too, that even in Africa the fortunes of war may be fickle; take warning from your own house, from your father and uncle, killed within thirty days of each other."

Fabius's attack became fiercer. "You claim that your object in going to Africa is to draw Hannibal after you. So whether you fight here or there, it is with Hannibal you will have to deal," he said, implying that Scipio was actually trying to avoid Hannibal. In a stinging cut, Fabius then reminded Scipio and the senate that Scipio's own father as consul, while en route to Iberia, had returned to Italy when Hannibal crossed the Alps. "You on the contrary, with Hannibal in Italy, are preparing to leave it, not because you think that such a move would help the country but rather that it would redound to your own glory and credit." Turning to the other senators again, Fabius harangued that the armies of Rome are "not for arrogant consuls who fancy themselves kings to whisk away to any part of the world they please."[18] When he took his seat, one could have heard a pin drop in the chamber.

Scipio got up and took a moment, just to show that he was in no hurry. Then he began, in an even-tempered voice, to rebut every point Fabius had made. As to his claim that Fabius was above jealousy, does not every great man—even and especially in old age—think beyond death to a legacy of glory? "I myself am convinced that the noblest minds compare themselves not only with their contemporaries but with great men in every age," said Scipio. "Nor do I pretend, Fabius, that I do not wish to rival your fame—indeed, if you will pardon my saying so, my ambition is to surpass it if I can." This disarming honesty had its desired effect and a few senators could not help but chuckle.

But how awful for Rome if its statesmen should start obstructing the younger generations for fear of their talent. "Jealousy like that would be harmful not only to its immediate objects, but the country as a whole—indeed to the world," said Scipio. With that said, why was Fabius, in his warnings about the dangers of an African invasion, suddenly so concerned for Scipio's safety, when he had voiced no such worries as Scipio set off for Iberia?[19]

Of course this war is all about Hannibal, continued Scipio, so let's talk seriously about him. Why would you want to keep fighting him here in Italy? Let me have my way and "you will hear at the same moment that I have crossed the sea, that Africa is ablaze, and that Carthage is already beset—yes, and the very sound of Hannibal's fleet making its preparations to sail."

Then Scipio turned directly toward Fabius and fixed his gaze on the old man. "Yes, Fabius, I shall have the antagonist you give me, Hannibal himself; but he won't keep me here, I shall draw him after me. I shall force him to fight on his native ground, and the prize of victory will be Carthage."

Turning back to the whole senate, Scipio said that he had no interest in belittling the achievements of Fabius as Fabius had belittled his own. "In moderation and restraint of speech, if in nothing else, you will see the young man surpass the old. Such has been the quality of my life and work that I am quite capable of saying no more."[20]

Scipio's composure under personal attack from the most senior Roman statesman in the chamber impressed those senators who were open to being impressed. But many still sided with Fabius. After tense negotiations, the senate came up with a pathetic bureaucratic compromise. Scipio would be sent to Sicily, but with a small and unimpressive force. The senate would give him permission "to cross to Africa if he judged it to be in the public interest."[21] It was as though the Roman senate were not sure whether it really wanted its consul to succeed.

Scipio, characteristically, wasted little time contemplating the pettiness of his country's political class. Instead he got busy raising and training volunteers in Sicily. The following year, 204 BCE, he crossed to Africa.

SCIPIO ARRIVED in Africa to discover that Syphax, the Numidian king who had hosted him, had reneged on his promise of support and had instead married the beautiful daughter of Hasdrubal Gisco, with whom he was now allied. Scipio pretended to try to negotiate with them. For several days, he sent his envoys in and out of the two enemy camps. At night, these Romans returned to make detailed maps of the camps. Scipio knew exactly where the soldiers slept, when the guards changed, and where the tents of dry reeds and boughs stood.[22]

Then, in the middle of the night, Scipio's archers shot flaming arrows into the enemy camps, which lit up like tinderboxes. The flames and smoke rose in a pink and orange plume into the African night sky. Just as he had promised Fabius in the senate, Africa was "ablaze." And as Scipio had predicted, there followed the "sound of Hannibal's fleet making its preparations to sail." The senate of Carthage, fearing for the city, recalled its greatest hero from Italy to save his native land. Scipio and Hannibal, after all these years, were at last about to meet.

You need to have a Fabius inside you to accept and absorb a disaster. But you need to have a Scipio in you to turn the disaster into a new and startling triumph. The Fabian part of you lets you survive and persist. The Scipionic part of you lets you imagine new realities and reinvent yourself. As men who lived twenty-two centuries ago, Fabius and Scipio clashed. But as metaphors for our psychological responses to disaster, Fabius and Scipio can work together in your mind to let you come back from tragedy and adversity.

The Fabian response necessarily comes first when disaster strikes, because you cannot reinvent yourself when you are still in denial, anger, or depression or are bargaining about your loss. First, you have to accept reality for what it is, to let it be, to "drift" with it as though it were Shackleton's Antarctic ice. Your inner Fabius is brave, cautious, and stoic. It bears what exists but does not create anything new.

The Scipionic response comes later. You recognize the Scipionic stage when you feel—perhaps to your own surprise—*liberated.* In the Scipionic phase you will get new ideas and new energies. A Scipionic reaction is passionate, bold, and, above all, innovative. Your inner Scipio has nothing left to lose and everything to gain, and in that knowledge sets out to create something new.

A Scipionic response is thus the precise opposite of the metaphorical *captivity* that success brought people such as Hannibal, Tennessee Williams, and Albert Einstein. They, being successful, felt that there was suddenly a lot to lose and not enough to gain by taking risks with their imagination. Hannibal did not *dare*, for example, imagine a bold evacuation of Italy; Williams during his captivity was unable to dream up new stories; Einstein was afraid to let go of what he believed were certainties in the physical universe so that he could become open to the *un*certain world of quantum mechanics. In the business world this is called the "innovator's dilemma"[23]—people who innovated in the past (with an invasion of Italy, *The Glass Menagerie*, or general relativity) no longer see the upside of subsequent innovation. By the same logic, people who have lost everything may see stunning opportunities in the world around them and feel free to seize them.

S teve Jobs met disaster at the age of thirty, when, having cofounded Apple and pioneered the era of personal computers, he was suddenly thrown out of his own company and his career seemed to be over.

Jobs grew up in the 1950s and 1960s with his adoptive parents in California's Silicon Valley, which "for the most part at that time was still orchards—apricot orchards and prune orchards—and it was really paradise. I remember the air being crystal clear, where you could see from one end of the valley to the other," Jobs later recalled.[24] There were engineers all around, and he began to tinker with electronics. Like Albert Einstein and Ludwig Erhard, however, he did not enjoy or do well in school. "I wanted to go outside and chase butterflies. You know, do the things that five-year-olds like to do," Jobs remembered. "I encountered authority of a different kind than I had ever encountered before, and I did not like it.

And they really almost got me. They came close to really beating any curiosity out of me."[25]

His curiosity intact, Jobs went to Reed College in Oregon for a semester, but then dropped out and audited only classes he liked. One of these was calligraphy, and it gave him the aesthetic ideas he would later use in the fonts available on Apple's computers. He was curious about many other things, and backpacked through India in search of enlightenment, coming back a Buddhist and a vegetarian.

As Meriwether Lewis met William Clark, and Paul Cézanne spent his time with Émile Zola, Jobs became close friends and soul mates with Steve Wozniak, "the Woz." They were complementary characters—Jobs had sharp features, an aggressive personality, and business savvy; Wozniak was pudgy, had a jovial nature, and was a gadget geek. Together they founded Apple in the 1970s. By the early 1980s, after launching the legendary Macintosh, the first mainstream computer that had a mouse to click with, they, and Jobs in particular, were gracing magazine covers. Jobs was successful, famous, on top of his game.

Jobs saw Apple rather as Lewis saw his quest to expand America or Shackleton his calling to cross Antarctica: "Apple was this incredible journey. I mean, we did some amazing things there. The thing that bound us together at Apple was the ability to make things that were going to change the world," Jobs later said. Comparing himself to Einstein and the quantum-physics revolutionaries, Jobs said, "We all worked like maniacs and the greatest joy was that we felt we were fashioning collective works of art much like twentieth-century physics."[26]

Computing was to Jobs an outlet for creativity just like art. "In the '70s and the '80s the best people in computers would have normally been poets and writers and musicians," Jobs said. "Almost all of them were musicians. A lot of them were poets on the side. They went into computers because it was so compelling. It was fresh and new. It was a new medium of expression for their creative talents. The feelings and the passion that people put into it were completely indistinguishable from [those of] a poet or a painter."[27]

As a company Apple was growing fast, and Jobs believed that he needed to find a professional executive, somebody with experience in corporate America, to run the company. In 1983, he asked the president of Pepsi-Cola, John Sculley, "Do you want to spend the rest of your life selling sugared water to children, or do you want a chance to change the world?" Sculley joined Apple as chief executive, and at first the two men appeared to get along fine.

THAT CHANGED in late 1984. The computer industry and Apple in particular entered a slump, and Jobs and Sculley started disagreeing about the proper response and strategy. Then they started fighting. As a friend and former colleague of Jobs's later recalled, "Steve Jobs had never suffered fools gladly, and as the pressure mounted, he became even more difficult to work with. Employees from every part of the company began to approach John with complaints about Steve's behavior. . . . John began to view Steve as an impediment toward fixing Apple's problems, and the board of directors were urging him to do something about it."[28]

Sculley and the board were not yet trying to push Jobs out of the company altogether. But Jobs, not a politically astute or diplomatic character, escalated with an all-out attack against Sculley, whom he now despised as passionately as he had admired him a year earlier. At a meeting in the spring of 1985 that extended over two days, the board sided with Sculley and against Jobs. Jobs was out of the company that he had founded.

JOBS ENTERED Elisabeth Kübler-Ross's grief cycle. Shock was followed mostly by anger and then depression. "What had been the focus of my entire life was gone, and it was devastating," he later said.[29]

Soon after the ouster, a friend went to see Jobs at his large and mostly unfurnished Spanish-colonial-style mansion in the hills of Silicon Valley for a vegetarian dinner with friends.[30]

"So what really happened at Apple?" he asked Jobs. "Is it really as bad as it looks?"

"No, it's worse," said Jobs, with a look of agony. "It's much worse than you can imagine." At least it was from his perspective.

Jobs blamed Sculley for absolutely everything. He felt betrayed, angry, bitter, his friend recalled, and seemed "more depressed than I had ever seen him before." In some ways, Jobs never got over his anger. Exactly ten years after the boardroom coup, Jobs said, with characteristic exaggeration, that "John Sculley ruined Apple and he ruined it by bringing a set of values to the top of Apple which were corrupt and corrupted some of the top people who were there, drove out some of the ones who were not corruptible, and brought in more corrupt ones."[31]

BUT JOBS WENT THROUGH the stages of his grief and came out at the other end. As Eleanor Roosevelt went to Rock Creek Cemetery to contemplate the statue *Grief*, Jobs went traveling in the summer of 1985, trying to figure out what to do next. As a female friend remembers, Jobs spent "only three or four months" paralyzed by what Kübler-Ross would have called his depression. And then something else started happening.

In several different ways, the disaster "freed him," recalls the same friend. In the years just before his ouster, she remembers, Jobs had increasingly been "pulled into being a bureaucrat"—managing, delegating, executing, all of which he considered excruciatingly boring. He had experienced this time before his ouster as an "imprisonment," she believes. Now, however, the prison door was unlocked. He was free again to do only what he wanted to do, which was to dream up gadgets that would change the world.

It also freed him in that the things he most wanted to do would have been too small for Apple, which was already a big company at that time, recalls his friend. One of Jobs's old extracurricular interests was movie animation, so he now bought a small animation studio across San Francisco Bay and renamed it Pixar. He hung out with its artsy types and got new ideas. He also developed a vision for computing that was too idiosyncratic for Apple at the time, so he founded a computer start-up called NeXT. As a commercial venture it failed, but it pioneered several cutting-edge technologies that Jobs, with his visionary zeal, believed were the future of computing.

Over time, he was also liberated emotionally, remembers his friend. "There was never any 'peaceful' there, but there was a bitterness that dissipated," she told me. Within a few years, Jobs married and started a family (he had fathered a daughter in the 1970s, but did not have a close relationship with her). With his new wife, he had three more children and now appeared to be a dedicated father. Even his new professional interests began blooming. Pixar released *Toy Story*, a movie about the tussle between two toys, an old-fashioned cowboy and a newfangled space ranger, for the attentions of their owner, a boy named Andy. It became an international hit, soon followed by others.

TWELVE YEARS AFTER his ouster, a stunning reversal occurred. John Sculley had left Apple, and Jobs's old company, under new management, bought NeXT, Jobs's new company, in order to use its technology as the foundation for a new line of computers. Suddenly, Steve Jobs was back at the company that had thrown him out. Apple was floundering at the time, and the board of directors ousted its then chief executive, Gil Amelio, making Jobs interim CEO. Not only was he back, Jobs was also back *in charge*.

And so Jobs started a second career at Apple. His greatest successes were yet to come. They were based on the ideas that he had had during his exile. The technology he had developed at NeXT evolved into the operating system of the next generation of Macs. Apple recovered, and in 2000, Jobs, with the charismatic showmanship for which he is famous, and to cheers from his audience, dropped the word "interim" from his title, becoming

Apple's CEO indefinitely again. In the following years, he turned the music industry upside down with the iPod and iTunes, and turned the cellphone industry inside out with the iPhone.

THESE ARE THE YEARS when I covered Apple for *The Economist,* and I remember Jobs striding triumphantly in his trademark mock turtleneck, jeans, and New Balance sneakers across the stage of the annual Macworld Expo convention in San Francisco. He was beaming with pride in his work, visibly fulfilled by it, going from success to success. He was still irascible and impatient, hot and cold, and often unbearable to those around him. And he became sick, looking gaunt by the end of the decade. But his twelve-year exile looked in retrospect like an apprenticeship for triumph. His disaster of 1985 now looked like a liberation.

Twenty years after his ouster from Apple, in 2005, Jobs delivered the commencement address at Stanford University. As I listened to Jobs speak, I thought of Scipio as he might have looked back at the death of his father and uncle. "I didn't see it then, but it turned out that getting fired from Apple was the best thing that could have ever happened to me," Jobs told the graduates before him. In being fired, "the heaviness of being successful was replaced by the lightness of being a beginner again, less sure about everything. It *freed* me to enter one of the most creative periods of my life."[32]

At some point Eleanor Roosevelt came out of Rock Creek Cemetery having traversed the grief cycle and *accepted* that her husband had cheated on her, that she had been betrayed, that her life as a docile wife, mother, and daughter-in-law had been a prison. And now she, too, felt a paradoxical and energizing sense of *liberation.*

Franklin and Eleanor had decided not to get divorced, in order to save his political career. But Eleanor also explained to him that they would henceforth have a new relationship. He was to have his sphere, and she was to have hers. They would remain allies in facing the public and partners in raising the children. But in their intimate lives and their intellectual pursuits they would be independent. Franklin understood and agreed.

Eleanor then fired all the servants in her Washington home. She may have believed them to be in collusion with Lucy Mercer or with her mother-in-law. From now on, Eleanor would hire her own staff. To the horror of her mother-in-law, she staffed the entire household with black servants. Eleanor did not care what anyone thought. She had changed her relationship to Sara. "Mama and I have had a bad time. I should be ashamed of myself but I'm not," she wrote Franklin.[33]

She took lessons in cooking, shorthand, and typing. She began writing newspaper articles. She took an open interest in politics and became associated with practically every progressive cause, from national health insurance to state pensions, from legislation against child labor to the new League of Nations, the forerunner of the United Nations. Among certain people, she began raising eyebrows for these "Bolshevik" leanings. But she did not care. With great passion and a sense of freedom, she connected with the feminist movement and made new and intimate friends.

She became close to a lesbian couple, Elizabeth Read and Esther Lape. Read was a lawyer who became Eleanor's personal attorney and financial adviser, and Lape was a journalist. Eleanor started spending almost all her private time at their apartment in New York's Greenwich Village. Nearby lived another lesbian couple, Nancy Cook and Marion Dickerman, who would also become her intimate friends. The atmosphere of these evenings reminded Eleanor of her happy days with Marie Souvestre, when she was in the company of strong women and reading French poetry or debating civil rights. Her new friends were outrageous and fun. They felt free to do and be anything they wanted.

In public, however, the Roosevelts maintained their image of the utmost propriety. And it was not fake. There still was a bond between them, but it was of a different kind. When Franklin contracted polio, in 1921, Eleanor cared for him. She bathed him, turned him, administered catheters and enemas, massaged him, brushed his teeth, and shaved him. Franklin would be in wheelchairs or leg braces for the rest of his life. Even so, Eleanor and Franklin were determined that he should continue his political career.

Watching Franklin accept *his* disaster, Eleanor became more impressed by her husband. She believed that polio "gave him strength and courage he had not had before. He had to think out the fundamentals of living and learn the greatest of all lessons—infinite patience and never-ending persistence"—things, in short, that she was learning herself.[34]

ELEANOR WAS NOW LIVING in two entirely separate but harmoniously overlapping worlds. One was her own world, shared with companions of her choice. The other was the world of family, which she never abandoned, but in which she defined a new role for herself. The two worlds were not only psychologically but also physically distinct. The world of family still centered on the grand estates of the Roosevelts by the Hudson River and the official residences—in Albany, when Franklin was governor of New York, and later the White House. Eleanor's own world centered on a new house, Val-Kill.

Franklin entirely approved of, and indeed financed and supported, the building of Val-Kill, a charming cottage built on the Roosevelt lands of Hyde Park, New York. Eleanor's mother-in-law detested Val-Kill, which made it even more fun for Eleanor and her friends Nancy Cook, Marion Dickerman, and others.

Val-Kill became more than a cottage and a guesthouse for anybody whom Eleanor liked. It became a venture of self-expression. Nancy Cook, a skilled carpenter, ran a furniture factory as part of it. They started a newspaper, the *Women's Democratic News*, which Eleanor edited. They ran a girls' school, Todhunter. It reminded Eleanor of Souvestre's school and she became the most popular teacher there.

Eleanor took up swimming, hiking, camping, running, and driving, which she did too fast. She played cards and became a rough and fun playmate for her children. She took flying lessons from Amelia Earhart. Her headaches and colds disappeared again. She gained weight and was often tan from spending so much time outdoors.

Simultaneously, Eleanor became a prominent political leader in her own right. She was one of the leading figures in the League of Women Voters and other feminist organizations, and became a hard-dealing party boss of the New York Democratic Party. When Franklin was elected governor of New York in 1928 and the family moved to Albany, Eleanor retained all these roles, which seemed revolutionary to many Americans at the time.

And she found love again. Earl Miller was a New York state trooper who had originally been assigned to protect Franklin. Miller was a natural athlete. He had won the navy's middleweight boxing championship and was an excellent horseman, marksman, and gymnast. Because Eleanor insisted on driving herself, Franklin appointed Miller her bodyguard. She was twelve years older than Miller. He taught her to ride horses and to play tennis, dive, and shoot pistols. They became completely relaxed around each other, and usually did not bother to hide their affection. Her arm is on his knees in some pictures, his on hers in others. Miller "gave her a great deal of what her husband and we, her sons, failed to give her. Above all, he made her feel that she was a woman," Eleanor's son James later said.[35]

Another love was Lorena Hickok, "Hick," a reporter for the Associated Press who was originally assigned to cover Franklin, but then followed Eleanor. Even though it compromised Hickok as a journalist, they fell madly in love. It was a bumpy ride, with jealousies and upsets, but the relationship filled another void in Eleanor's life. The day before Franklin was to be inaugurated president, Eleanor took Hickok to the holly grove to see *Grief*.

"Sometimes I'd be very unhappy and sorry for myself," Eleanor explained to Hickok. "When I was feeling that way, if I could manage it, I'd come out here, alone, and sit and look at that woman. And I'd always come away somehow feeling better. And stronger. I've been here many, many times." Hickok later said of the statue and perhaps also of Eleanor,

"I could almost feel the hot, stinging unshed tears behind the lowered eyelids. Yet in that expression there was something almost triumphant. There was a woman who had experienced every kind of pain, every kind of suffering . . . and had come out of it serene—and compassionate."[36]

EVEN AS FIRST LADY, Eleanor did not give up her new roles and new world. Officially a resident of the White House, she still maintained her own house in Greenwich Village, which she rented from Esther Lape. She was the first First Lady to give her own press conferences and to write her own newspaper column, which was syndicated to newspapers all over America. She visited coal mines and showed up at the breadlines of the Great Depression, concerned about the plight of ordinary people. She fought for the rights of African Americans, children, and the poor.

Looking back at that moment in 1918 when she had found those letters, she once said, "I faced myself, my surroundings, my world, honestly for the first time." Another time she spoke of that "painfully acquired self-discipline, which teaches you to cast out fear and *frees* you for the fullest experience of the adventure of life."[37]

TEN

THE THRESHOLD
OF MIDDLE AGE

Who does not know those touching old gentlemen who
must always warm up the dish of their student days,
who can fan the flame of life only by reminiscences of
their heroic youth, but who, for the rest, are stuck in a
hopelessly wooden Philistinism?

—Carl Jung

Three men stood in the heat on the African plain near a place called
Zama, five days' march southwest of Carthage in what is today Tunisia. They were alone except for two mighty armies looking on from afar.
For a few minutes, Hannibal and Scipio looked at each other in silence.
They were not angry. Far from it. They were, in fact, reverent. These two
enemies, each the greatest general of his nation, had long been curious
about each other. Hannibal had extended the invitation for a meeting, and
Scipio had immediately agreed. With them was a translator,[1] but both Hannibal and Scipio spoke fluent Greek and had no need for him, so the translator stood back, in awe of this moment, overwhelmed by the presence of
these men.

Hannibal was forty-five years old, visibly in middle age. His blind eye and the deep lines in his face were like a map of his fifteen years in Italy of soaring heights and plunging lows. Scipio was in his thirties, his skin still smooth and taut, his posture erect, his body lithe. He was respectful of his senior, and waited for him to speak first.

In my very first battle against the Romans I faced a noble general named Publius Cornelius Scipio, said Hannibal. How fitting that I should now come to Africa hoping to negotiate peace terms with another Publius Cornelius Scipio, the son and avenger of the former. Hannibal paused and Scipio nodded.

"I have learned by actual experience how fickle is Fortune, how by a slight shift of the scale she brings about changes of the greatest moment to either side, and how she sports with mankind as if her victims were little children,"[2] Hannibal continued, speaking more in the tone of a mentor than an enemy.

He had learned, Hannibal said, that "the greater a man's success, the less it must be trusted to endure."[3]

Hannibal paused, then continued: "But I fear that you, Scipio, partly because you are very young and partly because the whole course of events in Spain and in Africa has favored your plans, so that you have never yet experienced the ebb-tide of Fortune, will not be influenced by my words." And yet, Hannibal said, pointing to himself, Scipio could just look at his enemy, the same man who "after the battle of Cannae became master of almost the whole of Italy" and later "advanced to Rome itself, pitched camp within five miles of her walls, and there took thought as to how I should deal with you and your country." But today, Hannibal continued, he was here in Africa negotiating with Scipio for "my country's very existence and my own. Remember this change of Fortune, I beg you, and do not be over-proud, but keep your thoughts at this moment upon the human scale of things."[4]

Hannibal said that Scipio, too, would see reversals of fortune in his life. So why, since each respected the other, was it necessary to fight a battle now at all? They could instead make peace. Carthage would keep Africa;

Rome would keep everything Scipio had already conquered for it, including all of Iberia.

Scipio waited for a moment. Then he answered calmly that he had always contemplated Hannibal as his example and was very aware of "the fickleness of Fortune." As he spoke, there was no animosity. Instead, the two men felt a special bond at that moment. They understood each other and their situation; they shared a worldview and a story even though fate had put them on opposing sides of it. Both men had met with triumph and disaster and knew them to be impostors.

But in the present circumstances, continued Scipio, he could not conclude that the right course of action was to try to escape from this cycle of success and failure altogether, by not fighting one more battle. The goddess Fortune had put the two of them in Africa as enemies, Scipio said, and they had to accept their roles to play out her designs. There was no running from her. "The fact is that you must either put yourself and your country unconditionally into our hands, or else fight and conquer us," said Scipio firmly.[5]

Hannibal nodded. The two men parted in mutual, solemn, and terse reverence, each accepting that it had to be this way.

THE BATTLE TOOK PLACE the very next day. Both sides knew that this day would be a turning point in history, a day that would see either Carthage or Rome rise to dominance over the known world. All the soldiers in both armies also knew something else: that this was the first time in this war, and possibly in all of history, when *both* sides had a genius as commander. Both Hannibal and Scipio were undefeated, but they had each so far confronted only men of clearly less ability. Today, however, would be a clash of titans.

Both sides were also aware of an eerie symmetry with the past. When Hannibal and his army had emerged from the Alps, he had told his men that they now had only two options, to conquer or to die, since going back was out of the question. Now it was Scipio who told his troops that they could either "win for yourselves and for Rome the unchallenged leadership and sovereignty of the rest of the world" or "meet a death that is made forever glorious," because fleeing across the hostile landscape of Africa was out of the question.[6] Hannibal, by contrast, appealed to his veteran troops by recalling all their victories together, and pointed out that this time it was they who outnumbered the enemy. At the same time he knew that a lot of his troops had been recruited in a great hurry after his landing in Africa and were as untrained as the Roman soldiers had been sixteen years earlier.

Hannibal lined up his infantry in three thick lines, flanked by his cavalry. In front, he placed eighty war elephants, knowing how much these frightened the Romans. Scipio placed his Roman legions in the center, also flanked by his cavalry. Aware of Hannibal's elephants, Scipio positioned the troops in columns so that they could form lanes through which the elephants might be tempted to run.

As expected, Hannibal began by unleashing the elephants in a terrifying charge. But Scipio had prepared for this and ordered a blast of all the Roman trumpets just as the elephants were about to reach the Roman soldiers. The sound startled the animals, and some elephants turned back and started crushing Carthaginians instead of Romans. The other elephants took the path of least resistance and stampeded right through the lanes the Romans had formed for them and out the other end, where they dispersed, without the deadly effect that Hannibal had hoped for.

While this was going on, the cavalries clashed on both flanks, but this time the outcome was the reverse of what it had been at Cannae fourteen years earlier: the Roman horsemen drove the Carthaginian riders off the field and set off in pursuit. The battle now became a grinding and bloody clash of infantries. Hannibal had foreseen this and had placed his fresh recruits in the first two lines to wear down the Romans and, literally, to take the sharp edge off of the Roman swords, so that he could throw his more experienced soldiers into the battle at the very end, when they would be still fresh and their swords sharp.

Scipio understood this and responded with a difficult and bold maneuver. In the heat of the fighting, he ordered his trumpets to sound a disciplined retreat. His exhausted soldiers stopped and withdrew for a few hundred yards. Scipio changed the formation, turning his army into one long line facing the Carthaginians. And then, with cool confidence, he simply waited.

For what seemed a tense eternity, the two armies, drenched in blood and sweat, stared at each other across the corpses of the first clash. Finally, they attacked again. It was a desperate charge for both sides, as the warriors waded through the bodies of those already fallen and slipped in their blood. Then, just as the elite troops of both sides engaged, the Roman cavalry returned to the battlefield, tearing into Hannibal's troops from the rear and routing the Carthaginians. Hannibal, for the first and only time in his life, fled the field.[7]

THE BATTLE'S AFTERMATH was very different from that of the battle at Cannae. At Cannae, Hannibal had not followed up on his victory by marching straight to Rome. At Zama, Scipio immediately seized the momentum of his victory and moved toward Carthage itself. The city's elders, in shock that Hannibal had been beaten, asked for Scipio's terms.

Scipio's conditions were strict but humane; his motivation was not bloody revenge for all the years of war but rather a stable and lasting peace that both sides could live with. He imposed reparations to be paid for fifty years and took away Carthage's right to an independent foreign policy. Otherwise he allowed the city to remain autonomous.

It was, in fact, Hannibal who brought events to a close. He had escaped from the battle and returned to Carthage, which he had last seen decades earlier. Suddenly, as an old man, he was again walking among the temples and buildings that were so familiar and yet so alien. He had always assumed he would return as victor, but here he was, an old and vanquished man.

Emotionally, he was numb as he took a seat in Carthage's Council of Elders and listened to the senators debate Scipio's terms. A senator named

Gisco rose to speak against accepting Scipio's conditions. Hannibal sat up. He could not believe his ears. This man did not understand. Carthage had no army left and no way to draft a new one. Hannibal's brothers and most of the other generals were dead. The will of his few remaining troops was broken. It was obvious to Hannibal, if not to Gisco, that Scipio had replaced Hannibal as the invincible hero in the popular imagination. Gisco also did not understand that losing to Scipio was infinitely preferable to surrendering to any other Roman general. Scipio had the foresight and wisdom to make the peace terms clement enough to allow Carthage to survive and prosper. Rejecting his offer now would invite an even worse disaster.

As Gisco was speaking, Hannibal jumped up, bounded to the podium before the council, grabbed Gisco, and hurled him down. For a moment, the elders were shocked. As a stunned Gisco picked himself up and adjusted his toga, the chamber erupted at this outrage. How dare Hannibal besmirch the ancient traditions of the council!

Hannibal stared back at the elders screaming at him from all sides. He was at a loss. Nobody had ever dared challenge him like this. His anger turned to shame and bewilderment at this new situation and at his own behavior. What was he doing here? What was his role here, in the city of his birth and in this chamber? He did not know. It was not like him to lose self-control.

Hannibal apologized to the council, reminding the elders that he had left Carthage as a boy and had since then known only the rough world of camps and battlefields. Once the council returned to calm, Hannibal explained: "If you had been asked only a few days ago what you expected your country would suffer in the event of a Roman victory, the disaster which threatened us then appeared so overwhelming that you would not even have been able to express your fears."[8] Everybody in the chamber knew what those fears were. Usually, the Romans killed conquered populations or sold them into slavery. Carthage was therefore lucky if, in Scipio, it had a conqueror who actually wanted Carthage to survive and prosper, even if he required submission to Rome. The elders turned solemn and began nodding.

So the Carthaginians surrendered. Scipio ordered all but ten of the five hundred remaining Carthaginian ships rowed out into Carthage's harbor and burned. The entire population lined up on the shore to watch the inferno lighting up the sky, as if they were witnessing their own funeral pyre or that of their legendary ancestor, Queen Dido, when she threw herself into the fire after her lover, Aeneas, left her to found Rome. Soon it was time to pay the first installment of their indemnity to Rome, and the rich merchants and elders of the city wept as they handed over their fortunes.

As this happened, Hannibal was seen sitting forlornly on a bench, doing something extraordinary. He was—incomprehensibly—laughing. He could not stop. He howled uncontrollably, as if he were a madman. One elder walked up to him and screamed at him to be quiet. How dare he laugh while his own people wept, especially since he was the cause of their tears! But Hannibal kept laughing, with tears running out of his one eye.

"If eyes could see the mind within as they do the expression of a face," he stammered between heaves, "it would soon be apparent to you that this laughter you condemn springs not from a happy heart, but from one which is almost beside itself with its misfortunes."[9] Outwardly, the great Hannibal had turned into a guffawing wretch. Inwardly, his world was collapsing. Go and weep over your money, he screamed at the merchants and elders. As if your money were what this is about!

AND THEN HANNIBAL DISAPPEARED. He withdrew from public life and went into a kind of domestic exile, probably at his ancestral estate on the African coast. For five years, he stayed almost invisible, keeping the company of only a few old comrades with whom he planted olive trees.[10] Perhaps he tried to find his wife, Imilce, and his son, whom he had last seen in Iberia when he put them on a boat to Carthage before invading

Italy. But he never found them. His brothers were dead, as were most of those who had shared his confidence and gained his trust during the long years in Italy. He had nothing left: no power, no command, no office.

Day after day, he woke up, ate, spent his time thinking, and went back to sleep again, in a country that, once proudly independent, was now a docile subject of Rome. Perhaps he looked through the belongings and old weapons his father, Hamilcar, had left behind and remembered how the two of them had sworn their oath to be eternal enemies of Rome. He kept imagining what Hamilcar would say now.

Again and again, Hannibal saw in his mind the severed head of his brother Hasdrubal when the Romans catapulted it at his feet. He also kept seeing the screaming women, frightened children, and dying men who had filled his existence. Hannibal asked himself: What had his life been about?

THEN, at the age of fifty-one, he reappeared. He was still the hero of the common people of Carthage, and so he entered politics. He was elected suffete, the Carthaginian equivalent of a Roman consul. Hannibal did not intend to wait out his remaining years in a sinecure. After five years out of the public gaze, he wanted to remake himself and to rededicate his life—to creation instead of destruction. If Carthage was now a vassal of Rome, Hannibal wanted to help change and purify the city itself, to make it prosper, to make its people happy.

He set his sights on one cause of widespread unhappiness. There was an elitist institution called the "order of judges" in Carthage. It consisted of 104 members for life who had unchecked power over the lives and property of ordinary Carthaginians and who were themselves immune from the law. Hannibal felt that no Carthaginian should be above the law. He ordered the arrest of an arrogant and corrupt state treasurer who was about to enter the order of judges and brought this man before an assembly of the people, where Hannibal lashed out against the man and that venal institution. The crowd roared with approval and voted for Hannibal's proposal to limit the order's arbitrary powers. Carthage's aristocrats saw this as a challenge to their privileges and seethed with resentment. But they were outnumbered, and Hannibal scored a small victory of idealism.[11]

He was not done yet. Hannibal was looking for a new identity and purpose, and he believed he had found it. He started looking through the financial accounts of the city. It was tedious work, the sort he had always despised as a young man. But as he examined the revenues from customs on land and sea and the government's expenses, he discovered that the mighty economy of Carthage was one big racket in which the leading merchants, many of them in the Council of Elders, were embezzling the wealth of the country to make themselves rich.

Hannibal was outraged. These were the same men who had wept when they had to pay Scipio the indemnity. But they had been robbing the Carthaginian people for years while Hannibal was fighting for them in Italy.

Hannibal called another public assembly and exposed what was happening in detail. If Carthage simply cleaned up the graft of its own elite, he argued, it could pay the Roman indemnity every year without even taxing ordinary citizens at all. As he expected, the wealthy were outraged but the common people loved him. Hannibal scored another small victory and cleaned up the graft.[12]

FOR THE ELITE of Carthage this was too much. The city's elders and wealthy now regarded Hannibal, not Rome, as their foremost enemy, and the enemy of their enemy had to be their friend. Carthage's aristocrats and merchants started writing obsequious letters to powerful contacts in Rome, stoking Roman suspicions and fears of Hannibal. They alleged that Hannibal had sent messengers and letters to Antiochus, the king of the mighty Seleucid Empire in the east (in today's Turkey, Syria, and Lebanon). They said that Hannibal was plotting to help this foreign king launch a new invasion of Italy, that Hannibal was "like one of those wild beasts which cannot be tamed by any method."[13]

For a while, these Carthaginian slanders fell flat in Rome, because

Hannibal had one loyal and credible defender there: his nemesis, Scipio. Scipio kept reminding the Roman senate that these allegations were certain to be trumped up by the Carthaginian kleptocrats for their own political ends and that it would sit "ill with the dignity of the Roman people to associate themselves with the animosities of Hannibal's accusers."[14] But the Romans' paranoia about Hannibal, that scourge of Italy for so much of their lives, was overwhelming. Many Romans felt that they had a personal score to settle with Hannibal. So the Roman senate sent a mission to Carthage to indict Hannibal before the Council of Elders.

Hannibal's informers tipped him off. He realized that his enemies in Carthage were now too powerful and numerous. He prepared to escape. On the day the Roman delegation arrived in the city, he walked through the market as if conducting business as usual. But that night he went to one of the city's gates, met two old friends, and left with them. They found horses waiting for them and galloped through the night across the African plain to his estate by the coast, where a ship was waiting. For the second time in his life, he sailed away from the African coastline, this time knowing as he left that he might never see it again.

HANNIBAL SOON reached an island where Phoenician trading ships were anchored in port. He was afraid that the traders would leak his whereabouts back to Carthage. So he suggested that they all throw a big feast, and that the Phoenician captains bring their sails to make a huge tent to keep out the sun. Everybody drank late into the night, and Hannibal sneaked away and set sail. By the time the Phoenicians woke up, recovered from their hangovers, and untangled their sails, Hannibal was well on his way to Tyre, the Phoenician city in Lebanon that had founded Carthage as its colony centuries earlier.

Hannibal arrived there a refugee. He was literally and metaphorically drifting through midlife, still searching for a purpose, with no assurance that he would ever find one. Because Phoenicia was then part of the vast and mighty Seleucid kingdom, one of the successor empires to Alexander the Great's, Hannibal decided that he should introduce himself to the king, Antiochus, at his capital, Antioch. Hannibal traveled to the royal court, but the king was away. The king's son told Hannibal to travel to Ephesus, a beautiful Greek town in today's Turkey, and there Hannibal met Antiochus.

The Seleucid king was thrilled to meet this exotic war hero from the west. He had heard tales of his exploits and triumphs for many years. He began to tell Hannibal about his own plans to wage war on Rome, which he considered a barbarian city. Would Hannibal consider advising him?

We do not know what went through Hannibal's mind when he heard Antiochus's offer. Hannibal was fifty-two years old at the time. His own country had just betrayed him by concocting the lie that he had been scheming with this man, Antiochus, against Rome. Now that same king was actually proposing just that. Hannibal might have declined politely, kept traveling, and found a peaceful life in old age and obscurity. But he didn't. Having failed at making a transition to a new identity, Hannibal agreed to help Antiochus fight a new war against Rome.

What Hannibal experienced in his late forties, after his defeat by Scipio, was what we would today call a midlife crisis. The psychologist Carl Jung believed that, in the grand arc of a life story, such a crisis is not a failure but a necessary transition that all people need to make. Jung thought that all stages of life were important in the development of a person, but that the years roughly around age forty—what he called the "noon of life"—were crucial. If the psychological journey of a person during these years is healthy, it can lead to a new and prolonged success in the afternoon of life; if the journey leads the traveler astray, it can lead to failure.

THE WAY YOU SUCCEED in your midlife transition, as Jung saw it, begins with dropping the persona of your youth. When you were young, you inevitably tried to live up to the expectations of society—your parents, friends, teachers, bosses, lovers. So you assumed a role and projected a personality to help you do that. This is your persona. It is a mask that young people wear to fit in, said Jung, "a compromise between individual and society as to what a man should appear to be. He takes a name, earns a title, exercises a function, he is this or that. In a certain sense, all this is real. Yet, in relation to the essential individuality of the person concerned it is only a secondary reality."[15]

For example, a woman like young Eleanor Roosevelt might attend the debutante balls and social parties that her mother and her class valued, even though she secretly hated such events. She might start a family and become a submissive wife and daughter-in-law, even though she might dream of traveling and becoming involved in politics.

A different person, in a different social class, culture, or time, might take on a different persona. Amy Tan in her youth responded to modern Western ideals of rebellion, travel, and adventure, as when she got herself a dope-smoking German boyfriend in Switzerland to shock her mother and to feel cool. Meriwether Lewis assumed the persona of an adventurer and explorer, even though he might secretly have yearned for a quiet and happy family life. Young men such as Hannibal, Hasdrubal, and Mago became generals to fight the enemies of their fathers because society expected it of them.

BY DISCARDING THIS PERSONA in midlife, you as a more mature person have an opportunity, through inner crisis and upheaval, to build a new identity that is more authentic and natural. Jung called this process *individuation* to indicate that you now become "indivisible" and integrated—simultaneously new, whole, and distinct.

For example, Eleanor Roosevelt might cease defining herself solely as a wife, mother, and daughter-in-law and become an activist, politician, diplomat, traveler, and iconoclast. She might care less about accommodating and pleasing the people around her, and a lifestyle that once might have seemed eccentric or disallowed now feels right.

As part of individuation, Jung believed, you must confront those aspects of yourself that you have repressed in your previous persona. This includes whatever is vulgar or negative about your personality, as well as whatever traits society might frown on, which Jung called the *shadow*. If you are a woman, you might discover your assertive and masculine side, which Jung called the *animus*, which you may have suppressed in your youth to wear the mask of alluring femininity. Thus Eleanor Roosevelt discovered, or admitted, only in midlife that she liked driving fast cars, flying airplanes, shooting pistols, hiking up mountains, and negotiating with tough-as-nails party bosses.

If you are a man, you may have to meet and acknowledge your feminine side, which Jung called the *anima*. Hannibal, whose identity was based on power, strength, and courage, was almost certainly scared by the weakness and vulnerability he felt after his defeat by Scipio. Jung would say that Hannibal regarded being submissive—to Rome, to the Carthaginian Council of Elders—as feminine and threatening.[16] Allowing such vulnerability to be part of his personality would have been part of his individuation.

WHAT MAKES INDIVIDUATION so difficult—a "crisis"—is that, psychologically and metaphorically, you must let the young hero in your persona "die." This makes you feel your mortality more keenly than you have ever felt it. As a young hero you probably felt immortal, and this delusion made you bold and courageous. Hannibal and Meriwether Lewis, as they set out on their youthful adventures, knew in a theoretical sense that they might die but probably never actually believed it. But midlife brings constant reminders of death. Hannibal reached middle age with his father and both his brothers, and countless friends and loved ones, dead. Eleanor Roosevelt had lost both her parents and one child by middle age. Middle-aged bodies begin to creak and ail, whispering that their time is limited.

The ancient Greeks and Romans associated the feeling of transition in midlife so closely with the fear of death that they assigned both to the same god. The Greeks called him Hermes, the Romans Mercury, and his domain was "liminality."[17] *Limen* is the Latin word for threshold, and transitions, journeys, and death have in common that they are states of psychological suspension. Thus Hermes appeared to guide a middle-aged Odysseus, struggling on his long journey to return home to Ithaca after his youthful adventures in the Trojan War, to Hades, the underworld of the dead, and back again to remind him of his mortality. As Mercury, the same god also took middle-aged Aeneas, one of the Trojan survivors of the same war, to visit the realm of the dead.

Even the loss of a job or a demotion, divorce or separation, bereavement, and illness can represent such brushes with mortality. Traumatic at any age, these events can have the effect of "splitting the block"[18] in middle age, cracking the brittle identity you have built for yourself in your youth; in Hannibal's case, it once made him wail uncontrollably with deranged laughter.

A COMMON and positive response to this heightened sense of mortality in middle age is a new yearning to leave behind a positive and creative legacy. Young heroes might occasionally define success as destruction. For Hannibal success was the subjugation of Rome, for Theseus the slaying of the Minotaur, for young Odysseus the destruction of Troy. But as the same person during his midlife transition becomes aware of his own destructibility, he redefines success as creation, which suggests a metaphorical immortality.[19]

For example, you may get more involved in the lives of your children and *their* successes. You may discover altruism and philanthropy, or change jobs to enter a more creative field. In Hannibal's case, he planted olive trees and then threw his prodigious energies into creating a better Carthage, which he hoped would become his positive legacy. Albert Einstein discovered interests far beyond physics and became a Zionist and a proponent of a "world government" to assure peace among the nations. Eleanor Roosevelt dedicated herself to fighting racism, poverty, and misogyny, and gave her time to help the fledgling United Nations.

WHEN THE JOURNEY goes well and the midlife transition is a success, the best years of life are often yet to come. This seems to be the case for most people. Life expectancy is longer today in rich countries, so Jung's "noon of life" may now occur in the mid- to late forties. But research shows that well-being and happiness are still "U-shaped" throughout an average life in America and Europe. American men tend to hit their low point at age forty-nine, American women at forty-five, and European men and women slightly earlier. But after this "liminal" decade in their lives, Americans and Europeans report gradually becoming happier again.[20]

A good example of a midlife transition that has its share of upheaval but ends in success is, in fact, the journey of Carl Jung.

He was born in 1875 into an intellectual Swiss-German family. His grandfather had been a famous medical professor, poet, freethinker, and possibly an illegitimate child of Goethe.[21] His father, Paul Jung, was a vicar in the village where Carl was born.

Carl Jung grew into a large young man, but he was not yet impressive in other ways. He was introverted. At school, people teased him. Like Albert Einstein, he was a mediocre student, struggling especially in math and grammar. And as the Romans considered young Fabius dim-witted, Jung's teachers also thought Carl was slow. But he gradually improved. He wanted to be an archaeologist, but his father found that impractical and preferred medical school, rather as Amy Tan's mother did. So Jung studied medicine for five years in Basel, until his father died.

During his medical training, Jung discovered an interest in the paranormal. Odd things were always catching his attention. For instance, he was studying once when a sturdy walnut table cracked with the sound of a gunshot and split down the middle, without anybody standing near it. Two weeks later a sound came from a kitchen sideboard and Carl found that the steel blade of a bread knife had shattered into three distinct pieces. He took the broken knife to a cutler, who told him that the metal was in perfect order and could have been broken only deliberately and with effort. Jung realized how little we understand about the world, and he kept the pieces of the knife for the rest of his life.[22]

He titled his doctoral thesis "On the Psychology and Pathology of So-called Occult Phenomena." Then, just before his final exam in medical school, he skimmed a psychiatry textbook. He was fascinated and decided to become a psychiatrist. Psychiatry was regarded as just short of snake charming at the time, and his teachers and friends were shocked at his decision. But Jung didn't care.

He began his work with the mentally ill. He tried new treatments, such as word associations. He would say a series of words and analyze the responses of his patients to intuit their unconscious thoughts. When he discovered an emotionally charged tangle of associations, he called this a "complex." Jung's career was taking off, as was his family life. He married the daughter of a wealthy Swiss-German industrial family and they had three children in quick succession, followed by two more later.

Meanwhile, he put out feelers to Sigmund Freud, already the most famous psychologist at the time. Jung was thirty when he sent Freud, who was turning fifty, some of his work about associations. Freud took an interest and mailed a bundle of his own research back. There was an immediate and strong intellectual and emotional attraction between the two. When they first met at Freud's home in Vienna, in early 1907, they spent thirteen hours engrossed in conversation. They both viewed themselves as explorers of the human mind, with Freud playing the role of the mentor and Jung that of disciple.

"Freud was the first man of real importance I had encountered in my experience up to that time; no one else could compare with him," Jung recalled decades later. In turn, Freud was soon calling Jung his "scientific heir" and appointed Jung editor of the new journal of Freudian psycho-analysis.[23] He began talking about Jung as his "successor and crown prince." Everything was looking up for Jung.

THEN THE RELATIONSHIP took a wrong turn. There had been under-currents of tension for a while, which both men chose to ignore. Then, in a conversation Jung and Freud had in Vienna in 1910, the tension came to the fore. "My dear Jung, promise me never to abandon my sexual the-ory," Freud demanded in one confrontation, as Jung later recalled.[24] "That is the most essential thing of all. You see, we must make a dogma of it, an unshakable bulwark."

Taken aback, Jung replied, "A bulwark—against what?"

"Against the black tide of mud," answered Freud, adding, "of occultism."

"First of all, it was the words 'bulwark' and 'dogma' that alarmed me," Jung later said, "for a dogma, that is to say, an undisputable confession of faith, is set up only when the aim is to suppress doubts once and for all. But that no longer has anything to do with scientific judgment; only with a personal power drive. This was the thing that struck at the heart of our friendship."

As Jung recoiled and Freud noticed resistance in his protégé, they lost trust in each other. Jung began noticing Freud's "bitterness."[25] Freud, when once he fainted at a meeting of the two, accused Jung of having "death-wishes" toward him.[26] The tension and alienation kept building. Jung dared to dispute Freud's most cherished ideas, wondering, for instance, whether spiritual rather than sexual motives might be the foundation of the psyche. He denied that Freud's famous Oedipus complex—which would compel a man to want to kill his father and have sex with his mother—was in fact universal.

In turn, Freud began publicly ridiculing Jung's writings. He dismissed Jung's ideas as superstitious nonsense, the "occultism" he had warned Jung about. "As regards Jung, he seems all out of his wits, he is behaving quite crazy," Freud wrote to a colleague. "Take no more steps to his conciliation, it is to no effect."[27] As Jung realized he was in fact being excommunicated from the Freudian clique in psychoanalysis, he resigned the titles that he had won with Freud's blessing: the editorship of the psychoanalytic journal and the presidency of their international association.

For Jung's career, this break was a disaster. "After the break with Freud, all my friends and acquaintances dropped away. My book was declared to be rubbish; I was a mystic, and that settled the matter,"[28] Jung later recalled. He was thirty-eight years old at this time, at the threshold of midlife. He had always been clearly junior to Freud and professionally vulnerable. Now his flow of patients dried up. People deserted him. He was isolated.

Outwardly, Jung may still have looked like a picture of success: "an affluent physician with a wife and a brood of children, even a large beautiful house on a lake. Inwardly, though, none of that was what it seemed." He had extramarital affairs. He couldn't bear the noise and company of his children.[29] He was in "a state of disorientation," he later remembered. "I felt totally suspended in mid-air, for I had not yet found my own footing."[30]

FOR SEVERAL YEARS, Jung had a full-blown midlife crisis. But although he suffered, he also observed the changes within himself with great interest. He thought long and hard about his dreams during this time. He recorded even and especially his wildest fantasies and fears in a diary, and kept another journal, which he called the Red Book, in which he wrote in medieval script. He resigned from his teaching position at the University of Zurich and did something he felt slightly embarrassed by: he started building toy castles and towers. He spent hours each week by the lake near his house making villages out of stones. He found this childlike play strangely calming, and it gave him ideas about using art as therapy for patients.[31]

Jung occasionally wondered whether he might be going insane. He "heard" and "saw" characters that were communicating with him. At first, he saw two specific figures, a young woman and an old man. After a while, these characters reminded him of reports he had read about the fantasies of a schizophrenic woman. They also reminded him of motifs in the Eastern philosophies and religions he had studied, and of the ancient and Nordic myths.

He began to suspect that all human beings have a natural tendency to create myths out of their own experience, and that his life was indeed just such a story. He became convinced that we have not only an individual unconscious, as Freud believed, but also a "collective unconscious." And the figures he was seeing were universal "archetypes" roaming around inside it—the Hero on a Quest, the Wise Old Man, and so on.

So Jung starting seeing his midlife crisis in a new way. "Without this painful self-analysis, which lasted from three to six years," he later said, he "could never have hit upon and developed" the discoveries he would subsequently make.[32]

Jung thus emerged from his midlife crisis with a new identity. He left the episode with Freud behind him and achieved a new success entirely for his own ideas. He opened himself to the world and soaked it in. He traveled to exotic places, to Hannibal's homelands in Tunisia and Algeria, to New Mexico, and to India to practice yoga and learn from its gurus. He went up the Nile to Egypt and Sudan, where Cleopatra had taken Caesar. Once, he participated in an ecstatic ritual dance in Sudan so powerful that it frightened him.[33] By the time he was fifty, he had lost his old appearance of a rather stiff Prussian officer and looked more like a relaxed, somewhat disheveled, and professorial guru meditating on his chakras.[34]

He was writing and publishing more prolifically than ever. He was constantly producing new ideas that would transform the world of psychology. He pioneered art therapy, in which his patients drew or sculpted figures out of their imagination. He ditched the Freudian couch and sat across from patients in chairs. He came up with the idea of "synchronicity," the meaning in patterns of events that seem coincidental. He developed an understanding of psychological types. Individuals might be more given to introversion or extraversion, to thinking or feeling, sensation or intuition, and so on. Jung's categories are used to this day in the Myers-Briggs personality test.

Jung's last decades were the most productive and intimate of his life. Friends, disciples, patients, children, and grandchildren surrounded him right up to the end. When he set up a research center, his students insisted, over his objections, on naming it the C. G. Jung Institute. On the day of his death, Jung's favorite garden tree was struck by lightning and the bark was stripped off, but the tree was not destroyed. Jung, who regarded trees as symbols of life, would have considered this a synchronicity.[35] Aged eighty-six, he died happy and successful, the embodiment of the Wise Old Man he had seen appearing in his fantasies half a life earlier, during his midlife crisis.

E rnest Shackleton is an example of a midlife journey that failed—that did *not* lead to individuation but left Shackleton stuck in the liminality between youthful heroism and old age and that led not only to a *sense* of mortality but to actual and premature death.

Shackleton's expedition to the Antarctic in the *Endurance* had failed, but his heroic rescue of his entire crew, without a single man lost, should have counted as a much greater success. He was forty-two years old when he rescued his party from Elephant Island.

Shackleton was in middle age, although he looked and felt much older. The ordeal on the ice and in the lifeboats had taken an enormous physical toll, and he began to feel heart pains during the crossing of South Georgia. After coming so close to death so often, he felt his mortality keenly. At an event in Australia where he was asked to recruit volunteers for World War I, he told a crowd of young men, "Death is a very little thing, and I know it, because I have been face to face with it for twelve long months. All I know is that if a man can save his own soul and be true to himself and his manhood, that is what counts."[36] As Shackleton, after being totally cut off from civilization, caught up on world news, he read about the millions of men dying in the trenches of Europe. Everything was reminding Shackleton of death.

Shackleton's response seems to have been denial. He allowed no doctor near his heart with a stethoscope. Again and again, until the hour of his death, he refused to undergo a medical examination. It was as though he knew that his heart was failing and chose to ignore it. Instead, he began drinking and eating and smoking excessively. But he did admit that he felt "old and tired," as he wrote in a letter to his wife, Emily. "I am quite grey at the temples and threads throughout: but *de rien* it is all in the day's work. Anyhow you & I have the children who live our lives over again and that should help a good bit."[37]

But Shackleton was exaggerating the bond between him and his wife and three children. He had long been an absentee husband and father, and he did *not* now yearn to change that. He had long been estranged from his wife, writing her affectionate and tender letters whenever he was at sea but neglecting, arguing with, or being depressed by her whenever he was at home. "I do not think that ever again will I venture far from the homeside and your love," he wrote to Emily, even though he knew that he would try everything to venture far from the homeside again as soon as possible.[38]

Emily appeared resigned to the façade of her marriage. When Shackleton arrived home in England on May 29, 1917, he rekindled an old affair with Rosalind Chetwynd, an actress whose stage name was Rosa Lynd. At thirty-three, she was a decade younger than Shackleton and gave him the thrilling illusion of youth again. Shackleton also had a deep relationship with another woman, Janet Stancomb-Wills, who was a confidante and soul mate, not to mention wealthy, and helped Shackleton and his family with money, as they were deep in debt.[39]

Otherwise, England and his life there bored and frustrated Shackleton. The domesticity of his marriage made him claustrophobic. To make money, he gave lectures about his expedition, but he found that England after several years of modern warfare had lost its fascination for heroic exploration, and the audiences were small and lackluster. "He is getting restless—& chafing to be off," Emily wrote to a friend, "so for his sake I shall be glad when he gets his billet."[40]

But Shackleton did not get his billet, even though he desperately wanted to enlist and fight in the war. He was too old for Britain's wartime draft, and even when standards were lowered because of the dreadful casualties on the front, he would have had to get a medical exam, which he knew he would fail and refused. Rebuffed by the British war office, Shackleton found an influential patron who arranged for him to go to South America, where he was still a celebrity, to craft a propaganda strategy that might convince Chile and Argentina to drop their neutrality and join the Allies.

Shackleton, now bitter and wallowing in self-pity, resented the fact that the admiralty did not give him naval rank on this mission or a salary, but he went, glad to be away from home again. As soon as he was at sea, he resumed writing affectionate letters to Emily, telling her that he was "an absolute teetotaler," when in fact he was drinking far too much.[41] In South America, Shackleton threw himself into work, but his mission was rescinded and he had to return home again.

Ever more desperate to resume collecting youthful adventures, Shackleton did his best to join another, and somewhat sketchy, scheme. A private company was preparing an expedition to Spitsbergen, an island north of Norway whose ownership was disputed. The British feared it might fall into either German or newly Bolshevik Russian hands, and Shackleton was asked to take a ship there. He went, but on the way he "changed color very badly," as his doctor put it, suspecting a heart attack, although Shackleton refused to let the doctor listen to his heart.[42] Shackleton had to turn around and go back to England.

Soon he spotted another opportunity to leave the country. The British military wanted to open what it called "a sideshow" of the war in northern Russia and chose people who were unfit for duty on the main fronts to go to Murmansk, a Russian port north of the Arctic Circle. Shackleton was asked to go not as a commander or even an officer but as "staff officer in charge of Arctic equipment"—in effect a glorified storekeeper.[43] Shackleton desperately clung to his fantasy of heroic exploits, writing to a friend that this was a "job after my own heart, winter sledging with a fight at the end."[44] But Shackleton was employed mainly in the office in Murmansk and knew that he was being kept out of real action.

Shackleton's emotional state by now was a volatile mix of turmoil and denial. "The lord knows what I will do when this show is over," he wrote to Emily. "I don't want to go lecturing all over the place."[45] That—a calmer, perhaps more reflective life—seemed to him not mature but unworthy of an Antarctic hero. There was boastful posturing in some of his letters. "If I were rich," he wrote to Janet Stancomb-Wills, "I would do some good exploration when this is over before I grow too old, not that I feel a bit old now."[46] In other letters, he appeared resigned and depressed. "I have not been too fit lately," he wrote Emily, "I am tired darling a bit and just want a little rest away from the world and you."[47]

In another letter to his wife, Shackleton said that "sometimes I think I am no good at anything but being away in the wilds just with men and sometimes I grow restless and feel . . . part of youth is slipping away from me and that nothing matters. I want to upset everybodys calm and peace of mind when I meet calm and contented people." And throughout he was lying, if not to himself, at least to his wife: "I am strictly on the water wagon now," he wrote just after another bout of drinking.

Two weeks after Shackleton arrived in Murmansk, World War I ended, and soon after that the Bolsheviks consolidated their hold on Russia and Shackleton returned to London again. It was March 1919, and Shackleton had to support himself, so he resumed lecturing, which he dreaded. Adding insult to his already injured ego, the British public adored his old rival, Robert Scott, who had reached the South Pole in 1912 but died during the return, and who now fit the public fascination with the glorious death. Shackleton, by contrast, had failed and survived, which seemed less interesting.

Shackleton had constant pains across his shoulder blades but ignored them. He spent time around the theater where his lover, Rosalind Chetwynd, was performing, until he was told that his presence was bad for *her* publicity. Emily and the children were left to fend mostly for themselves in financing the household and schools. Shackleton was again thinking about only one thing: taking another ship to the Antarctic.

SHACKLETON STILL had a charismatic personality and wealthy and powerful acquaintances, and he persuaded an old friend to finance another expedition. He bought a ship that needed repairs and renamed it the *Quest*, making explicit that he still saw himself as a youthful hero on a mission.

He gathered some members of his *Endurance* expedition and formed a new crew. In September 1921, London's Tower Bridge opened to let the *Quest* sail through and down the Thames. Shackleton's wife, Emily, had not seen him off, although his mistress, Rosalind Chetwynd, had stopped by. As soon as he was at sea, however, Shackleton resumed writing his affectionate letters to Emily.

Everything about the new expedition seemed haphazard and unconvincing. It had no clear goal, and the crew began guessing that it was simply Shackleton's pretext for escaping from home and middle age. Shackleton had vaguely proposed to his financier to sail around the Antarctic to look for undiscovered islands. The onboard geologist was led to believe that Shackleton "hoped to find some mineral deposit that would get him out of his financial straits."[48] An Australian on board saw through Shackleton and said that this trip was "a long, but not entirely selfish joy ride . . . a last expedition [Shackleton] was determined to have."

To the crew members who had known him before, Shackleton was a different man. He was morose, pale, and clearly sick, but he still fended off attempts by the ship's doctor to examine him. While stopping in Rio de Janeiro, Shackleton had a massive heart attack. Nonetheless, he resumed drinking champagne in the mornings and more alcohol later in the day. He was bitter about his old nemesis, Robert Scott. He wrote to Stancomb-Wills that "the years are mounting up. I am mad to get away."[49] And yet he seemed to be getting away precisely because the years were mounting up.

When the *Quest* finally pulled into the harbor of South Georgia, he was briefly his old self again, reminiscing about arriving at the same spot with the *Endurance*. But that night, Shackleton had another heart attack. The doctor told him bluntly that if he wanted to continue to live, he had to change *how* he lived. "You're always wanting me to give up things, what is it I ought to give up?" Shackleton demanded of his doctor in his curmudgeonly, defiant tone.[50] A few minutes later, Shackleton was dead. He wasn't yet forty-eight years old.

A ship departed for England to bring Shackleton's body home, but Emily cabled that her husband should be buried in the Norwegian cemetery of South Georgia among the dead whalers in whose company he appeared most comfortable. The ship turned and left Shackleton in the place where he had once achieved a heroic triumph, the *Quest* anchored nearby.

Carl Jung could have been speaking about Hannibal or Ernest Shackleton when he said, "The very frequent neurotic disturbances of adult years all have one thing in common: they want to carry the psychology of the youthful phase over the threshold of the so-called years of discretion." As though observing Shackleton on his *Quest*, Jung asked, "Who does not know those touching old gentlemen who must always warm up the dish of their student days, who can fan the flame of life only by reminiscences of their heroic youth, but who, for the rest, are stuck in a hopelessly wooden Philistinism?"[51]

And as Jung knew, the risk is greatest for the likes of Hannibal and Shackleton, precisely because they have been successful and are talented. "For people of more than average ability—people who have never found it difficult to gain success and to accomplish their share of the world's work—for them the moral compulsion to be nothing but normal signifies the bed of Procrustes*—deadly and insupportable boredom, a hell of sterility and hopelessness."[52] Even new success only makes such a man "feel deflated as he realizes that this new contribution will never be as monumental as the omnipotent young man might have wished, nor will it give him the expected happiness."[53] To feel this way is to fail in one's midlife transition, and possibly in life.

---

*Procrustes was a villain living near a road to ancient Athens. He invited passersby to take a break from their liminal journey by spending the night sleeping in his bed. Then, as they slept, Procrustes would brutally adjust his guests to fit the bed's iron frame, amputating legs of the tall ones and stretching short ones on the rack. A former hero in midlife sometimes might feel that midlife is just such a bed—that he is being amputated or stretched.

ELEVEN

POLITICAL DEATH

Hell is other people.

—Jean-Paul Sartre

By his mid-thirties, Scipio had vanquished the invincible. He had subdued the deadliest enemy Rome had ever known, conquered Spain
and Africa, and won Rome's struggle against Carthage. To many of his
countrymen this made him the single greatest Roman who had ever lived,
not only the very embodiment of a youthful hero but also a wise statesman
and man of culture. Scipio was Rome at its best, and Italy could not wait
to celebrate him.

Vast crowds greeted him as he debarked on the southern tip of Italy to
make his return trip to Rome by land. Everywhere he went, peasants lined
the roads to cheer him. When he passed through a town, the entire
population turned out to catch a glimpse of the handsome conqueror
and savior. Scipio accepted gifts, gave blessings, winked thank-yous, patted
backs, flashed smiles.

When Scipio reached the banks of the Tiber, the Roman elite welcomed
him to prepare his formal triumph through the city. They opened a gate
used only for triumphal processions and the vast train began entering the
city and snaking through the frenzied crowds that squeezed into the streets
and hung from every roof, beam, and column. First went all the senators

and magistrates. Behind them marched the trumpeters, who answered the cheers of the mob with their high-pitched blasts of victory. Then a long procession of wagons and carts filed by, bearing exotic art and treasure from Carthage and Africa as well as mountains of silver.[1] Beautiful white bulls followed, on their way to being sacrificed. Then soldiers paraded past, carrying the battle standards and arms taken from the defeated Carthaginians. As the triumph progressed, the crowd grew ecstatic in anticipation of its hero.

Then Scipio entered. He stood on a sumptuous chariot pulled by white horses. His face was painted bright red, the color of Jupiter. He had donned a special toga that was dyed a dark and luminous purple and embroidered with gold. In his right hand he held a laurel bough and in his left a scepter. A slave stood behind him on his chariot, holding over his head a golden laurel wreath, as though it were a halo. "Remember, thou art mortal," the slave whispered into Scipio's ear again and again as part of the ritual. Behind Scipio came his army, in togas and without their weapons. Through a rain of flowers, Scipio rode up the Capitoline Hill and to the temple of the great Jupiter. He dismounted and slaughtered the white bulls as a sacrifice to the god.

It was the greatest triumph Rome had ever celebrated in her history, and the feasts and parties continued throughout the city. Scipio was given a new name, Africanus, for the continent he conquered, starting a new tradition for victorious generals for centuries to come. The people so adored him that they demanded that statues of him be erected all over Rome. Out of the question, said Scipio, and his modesty earned him even more adulation. All of Rome was in love with its hero.

ALMOST ALL, that is. For great Scipio also had enemies. They had been there all along, all through his astonishing and envy-evoking rise to success. There had been some early warning signs when Scipio was in Sicily, preparing for his invasion of Africa. A complicated and sordid scandal broke out in a town in southern Italy, when a sadistic Roman commander committed atrocities against the local population. It involved Scipio only tangentially, but he had made the mistake of visiting the town, called Locri, and this gave his enemies in Rome an opportunity to try to associate him with the scandal.

The most powerful political enemy was still old Fabius, who demanded that Scipio be recalled from his province of Sicily for the crime of leaving that island and sailing across the straits to Locri without the permission of the senate. The other senators considered this excessive and did not recall Scipio. But it was a sign of what was to come. Scipio now had enemies who wanted to bring him down and were willing to make their hostility public.

Other senators chimed in with Fabius to insinuate that Scipio had "gone Greek." They insinuated that Scipio was becoming soft, decadent, and un-Roman; that he was probably lounging around in Sicily's Greek gymnasia getting oiled and massaged and fraternizing with effeminate philosophers; that he was growing his hair long, in the Greek style, and letting his men carouse with wine and women; that he was spending his time admiring Hellenistic sculpture and art when he should be drilling his troops in swordsmanship and battle maneuvers; and whatever else the fertile imaginations of his detractors conjured up.

SCIPIO'S MOST FEROCIOUS and tireless attacker was a young Roman senator named Marcus Porcius Cato. He was not an aristocrat, but what the Romans called a "new man," a nouveau riche with a lot to prove. He had been drafted into the senate after the horrendous losses against Hannibal had decimated its ranks. In appearance, bearing, and style, he was the exact opposite of the sophisticated and cavalier Scipio.

Cato had piercing gray eyes and a ruddy complexion. He believed that "pleasure is evil's chief bait; the body the principal calamity of the soul." He ate only boiled turnips for dinner and made sure everybody knew it. He was said to use "living creatures like old shoes or dishes" and throw them away as soon as they ceased being useful; when slaves grew old, sick, or weak, he sold them. Encountering a fat man, he berated the man publicly, demanding to know "what use can the state turn a man's body to, when all between the throat and groin is taken up by the belly?"[2] Wherever Romans were having fun, he was quick to show up and make everybody feel guilty. His reputation as a killjoy was so widespread that a ditty about him made the rounds through Rome:

> *Porcius, who snarls at all in every place*
> *With his grey eyes, and with his fiery face,*
> *Even after death will scarce admitted be*
> *Into the infernal realms by Hecate.*[3]

This same ascetic, miserly, misanthropic, puritanical Cato had been a treasurer of the army and served under Scipio when he first left for Sicily. The two men mixed like oil and water. If it had been up to Cato, Scipio would have fed his army nothing but boiled turnips. But Scipio believed in treating his soldiers well. At one point Cato, though subordinate to Scipio, stormed up to Scipio with a bookkeeper's expression on his redder-than-usual face and accused him of "corrupting" the Roman army and giving the troops "means to abandon themselves to unnecessary pleasures and luxuries."

Scipio, with his usual brevity in such matters, replied that he had "no need for so accurate a treasurer" and probably added a reminder that everybody would do best to stay focused on the task of invading Africa and conquering Hannibal. Cato fumed and went back to Rome just in time for the Locri scandal and the insinuations by Fabius in the senate against Scipio. Cato eagerly weighed in, complaining of "Scipio's lavishing unspeakable sums, and childishly loitering away his time in wrestling matches and comedies, as if he were not to make war, but holiday."[4]

Most senators knew that envy and pettiness, rather than patriotism, were behind these charges and that the whole discussion was at its core ridiculous. But Fabius and Cato led a powerful faction and had to be assuaged. So the senate decided to make a bureaucratic gesture, sending a committee to Sicily to investigate the charges against Scipio. In effect, Scipio was being audited. This was clearly an insult, and it was meant to be so.

But Scipio, characteristically, wasted no time being insulted and gave the senate's auditors a gracious welcome to Sicily. He opened his accounting books to them, showed them the maneuvers and the barracks, and explained his strategy for winning the war. The visiting senators were impressed. What they saw was not even remotely what Cato's rants had described. They went back to Rome, where their report silenced Fabius and Cato for the time being. Scipio was confirmed in his command, his reputation still secure.

He went on to invade Africa and to win the war. And now, here he was again: back in Rome, celebrating victory over Hannibal, Rome's greatest triumph. Scipio's enemies hated him more than ever.

FOR THE MOMENT, Scipio's success was such that nobody could deny it or find fault with it without seeming ridiculous. His fame and popularity went some way toward protecting him from his enemies. In the coming years, he would hold the most prestigious offices, and as *princeps senatus* would for years rank as the equivalent of a senate president. As was his wont, he wore his power and fame discreetly. He introduced Greek culture and education to Rome and explained to the Romans his vision of their future, which was as large, sweeping, and clear as ever.

Thanks to Scipio's conquests, Rome was now the dominant military power in the western Mediterranean and was safe from attacks there. So Scipio began looking toward the Hellenistic world of the eastern Mediterranean that he so admired. As a diplomat, general, and statesman, he would influence all the momentous decisions the Romans would take toward the Greeks in the coming decades. It was Scipio, as much as any-body, who turned Rome into a superpower.

The Romans felt that after Scipio's victory over Carthage there were still scores to settle with the Hellenistic kingdoms in Greece and Syria, as well as threats to preempt and alliances to honor. One of the successor king-doms to Alexander the Great's empire, Macedon, had made an alliance with Hannibal while he seemed invincible, and the Romans were deter-mined to punish this treachery as an example to others. Simultaneously, two Roman allies in the eastern Mediterranean, the kingdom of Pergamum and the island of Rhodes, fed the Romans intelligence that Macedon was now colluding with the huge Seleucid Empire, ruled by King Antiochus. Antiochus was the most suspect ruler in the region because he was now hosting Hannibal himself at his court.

So the Romans began a long series of campaigns in Greece and what they called Asia (modern Turkey), rolling over the Hellenistic armies each time. At first, the Romans still wanted to show that they had no imperial ambitions in Greece. So, in 196 BCE, they declared all Greek cities free and completely withdrew from Greece. But this so-called freedom of the Greeks did not last long. The Greeks distrusted the Romans and invited Antiochus to come from Syria to Greece as their new protector. This was both an outrage and a threat to the Romans, especially since Antiochus was now employing Hannibal in his army. The Romans once again pre-pared for war and sought out their best commanders.

Scipio had in recent years been reelected consul, and it would have been unseemly for him to be consul yet again. He also wanted to give his brother Lucius a chance at achievement and pushed for him to become consul and lead the army against Antiochus. The senate didn't have much faith in Lucius, but it made him the official commander once his brother, Scipio Africanus, agreed to serve alongside him, nominally as his brother's second-in-command but in reality as chief strategist.

Together, the two Scipio brothers invaded the Seleucid Empire and defeated Antiochus. Africanus insisted that his brother Lucius get the public credit and the new name of Asiaticus. But everybody in Rome assumed that Africanus was the real victor. Scipio, now in his mid-forties, was yet again Rome's conquering hero. And his enemies hated him even more.

CATO WAS AS AGGRESSIVE and manipulative as ever. Boiling with resentment, he gathered a group of influential citizens and went after the Scipio brothers. The clique revived the old charges and insinuations against Scipio Africanus and spread every possible rumor about him, no matter how implausible. Then they decided to contest the Scipios' expense report. There was an allegation that funds had gone missing during the war against Antiochus, and that was the excuse they needed. Never mind that Scipio had saved Rome's existence and made it a superpower. Cato and his gang were determined to take him down by any means.

Scipio, now in middle age, was offended and hurt. As his brother, Asiaticus, stood before his accusers in the senate and held up the campaign's account books to defend himself, Africanus got up, took the papers out of his brother's hands, tore them to pieces, and threw them on the floor.[5] He wanted to show that this sort of forensic bean counting, in this political context and at his age, was beneath him.

The gesture did not help. He was put on trial for embezzlement. As it happened, the date of his trial fell on the anniversary of his great victory against Hannibal. Scipio walked to the *rostra*, the speakers' platform adorned with the beaks of the Carthaginian ships taken in the First Punic War, and addressed the crowd: "Tribunes of the plebs, and citizens of Rome, this is the day on which I fought with good success in a pitched battle against Hannibal and the Carthaginians in Africa. Therefore, since it is proper on this day that lawsuits and quarrels should be set aside, I shall straightway go from here to the Capitol" to offer sacrifices to Jupiter, Juno, Minerva, and the other gods. As Scipio walked away, the entire crowd spontaneously followed him across the Forum and up to the Capitoline Hill. Only the prosecutors, their slaves, and one herald were left, and they had no choice but to suspend the proceedings for the day.[6] The Roman people still loved and revered Scipio as much as ever.

BUT HIS ENEMIES kept hounding him. The trial was postponed a second time, indefinitely, and nobody showed an interest in taking the matter up again, but the charges were not officially dropped.

Scipio could not comprehend the pettiness of a few envious senators, their refusal to see the big picture and to sympathize with the large, indeed epic, vision for Rome to which Scipio had dedicated his entire life. He became depressed and, his cavalier nature notwithstanding, yielded to bitterness.

Alienated from his city and nation, Scipio voluntarily withdrew from Rome and from all political life and went to live in seclusion in his villa in the south of Italy. Here the records of his life stop. Perhaps he felt as Hannibal had felt when he had lived as a hermit at his villa in northern Africa, reliving in his mind the past with its triumphs and disasters.

At the age of about fifty-three, Scipio died in this self-imposed exile, probably in the same year that Hannibal died in another part of the Mediterranean. In his will, Scipio noted that his body was never to return to Rome. He left an epitaph inscribed at his villa: "Ungrateful fatherland, thou hast not even my bones!"[7]

How could Scipio not have seen all along what was happening? It was clear to everybody that certain people found his astonishing success threatening. Why not to him? Like so many other people who are blessed with talent, charisma, or vision, Scipio was unable or unwilling to acknowledge the petty resentment that drives most people some of the time and some people most of the time. Because he always looked far and aimed high, he habitually *over*looked the lowly and sordid aspects of human nature. Because he was large, he could not see that others were small. In common with many people of talent, he had an innocence about him that made him vulnerable.

This was his Achilles' heel. His enemies got out their magnifying glasses and crawled through the dust under Scipio's feet to find something they could use against him. In another era, they would have staffed the tribunals of the Spanish Inquisition, extracting false confessions from people accused by anonymous enemies, or lined up behind Senator Joseph McCarthy to execute his cold-war witch hunt.

Hell is other people, as the French existentialist Jean-Paul Sartre wrote. Hell is people like Cato. Hell is the school-yard bully, the master of office politics, the jealous neighbor, the woman scorned, and any mediocre man or woman who sees others succeed and hates them for it.

Every culture and era has its own metaphors for this hell. Some people speak of a crab mentality to describe those who sabotage others as crabs in a bucket pull down other crabs trying to climb out. Scandinavians speak about the Jante law, after the fictional town of Jante, whose burghers punished and humiliated anybody who dared stand out with great achievement. Australians and New Zealanders speak of the tall-poppy syndrome, which makes people want to cut down anybody who, like a tall poppy jutting out from its field, rises above the rest. Scipio was just such a poppy.

Ludwig Erhard was also a tall poppy and cut down in much the same way as Scipio. He became economics minister and chancellor of West Germany even though he had never been interested in power for its own sake. "I have no political ambition," he said, and later added, "In my eyes power is always dull, it is dangerous, it is brutal and ultimately even dumb."[8] What instead drove Uncle Lulu was a big idea. This was the idea of freedom—in life, society, and economy. But like Scipio, Uncle Lulu had a naïve side. He was a man of vision, and simultaneously blind to the dangerous eddies of power politics.

His vision of freedom—classical "liberalism," as that word is properly defined—was far from a mainstream philosophy in the years following World War II. Most policymakers in Europe were subscribing to *il*liberal ideas. Communist and Socialist parties were gaining popularity all over Europe. The French yearned for their ancient traditions of state planning and economic nationalism. Even the centrist parties of Europe, such as the Christian Democrats in West Germany, favored cozy arrangements between big business, labor unions, and government. Indeed, even the American occupation forces believed that a planned economy, instead of capitalism, was necessary to rebuild Germany. Only a small group of optimists, intellectuals, and genuine liberals, including Ludwig Erhard, believed in free markets for goods, ideas, and values. And so Erhard set himself a goal in life, which was to demonstrate that freedom could work and to teach its values to his fellow Germans.

Adopting a phrase coined by a friend of his, Erhard named his idea the "social market economy." The phrase included the word *social* to steal some of the thunder from the various Socialist demagogues then in vogue, but Erhard emphasized the word *market.* "I hope you don't misunderstand me when I speak of a social market economy," Uncle Lulu once said to Friedrich von Hayek, the most prominent liberal economist and philosopher of his day. "I mean that the market as such is social, not that it needs to be made social."[9]

It was hard, exhausting work, but Uncle Lulu succeeded as brilliantly as Scipio once had. Under the Allied occupation, he became the architect of a currency reform that replaced nearly worthless money with a new currency. This revived the destroyed postwar economy almost at once. Even in the bombed-out rubble, some Germans had been hoarding whatever goods they still had—perhaps cigarettes, old paintings, or carpets. As soon as a new currency with credible value was circulating, they brought these goods out of hoarding, sold them, and bought other things. Impromptu markets appeared on the streets. Suddenly, it made sense again to build, invest, and do business.

Within a few years, West Germany had Europe's fastest-growing economy, and its citizens became more prosperous than they had ever imagined. People began to call the rebirth a *Wirtschaftswunder*, an "economic miracle," and Erhard its "father." Uncle Lulu's policies were not the only reason for the economic revival—American aid under the Marshall Plan, which extended to other Western European countries as well, also played a part. But in the popular imagination, Erhard became the embodiment of the *Wirtschaftswunder*. The DM became famous for its stability and a symbol of West Germany's new and robust democracy.

During the 1950s, Uncle Lulu traveled the country and continent to explain the ideas underlying his policies. He was jovial, good-natured, and persuasive. He discovered that his optimism was infectious and that he was an inspiring public speaker. He was the most popular politician in West Germany.

BUT JUST AS SCIPIO'S ENEMIES hated his success and began to plot against him, so did Erhard's. Erhard had never in his life joined a political party, and even when he was elected to represent one—the Christian Democrats—he refused to become an official member. A smaller party, the Free Democrats, which was closer to Erhard's beliefs, also asked him to join, but he declined. He considered himself outside of and above parties and factions, and he tried to emphasize always that he worked only for his ideals. His supporters loved him for it.

But this independence had an unexpected effect. It made him a political loner. While his rivals were conspiring inside their party structures, Erhard not only stayed outside of those structures but also refused on principle to conspire with anybody. Should he ever be attacked, he would have no group or faction—no political "clan"—to defend him. And that time would come.

Erhard's biggest rival—a modern Fabius and Cato rolled into one—was Konrad Adenauer, a Christian Democrat and a man with a commanding presence in postwar Germany. A generation older than Uncle Lulu, Adenauer had been mayor of Cologne before the war and was now chancellor of West Germany and thus the most powerful man in the country.

(Germany's president, like Britain's queen, is nominally the head of state but largely a figurehead.) Uncle Lulu, as economics minister, was a member of Adenauer's cabinet. Ostensibly, the two were thus on the same side, political allies. But their relationship was complex and turned increasingly tense.

As personalities, Adenauer and Uncle Lulu were opposites in every way. Erhard loved big ideas and delegated administrative details and management decisions to others; Adenauer micromanaged his underlings and tended to fight and win bureaucratic turf wars. Erhard shunned power games; Adenauer was Machiavellian and excelled at closed-door power maneuvers.

Erhard relaxed by having a whiskey (or four) while playing cards at night with his wife, whom I knew as Auntie Lu, and he loved his cigars (reminding my father with a wink that tobacco was a plant and thus contained essential vitamins and nutrients). Adenauer was an ascetic and a teetotaler; he hated the stench of cigar smoke and was disgusted by the ashes that sometimes clung to Erhard's lapel.[10]

Erhard was principled in politics and ran campaigns based purely on his ideas; Adenauer suspended principles for power and handed out favors and gifts to important constituencies before elections, even if the gifts—subsidies to a particular industry, for example—contradicted his own policies. Erhard was an optimist about human nature; Adenauer was a pessimist. Erhard vigorously debated with Adenauer about policy but never took these debates personally; Adenauer did take disagreements personally and, while using Erhard's popularity to win elections, was prepared to double-cross him at a whim.

Indeed, throughout the 1950s, Adenauer knew that he needed to keep the popular Erhard in his cabinet if he wanted to win reelection. Yet Erhard wasn't always comfortable being in the cabinet. Several times, when Erhard felt that Adenauer's policies compromised his principles, he offered his resignation. Adenauer, ever the realist, talked him out of it each time. But while pleading with Erhard to stay in the cabinet, Adenauer would simultaneously undermine him in public speeches and in secret meetings with Christian Democratic party elders.

In 1957, at the height of his popularity, Erhard was the main factor in a big electoral victory for Adenauer's Christian Democratic Union, or CDU. As a result, he became vice chancellor and the pundits started talking about him as the logical successor to Adenauer. This was the scenario that Adenauer feared. Stung by a sense of rivalry, Adenauer began scheming with his factions and cronies to prevent it.

For a few more years, Erhard remained so popular among voters that his enemies dared not risk an open attack, just as Cato was temporarily silenced in the years following Scipio's victory over Hannibal. In 1963, the CDU nominated Erhard for chancellor. This was remarkable, given that Erhard was still not even a party member (a convenient story took hold that he did in fact join, but nobody has ever found the paperwork that would have made his membership official).[11] On October 15, 1963, Adenauer stepped down. The following day, the parliament elected Erhard the new chancellor. Uncle Lulu was now, in theory, the most powerful man in West Germany.

UNCLE LULU'S TRIUMPH was an impostor. Erhard's decline began on the day he became chancellor. He still refused to pay attention to building himself a loyal political base and a network of allies that might become a bulwark against his enemies. Some party officials took this as a snub. He also decided not to become chairman of the CDU, and naïvely—graciously, in his mind—allowed Adenauer to take that post. And he consented to the nomination of Heinrich Lübke, who also conspired against Erhard, as West Germany's president. He had one or two supporters in his cabinet, but he allowed Adenauer to staff many of the other positions in the ministries with his cronies.

Erhard was now surrounded on all sides by his enemies. But in his dogged optimism and idealism, he refused to regard them as foes. They may have spoken badly about him, but he never stooped to returning the favor.

Erhard was not naturally good at reading, or even mingling with, people. Often he was downright awkward and clumsy, and anecdotes began circulating to reinforce that impression. Once, on his sixty-ninth birthday, a party was thrown for him at the chancellor's office. The usual list of well-wishers came to congratulate him and then ate, drank, and gossiped. But instead of mingling, Erhard went to sit in a corner and began to read newspapers as if he were alone in the room.[12] Those who knew him understood that he was being his eccentric and socially tone-deaf self, but others thought he was simply being rude.

He was also bad at diplomatic tactics. Erhard had always been enthusiastically pro-American. This was another bone of contention with Adenauer, who favored the closest possible ties with France as a way of reintegrating West Germany into Europe, even though the French wanted to exclude Britain and America from the newly emerging European federation to increase their own power. Erhard was against this and wanted to remain close with the United States in an open and inclusive world of free nations.

Erhard's big political mistake was to let everybody, especially the Americans, know this preference without qualifications. When Dean Rusk, who at the time was U.S. secretary of state, came to Bonn, Erhard gushed to his guest that West Germany would be lost without the United States.[13] Rusk reported this to President Lyndon Johnson, who immediately concluded that he would need to make no concessions to Erhard on any matter and took West German support for granted.

When Erhard later visited the White House, Johnson kept him waiting for half an hour. During another visit to Washington, Erhard was in the middle of a sentence when Johnson simply walked out on him before the interpreter had even completed the translation.[14] On another occasion, after a state dinner in the White House, Johnson took Erhard to a small room and verbally and physically bullied the aging and much shorter chancellor, who was recoiling on his clubfoot and lame leg. The American diplomats in the room were mortified with embarrassment.[15]

The anecdotes of humiliation by the American president made their way home, where Erhard's political enemies recycled and embellished them as they prepared to pounce. In 1966, Johnson demanded that West Germany pay huge additional costs to finance the American occupation of West Germany and the Vietnam War. It appeared that West Germany would have to raise taxes just as it was entering its first major recession and unemployment was climbing, a situation that sullied Erhard's image as an economic wizard.

The Free Democrats who were Erhard's coalition partners in parliament resigned from his cabinet, and Erhard had to govern with the support of only the Christian Democrats, who did not by themselves have a majority of the seats. Erhard's back was against the wall. His refusal to embrace the party and cultivate allies over the years now showed. The support he needed was not there.

Adenauer himself was too old to run for chancellor again but let it be known that he considered Erhard unfit for that office. Adenauer's supporters had found new champions, and new contenders and rivals stepped forward. After a flurry of meetings, whispering campaigns, coalition negotiations, motions, votes, measures, and machinations, the Christian Democrats chose a new candidate for chancellor, Kurt Georg Kiesinger, and demanded that Erhard resign. Two months before his seventieth birthday, he did. He had been chancellor for just over three years.

UNCLE LULU CONTINUED to have a seat in parliament and honorary titles, but he gradually faded from the political scene and withdrew to his house overlooking an Alpine lake, the setting in which I knew him. As always in his life, he found comfort and happiness in his family, playing cards with his wife and my father, or hiding eggs for me, a toddler, to find during Easter. He continued to give speeches and started a foundation to spread his ideas about freedom. But in the world of power—politics—he had failed and retreated for good.

P olitical death is usually a metaphor. But there is a shockingly literal example of political death that illustrates just how arbitrary and irrational a group or nation can become when the equivalents of a Fabius or a Cato manipulate the baser instincts of human nature. At about the time when Ludwig Erhard was hounded out of the chancellor's office in West Germany, Mao Zedong and his wife and henchmen launched the Cultural Revolution in China, which led to the gruesome deaths of gifted but naïve people such as Liu Shaoqi, the president of China.

For most of his career, Liu was one of China's faithful Communists and most revered leaders. In his twenties he and Mao and a few others founded China's fledgling Communist movement. Liu then studied in Moscow, at the time the world capital of communism, and returned to China full of revolutionary zeal. He organized miners and railroad workers and led strikes. In the 1930s, he fought the Japanese invaders and the Nationalists in China's brutal civil war. Liu was one of those who went on the Long March into the countryside to evade the Nationalist army of General Chiang Kai-shek.

It was a time of danger and hardship but also of romance, as the young revolutionaries lived in caves and formed tight friendships. And it was particularly romantic for Liu as he met, toward the end of the Long March, perhaps the most sophisticated young woman in all of China, Wang Guangmei. Her father had been a diplomat in America and Britain, and she spoke English, French, and Russian. She was discreet, charming, intelligent, and self-assured. She had earned a master's degree in nuclear physics and had turned down scholarships to Stanford and the University of Michigan to stay in China and fight for her country and for communism. Many men wanted to marry her, but she had set her sights on Liu. She was twenty-five; he was forty-eight, and a widower. They fell in love and married.[16]

They were a great couple. Liu already had children from his first marriage, and had four more with Wang. They genuinely believed that communism would improve the lives of farmers and workers in China and the world. In fact, Liu literally wrote the book on communism. It was called *How to Be a Communist* and became China's bestseller until Mao's *Little Red Book*, a collection of aphorisms more brandished than read, replaced it. Liu and Wang tried to *live* communism. They held so-called daily life meetings with their staff, in which they dutifully listened to maids, cooks, and drivers complaining about the price of fish or the lines at the canteen.[17]

From 1949, when Mao stood in Tiananmen Square in Beijing to proclaim the People's Republic of China, and throughout the 1950s and early '60s, Liu was one of the pillars of the new nation, along with Mao and a handful of others. Mao was the chairman of the Communist Party; Liu was his first vice chairman and ostensible successor. When in 1959 Mao stepped down as chairman of the government—president, in effect—Liu took the role. He was officially China's head of state.

He and his family lived with the other leaders in Zhongnanhai, a walled compound next to the Forbidden City in Beijing, with lakes and pavilions and villas and courtyards. Liu's villa, named the "House of Good Fortune," was so close to Mao's that the two buildings almost touched. During this time, his three older children with Wang, Pingping, Yuanyuan, and Tingting, were already in high school; the youngest, Xiaoxiao, was still in grade school. In the early 1960s, Liu's only worry was about his health. He was in his sixties and had diabetes. "If Karl Marx could give me ten more years," Liu liked to say, "we could build China stronger and richer."

HAD HE BEEN more perceptive, he might have worried about a lot more than his health. But Liu, like Scipio and Erhard, was too busy thinking about large ideas to notice the petty and base.

Liu might have noticed, for instance, that Mao's wife, Jiang Qing, was seething with envy whenever she saw the elegant and graceful Wang Guangmei by Liu's side. Jiang was Wang's opposite—vulgar, insecure, vengeful, and vindictive. She had been born to a prostitute and had grown up without parental love. As a teenager she became an actress and made her way to Shanghai, China's most bustling and sophisticated city. She played in various theaters and films and used her allure to marry or sleep with a succession of powerful men. "Sex is engaging in the first rounds," she once told an interviewer. "What sustains interest in the long run is political power."[18] Already she kept a mental record of anybody who had ever slighted, disdained, or obstructed her, to be used if ever she might have the power and opportunity for revenge.

At some point, Jiang joined the Long March and set her sights on Mao, ultimately seducing him. In 1938, they married, raising eyebrows among the then straitlaced Communist officials because Mao had not yet divorced his previous wife. After the Communist victory in 1949, Mao did not give Jiang major official roles, but she used her access to wield power. In the 1960s, Jiang persuaded Mao to let her be one of the primary executors of the Cultural Revolution, endowed with the power to persecute anybody she hated.

Wang Guangmei was not a rival for Mao's affection, nor did she give any affront. But she was elegant and sophisticated, as many people who had once looked down upon Jiang Qing were, and Jiang wanted to destroy her.

Liu Shaoqi might also have paid attention to Mao himself, who felt surprisingly insecure by the 1960s and envied Liu's popularity and stature, even if Liu had no intention of challenging Mao. A few years earlier, the Communist leaders had met to take stock of a disastrous ideological program called the Great Leap Forward, which was causing poverty and starvation throughout China. Liu was one of several leaders who pushed for more pragmatic policies. Mao, who saw conspiracies everywhere, took this as a slight and an insult. He wanted to get rid of everybody in the party he distrusted. And now he felt threatened politically by Liu, just as Jiang Qing felt threatened personally by Liu's wife.

As Fabius had Cato around, Mao and Jiang had sycophants who eagerly volunteered to do their dirty work. Two of these were Kang Sheng and Lin Biao. As Mao left Beijing for a city in southern China known for its beautiful flowers, he hinted with a few nods what might please him, and his henchmen did the rest.

A "Cultural Revolution" was launched, ostensibly to clean China of old customs, old culture, old habits, and old ideas—the so-called Four Olds of Maoist propaganda at the time. Nobody had any idea of what precisely that meant, and nobody seemed to care. What young people across China understood was that they had permission to dress up in red armbands, go out in gangs, and terrorize anybody they didn't like. Teachers, parents, doctors—anybody who irritated them suddenly represented the Four Olds and had to be punished.

Mao wanted anarchy and chaos, with himself sitting aloof from it like a god, and that's what he got as China disintegrated. Every student in China became a Red Guard and then joined the hordes ransacking and vandalizing schools, temples, and hospitals. They plastered walls with *dazibao*, posters with big Chinese characters that named and shamed an individual they were targeting next. Then they found that person and humiliated, beat, and sometimes killed him. New phrases entered the Chinese language, such as "being suicided," as the Red Guards made their targets jump out of windows or lie on train tracks. It was all in the name of protecting Mao and the revolution, in the name of eliminating "capitalist roaders."

LIU SHAOQI was genuinely puzzled by the Cultural Revolution. What on earth did it mean? He called Mao, still in his vacation retreat, by telephone and said that he was trying to understand what was happening. But Mao offered no advice. Liu and his wife began to get nervous. As they sat with their children at dinner in their safe compound, the children told them about the world outside the walls. Hysterical student meetings, rallies, large-character posters everywhere, deans and teachers being thrown out of windows.

Liu and a like-minded leader, Deng Xiaoping, finally flew to meet Mao in person. What were they supposed to do? "I have no plans to come," said Mao. "Solve the problem according to the situation in the movement."[19]

None the wiser, Liu flew back to Beijing and went to the high school where his daughter Pingping was enrolled. He told the students old tales of communism, about the Bolshevik Revolution and the Long March, but he had to admit that he wasn't quite sure what the Cultural Revolution was about. Then he returned to the compound. To his surprise, he was told that Mao had changed his mind and returned. He was in his office. Liu ran over to see him, but the guards told him that Mao was tired. Liu wasn't allowed to see him. He went home.

By August 1966, in Beijing's summer heat and dust, the huge Tiananmen Square in front of the Zhongnanhai compound was packed full of Red Guards. At dawn, as the sun was rising, they chanted, "The East is Red," then shouted slogans. Everywhere, Mao's *Little Red Book* was being waved. Then, to everyone's surprise, Mao himself appeared. He had been up all night and walked across the square to cheers, then vanished back into the compound.

A couple of hours later Mao returned, with other leaders. They stood on the balcony of the Gate of Heavenly Peace that gave the square its name. Mao and the other leaders were dressed in military uniform. All except two. One of them was Liu Shaoqi, standing slightly apart from the others. At the last minute, Mao had sent messages dictating the dress code to all the leaders, except Liu. Liu was expressionless. Below them was a sea of Red Guards, howling and cheering. Here on the balcony, nobody spoke to Liu and he spoke to nobody.

Mao himself did not bother to speak. Instead, his henchman Lin Biao screamed to the masses that they should "beat down" Mao's enemies, the "capitalist roaders," the traitors, and the Four Olds. Just after noon, Mao left the balcony, still having said nothing. The others followed one by one. But nobody beckoned Liu to come as well. Suddenly, he was left standing on the balcony all by himself. The mob below him was shouting to "bring back Mao." Why was Liu still there, alone? The mob wondered, and he wondered. After an excruciatingly long time, Liu decided not to wait for permission to go, and left, trying to maintain his composure.[20]

———

IT DID NOT TAKE LONG NOW. Liu was still officially the president of China. He still went to his office, his secretaries still showed up for work, but there were no more phone calls, no more memos in the in-box, no meetings, no knocks on the door with urgent business. His children brought stories from the outside into the compound. Like all youngsters, they were themselves Red Guards now, and were out and about smashing things. To their horror, they began seeing large-character posters denouncing their own father. The posters were calling Liu a "traitor" and the "Number One Capitalist Roader."

Then the telephone rang. Somebody claimed in a shrill voice that one daughter, Pingping, had been in a car accident and was in serious condition. Liu and his wife rushed to the hospital. Then they realized that it was a ruse. There had been no accident. The Red Guards were trying to lure them out of the compound. They turned and raced back to Zhongnanhai.

A few days later, Mao unexpectedly summoned Liu to his office. Liu was eager to make amends. He offered to resign, to take the family and go to the countryside, to take up farming, to disappear.

Mao didn't answer directly. He sat there, smoking his cigarettes. Do some reading, he advised Liu cryptically. Try Hegel or Diderot and "study hard," Mao said. Oh, and "take care of your health."[21] It was the end of the interview. Liu left and tried to figure out what Mao meant.

Two days later, Liu received the answer. A mob of Red Guards stormed Zhongnanhai and broke into his office. They plastered large-character posters on its walls and forced Liu and his wife to stand on the desks, balancing on one leg, as they shouted obscenities at them. They ransacked the office and ripped out the telephone lines, and put Liu and his wife under house arrest. Liu sensed that things were building toward a dreadful climax and told his wife and children, "Please spread my ashes in the sea as was done for Engels."[22]

The Red Guards dragged Liu and his wife outside, separated them, and began torturing them, forcing their children to watch. They picked Liu up as though he were a sack of sand and dropped him to the floor. They beat and kicked him in the face. They yanked his white mop of hair. When seven-year-old Xiaoxiao started screaming in terror and her older siblings tried to console her, the Red Guards became even angrier. They redoubled their efforts on Liu, leaving him on the ground as a bloody pulp. This went on for weeks, again and again.

Then, one day, an army truck pulled up and took the Liu children away, to separate "dormitories." From then on, the children received no information about what happened to their parents. They would not even know whether they were alive or dead.

Their mother was thrown into a prison. Liu himself, still in the compound, had only seven teeth left and could no longer chew the scraps of food he was fed. The Red Guards took away his diabetes medication. His muscles atrophied and his hands turned into claws. Then, one day, he was wrapped naked in a blanket and loaded onto an airplane. He was flown to a remote and forgotten part of China and dumped in a prison. Weeks later he was found there, lying naked in his own vomit on the floor. He was dead.[23]

For whatever reasons, Mao and Jiang Qing allowed Liu's wife to live. But her mother was tortured to death in another prison, refusing to testify that her daughter was a spy. Liu's eldest son from his first marriage was beaten to death, his corpse placed on a railroad track with a suicide note. The next son spent eleven years in prison, in a dark cell, and died shortly after he was released. Liu's daughter was beaten and sent to a primitive part of Mongolia but survived. Wang Guangmei herself also survived and was reunited with her children. For years, they and the world did not even know that Liu Shaoqi was dead.

TWELVE

AGING AND TRANSCENDING

What a man can be, he must be. This need we may call self-actualization.

—Abraham Maslow

When Hannibal was about fifty-four and Scipio about forty-three—
in 193 BCE, about ten years before both men died—they met
again. They were old enemies and yet thought of themselves as comrades
of a sort, a paradox that did not seem to bother them. They met far from
home, in what is today Turkey, where they were once again on opposite
sides—Scipio and his brother, Lucius, were leading a Roman army to war
against Antiochus, the eastern king who employed Hannibal as an adviser.
But none of that was of even the slightest interest to these two men when
they finally had an opportunity to be alone.

For each of them, there was nobody else in the world quite like the
other. When they were together, they felt that they understood, and *were*
understood, as at no other time. They bantered easily, teased each other,
laughed, and reflected.

Half seriously and half humorously, Scipio asked Hannibal whom he considered to be the greatest general of all time.*

Hannibal, who had a mischievous sense of humor, answered deadpan: "Alexander, King of the Macedonians, because with a small force he routed armies of countless numbers, and because he traversed the remotest lands. Merely to visit such lands transcended human expectation."

Fair enough, Scipio nodded. Alexander had indeed been a great general; in fact, they were at this very moment in the lands that Alexander had once conquered. Scipio then asked: 'Who do you think was the *second*-greatest general of all time, Hannibal?'

"Pyrrhus," replied Hannibal, without missing a beat and feigning a very serious face. "He was the first to teach the art of laying out a camp. Besides that, no one has ever shown nicer judgment in choosing his ground, or in disposing his forces."

Quite so, nodded Scipio, with a look of exaggerated seriousness. 'So who is *third*, do you reckon?'

'Well, I am, of course,' said Hannibal.

At last the dam broke and Scipio emitted a suppressed laugh. "What would you be saying if you had defeated me?" he asked Hannibal.

"In that case," said Hannibal, now with a big grin, "I should certainly put myself before Alexander and before Pyrrhus—in fact, before all other generals!"

They were both laughing now, and Scipio nudged Hannibal for the compliment. In his wry, understated way, Hannibal had said what they both knew. None of the other generals had ever met a general of the same caliber in his time. Together, Hannibal and Scipio were the greatest, but they formed *one* story, not two.

Hannibal and Scipio both understood that they had never fought each other out of personal hatred, but that they had followed what they believed was their calling and duty in life. If Hannibal kept fighting Rome now, as

---

*This conversation is based on Livy, XXXV, 14. I have put direct speech that appears in Livy in double quotation marks, and direct speech that is part of my interpretation in single quotation marks.

Scipio understood, it was not because Hannibal still expected to defeat Rome, but because he was meant to. It was his destiny.

Scipio, for his part, confided in Hannibal that he felt uneasy about what lay ahead for him, his current success notwithstanding. He had picked up strong currents of animosity against him and his brother from their political enemies in Rome.

'I still remember what you told me that day at Zama before our battle,' Scipio said to Hannibal. 'You said that I might be at the high point of my life and should not get carried away. When I won the battle, I knew that you were right. I knew that I could never achieve anything so great again.'

'And did that bother you?' asked Hannibal.

'Yes, it bothered me,' said Scipio. 'But I'm trying to get to the point where you are now, Hannibal, where I accept things for what they are. I do what I have to do, I do it as well as I can.'

For a while, they kept walking in silence. Then Scipio asked Hannibal: 'If you could turn back time to when you were a young man at Saguntum, but you already knew what you know now, what would you do?'

Hannibal turned to his friend and said: 'You already know the answer.'

'Yes, I do,' said Scipio. 'You would do it all again.'

THE FAILURE OF HANNIBAL'S midlife transition a few years before this conversation had been sealed by a cruel irony. While Hannibal was still in Carthage after his defeat by Scipio, he had *not* been in league with Antiochus, the king of the Seleucid Empire. Hannibal had *not* been, at that time, planning another war against Rome. Instead, he had been true to his word to Scipio and was acting in good faith toward Rome.

But too many people in Rome simply did not believe him. Knowing this, his political rivals in Carthage slandered him to make the Romans remove him. Presumed guilty, Hannibal fled to a place that would shelter him. And so he walked right into the arms of that same Antiochus, making the slanders against him come true retroactively.

Hannibal was now a refugee, not a commander of an army; older and weaker, and without power. He was at the mercy of powerful but petty men like King Antiochus, who had never proved himself in battle or in life and was as insecure as he was arrogant. It was such people—vain, fickle, often stupid—that Hannibal now depended on.

HANNIBAL'S EPISODE with Antiochus set the tone for all the kings who were to come. At first, Antiochus was thrilled to be in the company of Hannibal, the man the Romans feared more than any other. Hannibal explained to Antiochus that if he really wanted to cut the Roman Empire down to size, he would have to send a fleet of warships to invade Italy and simultaneously take his land army to Greece to threaten Italy from the other side. Hannibal would gladly command the invasion of Italy, he added.

Antiochus initially agreed to this, until a Roman delegation including Scipio came to visit and Antiochus was told that Scipio and Hannibal spent a lot of time talking in private. Suddenly, the king's paranoia flared and he wondered whether Hannibal was colluding with the Romans—the Romans!—behind his back. This was an absurd idea, but that didn't stop Antiochus. He pulled his support from Hannibal and the invasion plan that they had discussed.

Hannibal, when he heard why he had fallen out of favor, could barely believe his ears. He stormed up to Antiochus. I once swore an oath to my father, he screamed, his healthy eye moist with emotion. And because of it "I have fought for thirty-six years; this oath, in time of peace, has exiled me from my native land; this oath has brought me, banished from my country, to your court; with this oath to guide me, even if you fail my expectations, I shall go in quest of Rome's enemies throughout the world, wherever I know that there is military power, wherever I know that armed forces are to be found—and I shall find some enemies of Rome."[1]

Antiochus was impressed—and moved. But another wily Greek diplomat from the mainland managed to convince him that Hannibal was still a threat. If the plan worked and Hannibal succeeded, "the glory would attach to Hannibal, not to Antiochus," said this Greek diplomat. And then "what hope was there that Hannibal would be ready to live under a king, subject to one person, when he had scarcely endured the authority of his native country?"[2]

Antiochus got the point. With a wave of the hand, he canceled Hannibal's entire plan. Instead, Antiochus led a woefully ill-prepared army into mainland Greece. Everything went wrong. Antiochus convened all his allies and advisers for a crisis meeting, which Hannibal attended as well. His frustration was unbearable. He desperately wanted to beat the Romans, and here he was, having to hold his tongue as windbags who knew nothing about war interrupted one another to make pompous speeches.

The Romans, meanwhile, had mobilized with their usual efficiency and arrived in Greece. Unceremoniously, they threw Antiochus and his army out of Europe, and the king retreated to Asia Minor. The Romans then pursued Antiochus. And they were led by none other than Hannibal's nemesis and friend, Scipio Africanus. For bureaucratic reasons, Scipio's brother, Lucius, was officially the commanding officer, but Africanus planned the strategy. Many people in Rome were excited by what they saw as a rematch between the two greatest adversaries in history, Scipio and Hannibal.

But Hannibal knew what the Romans were not even able to imagine: he was now more like a midlevel clerk in the Seleucid military bureaucracy than a commander. As the Romans closed in on land and sea, Antiochus dispatched Hannibal to Phoenicia to commission another squadron of ships. As Hannibal was returning from his mission, he ran into a fleet from the island of Rhodes, an ally of Rome. Hannibal, a land commander by experience, was routed, and he and his ships fled. In yet another anticlimax, Hannibal thus did not even participate in the war between Antiochus and Rome that now broke out in Asia Minor. The Scipio brothers trounced Antiochus, divided his kingdom, and gave parts of it to allies of

Rome. Rome now controlled, directly or through proxies, even the eastern Mediterranean.

AND SO IT CONTINUED. Hannibal resumed his odyssey, sailing to Crete and thence to the Black Sea, where he worked for a while for the king of Armenia. He may have made other stops along the way. Eventually, he showed up in Bithynia, near modern Istanbul. Its king, Prusias, was bickering with a neighboring kingdom allied to Rome. Together Hannibal and Prusias laid out plans for a new capital on the southern shore of the Sea of Marmara, which would become modern Bursa.

And Hannibal led Prusias's fleet against the king's enemies, showing some of his old guile. He loaded large jars full of venomous snakes onto the triremes he commanded. As his ships approached the enemy, the fleet of Pergamon, on the glittering Sea of Marmara, Hannibal ordered the jars loaded onto catapults and flung onto the enemy ships, where they shattered in the open banks of oarsmen and spilled out their live payload. With the glee of children playing a prank, Hannibal and his admirals looked on as the enemy rowers started screaming and tried to get away from the snakes winding around their oars and legs.[3]

Hannibal was in his sixties when he was hurling these snakes into ships. He had far outlived the life expectancy of people in his time, and certainly of warriors such as himself. His one-eyed face was wrinkled and leathery from the Mediterranean sun. He looked even more like his Phoenician ancestors, those weathered sailors who had roamed the seas in centuries past seeking goods to barter.

Hannibal had long ago stopped hoping that he would actually fulfill the dream his father, Hamilcar, and he had had—to defeat Rome and avenge Carthage's humiliation, to return Carthage to her former glory, and perhaps more. Instead, Hannibal was now living out his own story, which had become separate from that of Carthage when his own city betrayed him. What Hannibal was doing in these years did not compare to the great feats of his youth. But he still had to continue being Hannibal.

BESIDES, HANNIBAL KNEW that it was only a matter of time before the Romans caught up with him. And so they did. They sent Flamininus, a former consul and famous general, who arrived at Prusias's court and got straight to the point: there was a rumor that Hannibal was now staying here. If true, Flamininus wanted Prusias to kindly hand Hannibal over.

Prusias took a long look at the Roman in front of him and understood the consequences. He paused for just a moment. Then he nodded.

A young man who does not fight and conquer has missed the best part of his youth," said Carl Jung, "and an old man who does not know how to listen to the secrets of the brooks, as they tumble down from the peaks to the valleys, makes no sense: he is a spiritual mummy who is nothing but a rigid relic of the past. He stands apart from life, mechanically repeating himself to the last triviality!"[4] Was Hannibal a spiritual mummy during the last two decades of his life?

Unfortunately, the ancient sources do not tell us enough to know how Hannibal thought about his own life. But it is conceivable that Hannibal may have done *both*, that he listened to the secrets of the brooks *and* continued to fight, because that is what he heard the brooks murmuring to him to do.

One word for the state of inner peace and fulfillment of somebody who has listened to the secrets of the brooks is *self-actualization*. It is the word that Abraham Maslow, an American psychologist, used when describing perhaps the ultimate kind of success in life, a success that he considered so rare that perhaps only 2 percent of people ever achieve it.

Maslow thought of human needs, or definitions of success, as a pyramid. If I am suffocating, the only need I care about is air. Only once I can breathe again, do I become aware that I am also thirsty. Once I have drunk, I yearn for food, then for physical security. Once these basic needs are taken care of, I crave love and belonging, friends, family, and community. If I have these, I desire esteem, from both others and myself.

And if I have even esteem and I am of a certain age, then I yearn for something even bigger: I want to fulfill my human potential, perhaps even transcend myself. As Maslow put it, "A musician must make music, an artist must paint, a poet must write, if he is to be ultimately happy. What a man *can* be, he *must* be. This need we may call self-actualization."[5]

MASLOW STUDIED BIOGRAPHIES, both historical and contemporary, to try to discover what those few people who did self-actualize in their later years had in common. People who had achieved self-actualization, he believed, included presidents like Abraham Lincoln and Thomas Jefferson; the pioneer social worker and winner of the 1931 Nobel Peace Prize, Jane Addams; the philosopher and psychologist William James; the theologian, physician, and winner of the 1952 Nobel Peace Prize, Albert Schweitzer; the seventeenth-century philosopher Benedict Spinoza; the English writer Aldous Huxley; as well as Albert Einstein and Eleanor Roosevelt. Such people share the following traits, Maslow believed:[6]

> They see reality as it is, discriminating between what is fake and what is genuine.

> They treat life's difficulties as problems demanding solutions, not as grievances to be depressed or angry about.

> They feel that means can sometimes be ends, that the journey is as important as the destination.

> They enjoy occasional solitude.

> They have deep connections to a few people, rather than shallow connections to many.

They feel autonomous and relatively independent of society and its norms.

They are nonconformist—unconcerned about whether they fit in or not.

They have a sense of humor, but one that is not hostile toward others.

They accept themselves and others, not dwelling on flaws that cannot be changed but savoring them as quirks.

They are spontaneous and simple.

They respect others, including people of different races, creeds, and inclinations.

They have a strong sense of a common humanity shared by all people.

They have an unconventional but strong sense of ethics.

They are able to see the world and ordinary things with wonder.

They are original, creative, or inventive.

They often have mystical or transcendent feelings, what Maslow called "peak experiences."

These are all good qualities, or virtues, but Maslow was not interested in declaring certain people saints. In fact, he also found that self-actualizers share flaws. They often suffer from anxiety or guilt. They can, in some situations, be ruthless and cold.

But their personalities as a whole allow them to transcend most of the conflicts that torment other people. As they grow older, they view their lives—on balance—as full of truth, beauty, integrity, and meaning.

As I contemplate the people I have studied who reached old age, I am struck how closely several of them fit Abraham Maslow's description of self-actualizers. My father and I are sure, for example, that Ludwig Erhard self-actualized and became who he was meant to be. Even after his own political party betrayed him and ejected him from power, Uncle Lulu was always convinced that his life had meaning and purpose and felt content.

Uncle Lulu was an incredibly simple man, with simple joys and pleasures that nobody could ever take from him. My father remembers sitting in the back of the car with him on the many long drives during campaigns or on the way to speeches or official functions. Uncle Lulu typically read in the car; he could block out all distractions and concentrate completely. When not reading, he loved playing word games, either with my father or alone. He would write a word that was long and complicated (and most German words are) on a piece of paper, and then my father and he would make as many anagrams out of the letters as they could. My father might come up with twenty words, Uncle Lulu with seventy.

Uncle Lulu had many acquaintances but relatively few friends, but he was very close to those he did have. He kept in touch throughout his life with the most important German economists of his time, such as Walter Eucken and Wilhelm Röpke, with whom he had a deep intellectual connection. But he felt happiest when he was with his family—his sister, Rose; his wife, Lu; his daughter, Elizabeth; his two granddaughters, Sabine and Susanne; and his godson and nephew, my father.

Uncle Lulu might come home from work—in his ministry, the chancellor's office, or, in later years, his foundation—and play skat for an hour or so. Skat is a popular card game in Germany, not unlike bridge in that it requires mental skill and agility. Typically, he played with his wife and my father, and when other, less skilled, family members wanted to join, he became somewhat cranky. While playing, Uncle Lulu had a few whiskeys, which seemed to relax rather than slow him, as my father recalls. Late at night, he would then retire to his home office to read and work.

His clubfoot and war injuries prevented Uncle Lulu from doing strenuous physical exercise, but he loved to go to soccer games with my father and knew every score in the league. If he saw children on the street, he would spontaneously kick a ball around, even with his orthopedic boots. He also loved to do the grocery shopping because, as an economist who had thought a lot about inflation, he was fascinated by comparing prices for various items.

He had other little hobbies that absorbed him completely. His daughter, and later his granddaughters, had little toy kitchens, and Uncle Lulu kept the tiny shelves stocked with elaborate marzipan replicas of potatoes, carrots, and the like, then placed his large body in the little kitchen to play with complete dedication.

His abilities to concentrate and be absorbed by what he was doing made him appear famously absentminded to many people. For years he had a driver, an older man who was almost blind in one eye but whom Uncle Lulu would not part with, who picked him up at the same exact parking spot every day. One day, a delivery van had taken the spot. Uncle Lulu came out of his office and went to the parking spot, opened the door of the vehicle that was there, took a seat, and sat in the van reading, until his driver came over and reminded him that this wasn't his car; his car was parked somewhere else that day.

The entertainments and diversions that came with his political offices, his fame and connections, made no impression on Uncle Lulu. He did not care for complex and refined food, and was happiest when eating Pichel-steiner Eintopf, a rustic stew of lamb and vegetables.

He had a wry and good-natured sense of humor. Once, when Uncle Lulu was economics minister, my father, a student at the time, had gone out and got drunk. My father's room was next to the front door, and the following morning, when Uncle Lulu was being picked up for work, my father hung out of his window and vomited very publicly. Uncle Lulu teased him about

it for years, but so gently that my father, far from feeling ashamed, shared
in the amusement and almost took a certain pride in the story. The most
characteristic expression on Uncle Lulu's face was a *Schmunzeln*, recalls my
father—a tender and compassionate smirk of amusement. Uncle Lulu did
not hold grudges, and accepted, even indulged, the people around him and
their foibles.

Similarly, he did not seem to care what others thought about him.
Coming from a textile family, he had the same suit tailored again and again
throughout his life, ignoring fashion entirely. Usually, his jacket was covered in tobacco ashes.

AMID THESE SMALL SIGNS of a nonconformist mind at ease with himself and his world, Uncle Lulu spent most of his days thinking, talking, and
writing about complex issues that affected his country and the world. If
he did not seem bitter after being ousted as chancellor, it was because he
continued to develop and spread his *ideas* just as passionately as he had
while in power. Through his foundation, but really through his personality,
he explained the concepts of market economics and the ideals of a free
society, and increasingly urged *Masshalten*, a modesty and restraint from
the vulgar consumerism and materialism that he thought was gripping
affluent West German society.

Uncle Lulu considered his ideas and vision larger and more interesting
than himself. My father remembers him as a man who was at peace and
optimistic, who believed that he had fulfilled his potential and become what
he was meant to be—as a man who achieved his own unique kind of success.

Eleanor Roosevelt resembled Ludwig Erhard in many respects. She was
very close with few people but good-natured toward all. She was simple and unconventional in her habits, curious about the world, and passionate about her ideas, which she felt transcended her own life.

She was sixty when her husband died, and she briefly thought that her public life might now be over. But Harry Truman, her husband's successor, recognized her wisdom and sought her advice while he was president. He appointed her as one of five American delegates to the first meeting of the United Nations General Assembly. The four male delegates maneuvered her onto what they thought was the least interesting committee, the one dealing with humanitarian, educational, and cultural questions. It turned out to be the most interesting. One of the most controversial questions for the fledgling United Nations was what to do about the millions of refugees of the recent World War. Thanks in large part to the efforts of Eleanor Roosevelt, the UN voted to let refugees choose their new homes, saving many of them from returning to repressive lands east of the Iron Curtain. In the process, Eleanor Roosevelt became known around the world as a spokesperson for human rights.

She went on to chair the UN Human Rights Commission, where she drove her committee members with charm and firmness to overcome their cultural differences and draft a universal declaration of human rights. When it was passed in 1948, she received a standing ovation in the General Assembly. Metaphorically, the whole world was paying its respects.

Her newspaper column, which she had been writing since she was first lady, was as popular as ever. She traveled all over the world in the interests of human rights, and met with kings and queens, presidents and prime ministers. And yet she stayed as unpretentious and simple as she had ever been. Once, when the airplane she was on was preparing to land, one of the other passengers tugged at her sleeve and pointed out the window to the large crowds waiting at the airport. "That's not for us," replied Roosevelt. "Someone important must be flying in." When they stepped off the plane, she was genuinely surprised that the crowd was waiting for her.[7] When a new assistant was hired, the woman was surprised by Roosevelt's unthreatening demeanor. "I expected some kind of royalty and here was a warm, kind, embracing person," the assistant recalled. "Her total simplicity was such a revelation to me, her lack of any feeling of self-importance."[8]

When not traveling, Roosevelt lived in her apartment in New York or her cottage at Val-Kill, near her old friends Marion Dickerman and Nancy Cook. Lorena Hickok moved to a small apartment in Hyde Park village to be close by. The guest rooms at Val-Kill were usually filled, and grandchildren were running around, often in dripping swimsuits. It was a small circle of intimacy. "There are a few close people whom I love dearly & who matter to me above everything else," Roosevelt once told a new friend, David Gurewitsch. "There are not so many of them & you are now one of them and I shall just have to try not to bother you too much!"[9]

Like Ludwig Erhard, Eleanor Roosevelt felt that her ideas and calling transcended her own life. "My philosophy has been that if you have work to do and do it to the best of your ability, you will not have much time to think about yourself."[10] For Roosevelt, self-actualization had begun with her midlife transition, what Carl Jung called individuation, and ended in success.

"It was not until I reached middle age that I had the courage to develop interests of my own," she later said. "From that time on, though I have had many problems, though I have known the grief and loneliness that are the lot of most human beings . . . I have never been bored, never found the days long enough for the range of activities with which I wanted to fill them. And, having learned to stare down fear, I long ago reached the point where there is no living person whom I fear, and few challenges that I am not willing to face."[11]

Albert Einstein is an example of a man who displayed some of the paradoxical flaws Abraham Maslow found common among people who self-actualize. Einstein, as warm and good-natured as he was generally, was also capable of reactions that seem cold and ruthless, especially toward those closest to him.

In 1902, Einstein and his lover, a Serbian woman named Mileva Marić, had a baby girl, Lieserl. They were not married, and Marić gave birth at her parents' house in Serbia while Einstein was in Bern, Switzerland. Einstein did not travel to see the baby, nor did he tell his parents or anybody else about the birth. It appears that he never in his life saw his daughter, who was left with her mother's relatives so that Einstein could maintain his bohemian and free-spirited lifestyle at the time.

Einstein married Marić and they lived in Switzerland. A few months later news came that Lieserl, then nineteen months old, had come down with scarlet fever, and Marić traveled to Serbia to see her daughter. Almost nothing is known about what happened next, the only clue being a cryptic letter by Einstein to his wife in which he said, "I am very sorry about what happened with Lieserl. Scarlet fever often leaves some lasting trace behind." There is no other sign of Lieserl's existence in any of Einstein's papers. Einstein and Marić destroyed any correspondence that dealt with their daughter.[12]

They also had two sons, Hans Albert and Eduard. Einstein and Marić later drifted apart, and Einstein was on occasion ruthless in pushing aside Marić, who tended toward depression, eventually divorcing her and marrying again. His relationships with his sons were also strained. Einstein tried unsuccessfully to prevent Hans Albert from marrying the woman of his choice, and tension between the two of them remained for years. Eduard was schizophrenic, and as his mental health deteriorated, it was again Marić who chose to remain close to her son, who was confined to an asylum in Zurich, while Einstein carried on with his career, his new marriage, and his other interests. After Marić died, Eduard was mostly alone. "There is something blocking me that I am unable to analyze fully," Einstein told a friend, trying to explain why he did not visit Eduard more often. "I believe I would be arousing painful feelings of various kinds in him if I made an appearance in whatever form."[13]

THESE ARE SURPRISING, even disturbing, aspects of Einstein's character. But rather than eclipse his otherwise remarkably open, good-natured, and moral personality, they seem to bring it into greater relief. "The most important human endeavor is the striving for morality in our actions," he once wrote a minister in Brooklyn, New York. "Our inner balance and even our existence depend on it. Only morality in our actions can give beauty and dignity to life." And the way to be moral, Einstein believed, was to rise above the "merely personal" to live in a way that benefited humanity.[14]

For many years, Einstein believed that pacifism was the best way to benefit humanity. In a speech in the United States during the 1930s, he urged people everywhere to dodge the draft. "Even if only 2% of those assigned to perform military service should announce their refusal to fight . . . governments would be powerless, they would not dare send such a large number of people to jail."[15] With characteristic irony, he told one interviewer, "I am not only a pacifist, I am a militant pacifist."[16]

When the evils of Nazism became fully clear to him, Einstein changed his mind about his categorical pacifism. In later years—especially after the dropping of the two atomic bombs, in whose development he played a marginal role but for which he felt responsible—he used his fame to plead for a world government, a supranational (as opposed to international) institution that would have a monopoly on violence and could force the nations of the world to settle their disputes peacefully. He was a Zionist but always empathized with the Arabs in Palestine as well. He was quintessentially cosmopolitan, with German, Swiss, Austro-Hungarian, and U.S. citizenships at different times of his life. "Nationalism is an infantile disease, the measles of mankind," he said, and urged the world to get beyond it.[17]

AS EINSTEIN kept himself occupied with issues larger than himself, he also remained, like Roosevelt and Erhard, simple in his daily life. He enjoyed being alone, and spent hours upon hours sailing—often just drifting, really—while thinking about his equations or the cosmos. On his fiftieth birthday, when he was already famous and still living in Berlin, he escaped from the attention of the press and fled to a gardener's cottage on an estate on the Havel River owned by a friend. For days, he lived there by himself, cooking his own meals, while journalists were looking for him everywhere. "Such a fuss about a birthday," he laughed to his lover.[18]

His quirkiness and eccentricity became famous. He slept naked, often did not wear socks, rarely paid attention to his white mane of hair, and had a generally rumpled look.[19] Once a friend was driving him around in a convertible when it started raining, and Einstein pulled off his hat and put it under his coat. When the friend looked quizzical, Einstein explained: "You see, my hair has withstood water many times before, but I don't know how many times my hat can."[20]

In Princeton, New Jersey, he lived his final decades in a modest white wooden house with his second wife, Elsa, her daughter Margot, his assistant, Helen Dukas, and, at various times, a parrot named Bibo, a cat named Tiger, and a terrier named Chico. When a group of twelve-year-old girls came over on Halloween to play a trick, they were astonished to find the famous man appear at the door with his violin to serenade them.[21] When an eight-year-old neighbor named Adelaide Delong rang his bell and asked for help with her math homework, he asked her in and explained it to her, accepting her homemade fudge and giving her a cookie in return. When Adelaide returned with two friends, he invited them into his office. "So he moved a whole bunch of papers from the table, opened four cans of beans with a can opener, and heated them on a sterno stove one by one, stuck a spoon in each and that was our lunch," she recalled. "He didn't give us anything to drink."[22]

EINSTEIN, like Erhard and Roosevelt, had relatively few close friends but had deep connections with the ones he did have. One friend was Kurt Gödel, a German-speaking immigrant and mathematician famous in his own right. The two men were very different—Einstein was good-humored, Gödel introverted and so logical as to be humorless at times. Together they took long walks in Princeton, talking about physics and mathematics and speculating on such matters as whether time existed at all.

Most of Einstein's mental energies were still devoted to physics, and in particular to his search for a unified field theory that would refute quantum mechanics and complete his life's work. This, of course, was where he got stuck, hopelessly stuck, and failed. But it remained his life's calling. One morning when walking to work with his assistant, Ernst Strauss, Einstein thought out loud about their interests in politics *and* physics. "But our equations are much more important to me," Einstein added. "Politics is for the present, while our equations are for eternity."[23]

IF HE HAD NO SUCCESSES with his equations in later years, Einstein nonetheless was able to get something arguably more important out of them: wonderment. At a dinner party in Berlin he once said: "Try and penetrate with our limited means the secrets of nature and you will find that, behind all the discernible laws and connections, there remains something subtle, intangible and inexplicable. Veneration for this force beyond anything that we can comprehend is my religion."[24] Another time he said, "The most beautiful emotion we can experience is the mysterious."[25]

This sporadic awe Einstein felt was what Maslow called "peak experiences." Once when Einstein was crossing by ship from Germany to America in the 1930s, a ferocious storm seized his ship. "One feels the insignificance of the individual," Einstein wrote in his diary, "and it makes one happy."[26]

Einstein perhaps summed up what Maslow meant by self-actualization when he wrote to his friend Max Born, then a professor in Edinburgh: "I simply enjoy giving more than receiving in every respect, do not take myself nor the doings of the masses seriously, am not ashamed of my weaknesses and vices, and naturally take things as they come with equanimity and humor."[27]

In another letter, he came close to defining success: "People who live in a society, enjoy looking into each other's eyes, who share their troubles, who focus their efforts on what is important to them and find this joyful— these people lead a full life."[28] It was ironic, and entirely compatible with the contradictions in self-actualizers that Maslow found, that Einstein wrote these words to his son Eduard, who was then in an asylum in Zurich where Einstein preferred not to visit him.

ERHARD, ROOSEVELT, EINSTEIN, and other people who self-actualize in their later years are not saints. They are not perfect, they cannot be role models in every way. They are likely to have suffered their disasters, defeats, and failures in life. But these setbacks did not define them. For that, they were too large as characters. They all became what they were meant to be, transcending disaster for a larger triumph. Hannibal *may* have been one of them. You should strive to be.

THIRTEEN

THE LESSONS
OF HANNIBAL

*With no desire for success, no anxiety about failure,
indifferent to results, he burns up his actions in the fire
of wisdom. Surrendering all thoughts of outcome, unperturbed, self-reliant, he does nothing at all, even
when fully engaged in actions. There is nothing that
he expects, nothing that he fears.*

—Krishna to Arjuna, Bhagavad Gita, 4.19–21

Hannibal had long known how it was likely to end. Sooner or later,
the Romans were going to catch up with him. The only question
was how. But Hannibal was not about to make it easy for them. While
living in a villa at the sumptuous court of King Prusias in Bithynia, he had
built an elaborate underground system of secret shafts and mines to serve
as his escape routes in an emergency. Seven secret doors in his residence
opened to seven passages that led in seven directions.[1]

When servants came running to him one day with the news that Roman
legionaries were approaching his villa, Hannibal entered the first shaft and
ran, then crawled through the mine, wheezing with the breath of a sixty-
three-year-old. But when he saw the light at the end of his escape tunnel, he

froze. Bithynian soldiers were standing guard outside the exit, blocking his escape. He crawled backward, then turned around and ran back into his residence. He entered another secret door and set off down another mine, but it, too, was blocked by Bithynian soldiers. Hannibal tried another escape route, to no avail. Prusias must have known about the tunnels and, collaborating with the Romans, had placed guards outside all seven of them.

Hannibal understood that the moment—*that* moment—had finally arrived. He could already hear a Roman centurion in the vestibule of his house, barking orders to the villa's servants in that matter-of-fact, ruthlessly efficient Latin that Hannibal had heard so often in his battles against the Romans. It would only be minutes now before young Roman soldiers would come streaming through the chambers, looking for their prey, for the man who had once slaughtered their fathers and whose very name they had grown up fearing, but who was now helpless before them.

This was what Hannibal had prepared himself for. He was no longer afraid of death. His father had once given his life so that Hannibal and his brother Hasdrubal might live. His brother Hasdrubal had later given *his* life when, knowing the Romans had closed in on him, he charged straight into their lines to a glorious death. Hannibal also wanted to die on his own terms.

He did not make a fuss. There was no melodrama. He dismissed his slave, wanting to be alone. He took from his finger a ring that contained a small but lethal dose of poison. He popped it open and poured the powder into a cup. He drank it. He waited for the poison to do its work, even as he heard the clink of Roman helmets, shields, and spears draw nearer. He felt his body stiffen and he lost consciousness. He died.

The unsurpassed triumphs of Hannibal's youth appear to have been impostors. His life appears to have ended in failure. He had been on a quest to overcome Rome and to restore Carthage to glory. Instead, paradoxically, the war Hannibal launched *caused* Rome to become the greatest power of the ancient world and led to Carthage's extinction.

For the Romans never forgot what Hannibal had done to them. *Ceterum censeo Carthaginem esse delendam.* "Furthermore, I think Carthage must be destroyed," the old senator Cato said at the end of almost every speech he gave. Thirty-seven years after Hannibal's death, the Romans did exactly that. They destroyed Carthage, by now a largely submissive city, erasing one of the great civilizations of the ancient world. Hannibal's suicide, it appears, punctuated not just *a* failure, but one of the most consequential in all of human history.

AND YET THAT is not the conclusion I draw from his story. Instead, I have always read the remarkable tale of Hannibal, Fabius, and Scipio— with all its twists and turns, its suspense and mystery, its revelations about character—as a metaphor for life in general. As Carl Jung wrote, "Ultimately, every individual life is at the same time the eternal life of the species." Aspects of Hannibal, Fabius, and Scipio must therefore be present in everybody else in history, and in all of us today, in you and in me.

Trying to spell out the lessons of the past is a bit like trying to jump on your own shadow. You know it is there because you see it, but when you jump, it moves out of reach. Thus it is often said that those who don't learn from history are doomed to repeat it. But it is just as true that those who *do* study history but *mis*interpret its lessons—by taking them too literally or selectively—fare just as badly.

Hannibal and Sosylus, for example, knew history very well as they were debating (in the conversation I imagined in Chapter 6) what the best strategy might be against Rome. The difficulty was to discern *which* part of the history they had studied was relevant to their particular situation. Should Hannibal have looked to the Trojan War, to the Greco-Persian wars, to Alexander the Great's campaigns, to Pyrrhus's invasion of Italy, or to some other war for his lessons? Somehow, he and Sosylus had to distill out of *all* of these stories insights that were (a) specific enough to be useful and (b) general enough to fit a new situation, *their* situation.

Each chapter in this book came with one overarching insight. But ulti-

mately you must draw your own insights, moments of recognition or lessons from Hannibal, Fabius, and Scipio, and from all the other lives in
these pages. Each of us must do this differently. Here are some possibilities.

1. Stay balanced when others lose their balance.

By far the simplest and most obvious lesson of Hannibal arises out of his
stunning battle victories. Hannibal was the military equivalent of an aikido
master like Morihei Ueshiba. Both knew that the most immediate kind of
success—winning—is not about being stronger than others but about
being more balanced and calm and then *letting* opponents throw their own
weight around and in the process defeat themselves. So show your rivals
the bulging Gauls in the middle of your lines (as at Cannae), give them a
point to fix their attention on, let them charge into you with full force,
then observe as they become unbalanced, and allow them to fall.

You may one day find yourself attacked—verbally, emotionally, psychologically; in a debate, a negotiation, a court room. And then you might
remember Hannibal and Ueshiba, who showed that we need not fear enemies who are stronger as long as we retain control over ourselves.

2. Never confuse means with ends, tactics with strategy.

Victories are merely tools and never the goal. Scipio's victories led to success because they caused Hannibal to leave Italy. Hannibal's victories led
to failure because they did not cause Rome to surrender. Cleopatra was at
first right in thinking that seducing one particular Roman (Julius Caesar)
would secure her life and reign in Egypt. But then she drew the wrong
conclusion that seducing *another particular* Roman (Mark Antony) would
sustain her success, when in fact she had to retain the support of the
Roman state, *no matter which* individual Roman might gain the upper
hand. Her tactics should have changed to fit her strategy.

Pointless or Pyrrhic victories may indeed be the single biggest threat to
talented and ambitious people—like Pyrrhus himself or Hannibal—for

they lead them away from where they actually want to go. Let me give a modern example.

Many educated people today, in sharp contrast to virtually all of our ancestors, *delay* having children in order first to achieve "success." Indeed, in many careers it helps enormously to be childless for a while, for you will be free to take foreign, risky, or inconvenient assignments and to keep bizarre hours, with little or no economic security. Children would interfere with all of this. So, male or female, you postpone having children.

At some point, however, you may reflect—or intuit—that you only wanted professional success as a *means*, the *end* being a big, happy family. So you must change your tactics—perhaps limiting your *professional* success by taking less interesting assignments or investing less time—and nurture a relationship and make babies. If you wait too long, this may turn out more difficult than you imagined because you might be older and less fertile (if you are a woman) or older and married to somebody less fertile (if you are a man). If you forget to change your tactics altogether, you might find yourself becoming chief executive of this or president of that and yet feeling like a childless failure. And ironically, it will have been your "success" that led you astray.

3. Have "young" ideas while you're young and while you're old.

As you get older, it becomes ever easier to think of reasons not to try something, not to think a thought, not to dream a dream, not to keep simple things simple. That is called *experience*. It is an awareness of the complexity of the world. So young heroes like Hannibal, Picasso, and Einstein have the advantage of *in*experience that we call freshness. They have a bold idea (an Alpine crossing) and actually do it. They imagine a shocking new way of painting (*Les Demoiselles d'Avignon*) and put it on the canvas without further ado. They keep pondering childish mind puzzles (What would happen if I rode alongside a beam of light at the same speed?) and stumble on new insights to our world.

For many people, freshness wilts with age, as it did for Hannibal,

Picasso, and Einstein. But it is possible to stay, or even become, fresh in later years. Jung did it. Only after a major crisis that punctuated the first and relatively conventional half of his career did he discover the playful, spontaneous, and iconoclastic habits and intellect—building toy castles by the lake, drawing fantasy creatures, following his occult ideas wherever they took him—that led to the success we remember him for. Eleanor Roosevelt, too, became her adventurous and authentic self only after the trauma of her marital crisis. Ludwig Erhard, though reaching power late in life, was nonetheless able to formulate a bold and simple—his rivals said "naïve"—vision of freedom for Germany, the social market economy.

It can be difficult to keep thinking young thoughts in later years. One of the stories I find most perplexing is the conservative turn in Albert Einstein's mind after his great breakthroughs in physics. This thinker who was quintessentially free—even "impudent"—in his youth allowed certain prejudices (that "God does not play dice with the universe," that uncertainty can have no role in science) to imprison his imagination in later years and closed his mind to the "young" ideas of quantum physics.

When that happens—when experience or success becomes a prison of the imagination—what can you do? First, recognize it. Then, make a change of some sort. Tennessee Williams eventually overcame his "catastrophe of success" by leaving the country and going for a while to Mexico, a new setting where his success did not matter and he became his old self again. Amy Tan had writer's block after *The Joy Luck Club* became a bestseller, but eventually told herself: "Don't think of what's going to happen afterwards. If it's a failure, will you think what you wrote was a failure, that the whole time was wasted? If it's a success, will you think the words are more valuable? . . . It took me a long time to get over that, [to be] able to breathe again and say, 'What's important? Why are you a writer? Why did you write that book in the first place? What did you learn? What did you discover?'" To regain her freedom she had to relearn her inexperience.

4. Start maintaining an "old" self-discipline
even while you're young.

By contrast, the advantage some (though by no means all) older people have is that they are somewhat less likely to be corrupted by the trappings of success, should it present itself. Harry Truman, after a life of setbacks and disappointments, was famously undazzled by the power and pomp of the presidency, and stayed the simple boy from Missouri whether he was negotiating with Winston Churchill and Joseph Stalin over the fate of the world or slipping out of the Oval Office to have a quiet lunch with his wife. Ludwig Erhard, as economics minister or chancellor, couldn't wait to leave the crowds of adoring fans at campaign rallies to have Pichelsteiner Eintopf and a game of cards with Auntie Lu and my father. Paul Cézanne, long after he had achieved success and fame as a painter, kept working on his canvases and practicing his technique as though he were the unsure novice of his twenties.

Young heroes, on the other hand, have had much less time to prepare for success. Some, like Meriwether Lewis, might suffer delusions of grandeur, then crushing disappointment at the banality of their life after triumph, and literally fall apart. Others will succumb to that old temptress hubris, thinking they are above the law, morality, or reproach. Tiger Woods became successful through tactical and strategic discipline on the golf course, but then lost all self-control in his sexual life and nearly came to ruin. So in your personal habits and humility, be "old." Seek the company and counsel of older mentors, study those who came before you, take the long view of your success, stay in control of yourself.

5. When disaster strikes, try to be
"Fabian" first and later "Scipionic."

Sooner or later, every life suffers a setback or disaster. Most of these are not fatal and can be overcome. If you lose your job or your house or your spouse, or you are diagnosed with cancer, it is normal to be angry, or to live in denial for a while, or to become depressed. But it is also possible to recognize after a while that these are unhelpful reactions and to let them go. Resilience begins with accepting the setback, as Fabius accepted Hannibal's invasion or as Roosevelt accepted her husband's infidelity. And accepting often means "doing nothing," as Fabius did *not* fight Hannibal in battle or as Ernest Shackleton did *not* attempt to march his men over the Antarctic ice but instead stayed put and floated with it. It may mean *not* fighting the employer who laid you off, *not* fighting the bank that foreclosed on you or the spouse who divorced you. This is not passivity. It merely means letting go, until you see that the situation has changed and renewed action makes sense.

When that occurs, however, you may feel the paradoxical and energizing sense of liberation that Scipio and Steve Jobs and Roosevelt experienced. After all, once the worst has happened, what else do you have to fear? Why *not* switch careers? Why *not* start a new company? Why *not* mix with new people, try new things? That crazy idea you once had in the back of your mind but suppressed because it seemed just too crazy may now be just the thing to pursue. If so, disaster may end up giving you the boldness you once lacked and pointing you to the quest that will make you a new hero.

6. Part of success is adjusting your idea of what it is.

Over the course of a life, success and failure will mean different things at different times. When you are young, one way or another, you will define success in response to your parents—either by emulating them, as Hannibal did; or by filling a void they left, as Roosevelt did; or by rebelling, as Amy Tan did. By reacting to your background, you will form an identity or persona, as Jung called it, and this persona—the "explorer," the "conqueror," the "wife and mother"—will tell you what to strive for. There is nothing bad about that; it is inevitable and necessary. But it may also become necessary for you to update, refine, or even scrap that persona of youth when you grow out of it.

One of the stories I find most harrowing is the fate of the explorer-hero Shackleton. He is known today for calling the bluff on the impostors once, when his expedition on the *Endurance* turned into disaster, but he turned this into the greatest of triumphs by rescuing all of his crew. But he did not recognize the impostors the second time, when he held on so desperately to his persona of the explorer-hero that he could not grow into a new identity as an older man. He ignored his health, his family, and his home and kept redreaming—desperately—his old dreams until that killed him. If Shackleton had been like Roosevelt, he might have overcome the disappointment of returning to a changed Britain, found new and intimate relationships and new causes to believe in, and lived for a new kind of success.

7. See the best in people, but protect yourself against the worst in them.

Another lesson from these lives is that success requires the old-fashioned virtue of magnanimity toward other people. The two most enigmatic and inspiring relationships in this book are those between Hannibal and Scipio and Eleanor and Franklin Roosevelt. Life and history had cast Hannibal and Scipio as enemies. And yet Scipio never felt personal animosity toward Hannibal. Instead, he had respect for Hannibal, seeing nobility in him, learning from him, even defending him in later years against the slanders of both Carthaginians and Romans. In turn, Hannibal did not detest Scipio but recognized his talent and admired his integrity. None of this stopped them from fighting a brutal battle, but they never took the fight personally.

Something similar might be said about Eleanor and Franklin Roosevelt. It would have been entirely understandable if Eleanor, upon discovering that Franklin had betrayed her, had stopped loving and begun hating him forever. They might well have spent the rest of their years in bitterness toward each other. But Eleanor never hated, never demonized, never abandoned Franklin, nor he her. They merely changed their relationship.

And what a relationship it became. Although Franklin would have his lovers and Eleanor hers, they remained each other's best and most trustworthy ally throughout their lives. This went beyond their common interest in their children. Each respected the intellect, quirks, and, above all, the good intentions of the other. Each supported the other's dreams— Franklin, by financing Val-Kill, for example; Eleanor, by helping Franklin in his struggle against polio. Like Hannibal and Scipio, Franklin and Eleanor never pretended that nothing stood between them, but they also did not allow anything to keep them apart.

This is a lesson for all of us. It is naïve to think that there could ever be people in our lives with whom we will never have conflict, or who will never disappoint us. But that does not make them bad people or give us reason to reject them. Husbands and wives, political opponents, rivals in life's power games, ideological enemies—we all can choose to respect one another no matter what issues come between us. If, for example, we fight somebody on the field of ideas, the fight should *remain* about ideas, for there is nobility and ultimate success in this stance. As Eleanor Roosevelt once said: "Great minds discuss ideas. Average minds discuss events. Small minds discuss people." Greatness can bring people together even when events or people might separate them, and this is itself a kind of triumph.

By contrast, those who do personalize their frustrations, hatreds, or vendettas invariably end up playing the minor or unsavory roles in history and life. Hannibal had, throughout his life, a political enemy in Carthage named Hanno, who worked ceaselessly to destroy Hannibal's reputation and success. Scipio was pestered by Cato, who was as petty as Scipio was magnanimous. Wang Guangmei had Jiang Qing, perhaps the archetype of the vindictive plotter. The Catos and Jiang Qings of the world may score occasional "successes"—Cato hounding the Scipio brothers into court, Jiang Qing persecuting Wang Guangmei and countless other Chinese victims. But their legacy will be discord. After the Cultural Revolution, China put Jiang Qing in prison, then on trial—with Wang Guangmei observing in the courtroom. Jiang eventually committed suicide.

For the noble personalities, however, there is an associated lesson. It is that the Catos are out there. Magnanimity often bears the risk of naïveté. Scipio should have recognized the threat from Cato, Wang the danger of

Jiang. They should have protected themselves by making and maintaining allies. Ludwig Erhard probably should have joined a political party and cultivated specific individuals in parliament. Hannibal should have wooed members of Carthage's oligarchy before reforming the city as suffete. Personal alliances and political shrewdness need not be a sword that you choose instead of magnanimity, but they should be a shield to carry in case you need it.

8. Success means becoming a mensch.

Especially as you get older, success must include becoming a whole, integrated human being—a *Mensch,* in German and Yiddish. In essence, this means "self-actualizing," as Abraham Maslow described it. The people in this book who, in my opinion, did self-actualize seemed at a certain point to *transcend* conventional success and failure by achieving a separate peace with themselves and their world. Albert Einstein, Eleanor Roosevelt, and Ludwig Erhard maintained their quirky, simple habits, had their wry sense of humor, their childlike sense of wonderment and awe at the mysteries of the world and life—what Maslow called "peak experiences." They tried to make others happier, not just themselves, and they looked past façades to find authenticity in their lives.

This is the kind of success that a woman from Kansas named Bessie Stanley captured in a disarmingly simple little poem she wrote in 1905. She had entered a contest for the best answer in fewer than one hundred words to the question "What constitutes success?" and won the $250 prize money with these ninety-six words:

> He has achieved success who has lived well, laughed often and loved much;
>
> who has gained the respect of intelligent men and the love of little children;
>
> who has filled his niche and accomplished his task;

who has left the world better than he found it, whether by an improved poppy, a perfect poem, or a rescued soul;

who has never lacked appreciation of earth's beauty or failed to express it;

who has always looked for the best in others and given them the best he had;

whose life was an inspiration;

whose memory a benediction.[2]

What prevents this success? Pretentiousness, envy, and bitterness, among other negative emotions. Shackleton indulged his pretension to the explorer-hero identity; envied his nemesis, Robert Scott; and wallowed in bitterness that Britain no longer wanted and adored him. Even noble minds can fail at this highest rung. Great Fabius, after all his achievements, envied the young and charismatic genius of Scipio and tried to belittle and obstruct it when he should have supported and helped Scipio. Even Scipio himself, so magnanimous throughout his life and toward his enemies, eventually became bitter in his exile, unable to understand his "ungrateful fatherland."

9. Do your duty with equanimity.

The ancients believed that success meant in large part doing your duty to your best ability, fulfilling your purpose in life. The Romans called it *pietas*. The Indians in their ancient scriptures, such as the Bhagavad Gita, or "song of God," called it dharma. Hannibal, Fabius, Scipio, Roosevelt, Erhard, and many of the other characters in this book—even Cato, who may have considered it his duty to purify Roman public life—all dedicated their lives, at least at some stage, to what they saw as their duty.

Today, duty might seem to have gone out of fashion. But it hasn't, not really. It might mean caring for an aging parent or a sick child. It might mean helping others who confront a disease you have overcome, or dedicating yourself to some small thing that is overlooked, like preserving a plot of land or a river. You will know it is your duty not by how large or small it is but by perceiving it to be bigger than you, *beyond* you.

Once you find such a purpose in life, you might observe a change in your attitude. The fear of failure might seem less overwhelming, the yearning for success less consuming. This new attitude has nothing to do with indifference—you still do your best to succeed. Instead, this attitude might be called *equanimity*.

THE BEST DESCRIPTION in history of equanimity—and how incredibly hard it is to achieve—is probably found in the Bhagavad Gita, a story about a mythical war. Mohandas Gandhi, the leader of India's independence movement and an opponent of war, said of the Gita what I feel about the Second Punic War: "that under the guise of physical warfare it described the duel that perpetually went on in the hearts of mankind, and that physical warfare was brought in merely to make the description of the internal duel more alluring."[3] What is that internal duel? In essence, it is the daily and individual struggle we must all wage between our good states of mind—clear thinking, compassion, tolerance, courage, humility, and so forth—and our bad emotions, such as anger, hatred, greed, vanity, envy, arrogance, fear.[4]

In the story, two men steer their war chariot into the space between two hostile armies on the eve of a great battle, a bit as Hannibal and Scipio once stood on the African plain near Zama before their battle. One of them is an Indian prince named Arjuna. The other man, who is Arjuna's charioteer and friend, is Krishna.

Arjuna is one of five brothers, the Pandavas, who represent our positive emotions. And they have cousins, the Kauravas, who are vicious and devious and have stolen a kingdom from them. Now both sides, with their armies, have come to Kurukshetra to settle this dispute. Arjuna and the Pandavas know that they are fighting for justice.

But as Arjuna gazes from his chariot at the two armies, he suddenly loses his will to fight. Arjuna is scared. He is afraid of losing not only his own life, but also the lives of the "fathers, grandfathers, teachers, uncles, brothers, sons, grandsons, fathers-in-law, and friends, kinsmen on both sides" whom he sees lined up in both armies with their deadly weapons. For although this is a just war, it is still a war within a family. If the Pandavas lose, they die. But to win, they have to kill people they have grown up with. Arjuna drops his bow and arrows and sinks to the floor of his war chariot, sobbing like a frightened child.[5]

Because this is "a righteous cause, Arjuna, no matter what happens, you win," Krishna said, trying to console him. "If killed, you immediately enter heaven; if victorious, you achieve a great name and fame. Either way you triumph. So arise, Arjuna! Fight!"[6]

But Arjuna is too afraid. His mind, he tells Krishna, is "restless, unsteady, turbulent, wild, stubborn; truly, it seems to me as hard to master as the wind."[7]

Krishna stays firm. Life has put you here to fight this battle, and this is now your dharma, he says. So you must prepare your mind for what lies ahead. Don't dwell on what the outcome of the battle might be. Don't picture either you or your cousins lying in a pool of blood. You need to let your fears go, Krishna tells Arjuna. Bring your mind back from worrying about the future and focus on the here and now.

If you do that, Krishna continues, your mind will become calm. Arjuna, I'm telling you to become a man who "lets go of all results, whether good or bad, and is focused on the action alone."[8] You must be "content with whatever happens, unattached to pleasure or pain, success or failure."[9] And finally, Arjuna understands. He fights the war and leads the Pandavas to victory.

Rudyard Kipling, in a sense, gave us a riddle. "Meet with triumph and disaster and treat those two impostors just the same," he wrote. Just the same, yes. But how? The *ultimate* answer may hide in this story about

Arjuna and Krishna, as in the stories of Hannibal and Scipio, Eleanor and Franklin, Erhard and Adenauer, and the other people in these pages.

When Arjuna broke down crying in fear before the battle, when Hannibal once broke down in the crazed laughter of despair after his loss, when Eleanor Roosevelt wept before *Grief*, they each became all mankind and each one of us during those moments when the challenges and risks of life seem overwhelming. But at that same instant, Krishna became the inner voice that, although rarely audible, sometimes speaks to us all. Krishna reminds us to remember our purpose in life and to have equanimity in trying to fulfill it. It is much to ask, but perhaps there is nothing else to answer.

Don't agonize about success or failure. Just do what you must do as well as you possibly can. In the process you may eventually transcend triumph and disaster. *That* is how to meet those two impostors.

ACKNOWLEDGMENTS

This book would not have come about without Dan Mandel, who, after a brainstorm in a New York café, believed in the idea with passionate conviction and guided me through the bewildering process of getting it published. Thank you, Dan, for being a great agent. I'm also grateful to Jake Morrissey, my editor, for spotting the potential in the idea and then giving me such detailed and patient feedback on how to execute it better. Above all, thank you to my parents and to my wife for putting up with me during what was an exceptionally busy time in my life, complicated unnecessarily by the writing of a book. And thank you to my three little ones for reminding me always what matters, just by being there.

NOTES

ONE. HANNIBAL AND ME

1. Polybius, *The Rise of the Roman Empire*, trans. Ian Scott-Kilvert (London: Penguin, 1979), III, 117.
2. Adrian Goldsworthy, *The Punic Wars* (London: Cassell & Co., 2000), p. 315.
3. David McCullough, *Truman* (New York: Simon & Schuster, 1992), p. 43.
4. Ibid., p. 415.
5. Dan P. McAdams, "The Psychology of Life Stories," *Review of General Psychology* 5, no. 2 (2001): 100–122.
6. Serge Lancel, *Hannibal*, trans. Antonia Nevill (Oxford, UK, and Malden, MA: Blackwell, 1998), p. 55.
7. Such as Joseph Campbell, a scholar of mythology.
8. *The Wisdom of Carl Jung*, ed. Edward Hoffman (New York: Citadel Press Books, 2003), pp. 57, 66.
9. Livy, *The History of Rome from Its Foundation, Books XXI–XXX*, trans. Aubrey de Sélincourt (London and New York: Penguin Books, 1965), XXX, 30.

TWO. THE INFLUENCE OF PARENTS

1. Serge Lancel, *Hannibal*, trans. Antonia Nevill (Oxford, UK, and Malden, MA: Blackwell, 1998), p. 9.
2. Adrian Goldsworthy, *The Punic Wars* (London: Cassell & Co., 2000), p. 135; Lancel, *Hannibal*, p. 9.
3. Diodorus, *The Library of History*, XXV, 10. At http://penelope.uchicago.edu/Thayer/E/Roman/Texts/Diodorus_Siculus/25*.html.
4. Richard Miles, *Carthage Must Be Destroyed* (London: Allen Lane, Penguin Group, 2010), p. 160.
5. Ibid., pp. 36, 45.
6. Goldsworthy, *Punic Wars*, p. 50.
7. Ibid., p. 109.

8. Miles, *Carthage Must Be Destroyed*, p. 203.
9. Lancel, *Hannibal*, p. 21.
10. Ibid., p. 23.
11. Barack Obama, *Dreams from My Father* (New York: Three Rivers Press, 1995), p. 5.
12. Ibid., p. 220.
13. Ibid., p. xvi.
14. Ibid., p. 430.
15. Blanche Wiesen Cook, *Eleanor Roosevelt, Volume 1: 1884–1933* (New York: Penguin Books, 1993), p. 18.
16. Ibid., p. 62.
17. Ibid., p. 39.
18. Ibid., p. 85.
19. Ibid., p. 88.
20. Ibid., p. 115.
21. Ibid., p. 121.
22. Ibid., p. 131.
23. Ibid., p. 145.
24. Ibid., p. 146.
25. Ibid., p. 155.
26. Ibid., p. 157.
27. Ibid., pp. 174–75.
28. Ibid., p. 183.
29. Biography of Amy Tan at the Academy of Achievement, at http://www.achievement.org/autodoc/page/tan0bio-1.
30. Ibid. All direct quotes are from this interview, unless otherwise cited.

THREE. DO YOU NEED A GOAL?

1. Richard Miles, *Carthage Must Be Destroyed* (London: Allen Lane, 2010), p. 2.
2. Ibid., p. 54.
3. Patrick Hunt, *Hannibal*, Stanford University course ARC123 on iTunes University, lecture 1.
4. This description is taken almost verbatim from Polybius, *The Rise of the Roman Empire*, trans. Ian Scott-Kilvert (London: Penguin Books, 1979), III, 11.
5. Livy, *The History of Rome from Its Foundation, Books XXI–XXX*, trans. Aubrey de Sélincourt (London and New York: Penguin Books, 1965), XXI, 1. According to Livy, Hannibal swore to be "the enemy" of Rome; according to Polybius, he swore that he "would never become a friend to the Romans."
6. Ibid., XXI, 43.
7. Ibid., XXI, 4.
8. Plutarch, "Fabius," in *Lives*, trans. John Dryden (New York: Modern Library, 2001), I, 246.
9. Miles, *Carthage Must Be Destroyed*, p. 227.
10. That is, when he told the story of the oath to King Antiochus, in order to convince him that he could be trusted not to make any secret deals with the Romans.
11. Serge Lancel, *Hannibal*, trans. Antonia Nevill (Oxford, UK, and Malden, MA: Blackwell, 1998), p. 55.

12. Ibid., p. 50.
13. Livy, *History of Rome*, trans. de Sélincourt, XXI, 18.
14. Lancel, *Hannibal*, p. 55.
15. Miles, *Carthage Must Be Destroyed*, p. 252.
16. Livy, *History of Rome*, trans. de Sélincourt, XXI, 22.
17. Joseph Campbell with Bill Moyers, *The Power of Myth* (New York: Anchor Books, 1991), p. 158.
18. Daniel Levinson with Charlotte Darrow, Edward Klein, Maria Levinson, and Braxton McKee, *The Seasons of a Man's Life* (New York: Ballantine Books, 1978), p. 91.
19. Stephen Ambrose, *Undaunted Courage: Meriwether Lewis, Thomas Jefferson, and the Opening of the American West* (New York: Simon & Schuster, 1996), p. 22.
20. Ibid., p. 24.
21. Ibid., p. 59.
22. Ibid., p. 63.
23. Ibid., p. 13.
24. David McCullough, *Truman* (New York: Simon & Schuster, 1992), p. 192.
25. Ibid., p. 99.
26. Ibid., p. 151.
27. Ibid., p. 160.
28. Ibid., p. 195.
29. Ibid., p. 204.
30. Ibid., p. 214.
31. Ibid., p. 285.
32. Ibid., p. 342.
33. Alfred C. Mierzejewski, *Ludwig Erhard: A Biography* (Chapel Hill: University of North Carolina Press, 2004), p. 7.
34. Ibid., p. 10.
35. Jess Lukomski, *Ludwig Erhard: Der Mensch und der Politiker* (Düsseldorf: Econ-Verlag, 1965), p. 38.
36. Ibid., p. 49.
37. Mierzejewski, *Ludwig Erhard*, pp. 12, 15.
38. Lukomski, *Ludwig Erhard*, p. 55.
39. Ibid., p. 59.

FOUR. TOWERING PEAKS

1. Richard Miles, *Carthage Must Be Destroyed* (London: Allen Lane, 2010), p. 107.
2. Serge Lancel, *Hannibal*, trans. Antonia Nevill (Oxford, UK, and Malden, MA: Blackwell, 1998), p. 63.
3. Livy, *The History of Rome from Its Foundation, Books XXI–XXX,* trans. Aubrey de Sélincourt (London and New York: Penguin Books, 1965), XXI, 30.
4. John Prevas, *Hannibal Crosses the Alps: The Invasion of Italy and the Punic Wars* (Cambridge, MA: Da Capo Press, 1998), p. 126.
5. Patrick Hunt of the Stanford Alpine Archaeology Project believes this to be the likeliest pass. See http://traumwerk.stanford.edu/archaeolog/2006/11/alpine_archaeology_hannibal_ex.html. Other passes often mentioned include the Col du Petit Saint

Bernard, Col de Mont Cenis, Col de Montgenèvre, Col de la Croix, and Col de la Traversette. See also: http://www.livius.org/ha-hd/hannibal/alps.html.

6. Patrick Hunt, lecture "Hannibal in the Alps: Potential Passes," at 1 hour, 48 minutes, 28 seconds.

7. Livy, *History of Rome*, trans. de Sélincourt, XXI, 35.

8. Prevas, *Hannibal Crosses the Alps*, p. 146.

9. The climate in 218 BCE, known as the Roman Warm Period, was slightly warmer. See Hanspeter Hohlhauser, Michel Magny, and Heinz Zumbuhl, "Glacier and Lake-Level Variations in West-Central Europe over the Last 3500 Years," *The Holocene* 15 (6) (2005) 789–801.

10. According to Patrick Hunt at Stanford University, this is plausible because hydrochloric acid vinegar (acetic acid) reacts on carbonate rock, which can effervesce or even dissolve if heat also causes the rock itself to expand. See http://traumwerk.stanford.edu/archaeolog/2007/06/hannibals_engineers_and_livy_o.html.

11. Livy, *History of Rome*, trans. de Sélincourt, XXI, 36–37.

12. Polybius says that he started his ascent with forty-six thousand soldiers. Livy puts the number at fifty-nine thousand men.

13. Livy, *History of Rome*, trans. de Sélincourt, XXI, 40–41.

14. David W. Galenson, *Old Masters and Young Geniuses: The Two Life Cycles of Artistic Creativity* (Princeton, NJ, and Oxford, UK: Princeton University Press, 2006).

15. Ibid., p. 10.

16. Ibid., chapter 2.

17. John Rewald, *Cézanne: A Biography* (New York: Abrams, 1986), p. 16.

18. Ibid., p. 13.

19. Ibid., pp. 19, 22, 27.

20. Ibid., p. 25.

21. Ibid., p. 34.

22. Ibid., p. 159.

23. Ibid., p. 100.

24. Ibid., pp. 155, 192, 254.

25. Ibid., p. 265.

26. Galenson, *Old Masters and Young Geniuses*, chapter 2.

27. Stephen Ambrose, *Undaunted Courage: Meriwether Lewis, Thomas Jefferson, and the Opening of the American West* (New York: Simon & Schuster, 1996), p. 246.

28. Ibid., p. 197.

29. Ibid., p. 227.

30. Ibid., p. 421.

31. Ibid., p. 438.

32. Ibid., p. 460.

33. Ibid., p. 462.

34. Ibid., p. 463.

35. Ibid., pp. 471–76.

FIVE. THE ART OF WINNING

1. Livy, *The History of Rome from Its Foundation, Books XXI–XXX*, trans. Aubrey de Sélincourt (London and New York: Penguin Books, 1965), XXI, 42–43.

2. Polybius, *The Rise of the Roman Empire*, trans. Ian Scott-Kilvert (London: Penguin Books, 1979), III, 84.

3. According to Polybius, the Romans had eighty thousand foot soldiers and six thousand horsemen, the Carthaginians forty thousand foot soldiers and ten thousand horsemen.

4. Polybius estimates the number of Roman dead at seventy thousand, Livy at fifty thousand.

5. See for instance, Robert Greene, *The Art of Seduction* (New York: Penguin Books, 2003).

6. Kisshomaru Ueshiba, *A Life in Aikido: The Biography of Founder Morihei Ueshiba*, trans. Kei Izawa and Mary Fuller (Tokyo and New York: Kodansha International, 2008), p. 111.

7. Ibid., p. 59.

8. Ibid., p. 65.

9. Ibid., pp. 66–68.

10. Ibid., pp. 72–73.

11. Ibid., p. 74.

12. Ibid., p. 86.

13. Ibid., p. 107.

14. Ibid., p. 171.

15. Ibid., p. 174.

16. Ibid., p. 241.

17. Ibid., p. 188.

18. Ibid., p. 179.

19. Interview with Morihei Ueshiba O Sensei and Kisshomaru Ueshiba, as it appeared in the Japanese-language text *Aikido* by Kisshomaru Ueshiba (Tokyo: Kowado, 1957), pp. 198–219, trans. Stanley Pranin and Katsuaki Terasawa. Available online at: http://www.aikidofaq.com/interviews.html.

20. Interview with Morihei Ueshiba O Sensei and Kisshamaru Ueshiba, trans. Stanley Pranin and Katsuaki Terasawa. Available at http://www.aikidofaq.com/interviews.html.

21. Ueshiba, *A Life in Aikido*, pp. 252–53.

22. Ibid., p. 24.

23. Adrian Goldsworthy, *Caesar: Life of a Colossus* (New Haven, CT, and London: Yale University Press, 2006), p. 100.

24. Michael Grant, *Cleopatra* (Edison, NJ: Castle Books, 2004), p. 67.

25. Goldsworthy, *Caesar*, p. 66.

26. Greene, *The Art of Seduction*, p. 7.

27. Ibid., pp. 7–9.

28. Ibid., pp. xix–xxi.

29. Grant, *Cleopatra*, p. 96.

30. Plutarch, "Antony," in *Lives*, trans. John Dryden (New York: Modern Library, 2001), II, pp. 496–97.

31. Grant, *Cleopatra*, p. 127.

SIX. TACTICS AND STRATEGY IN LIFE

1. Livy, *The History of Rome from Its Foundation, Books XXXI–XLV*, trans. Henry Bettenson (London and New York: Penguin Books, 1976), XXIII, 7.

2. Ibid., XXIII, 11–13.
3. My primary source for Clausewitz is Michael Howard, *Clausewitz: A Very Short Introduction* (Oxford, UK, and New York: Oxford University Press, 2002).
4. Howard, *Clausewitz*, p. 16.
5. Ibid., p. 36.
6. http://web.tigerwoods.com/news/article/200912117801012/news/ (accessed on 1/4/2010).
7. Michael Grant, *Cleopatra* (Edison, NJ: Castle Books, 2004), p. 185.
8. Ibid., pp. 226–27.
9. David McCullough, *Truman* (New York: Simon & Schuster, 1992), p. 799.
10. Ibid., p. 802.
11. Ibid., p. 804.
12. Ibid., p. 806.
13. Ibid., p. 817.
14. Ibid., pp. 832, 835.
15. Ibid., p. 847.
16. Plutarch, "Pyrrhus," in *Lives*, trans. John Dryden (New York: Modern Library, 2001), I, 529–30.

SEVEN. DEALING WITH DISASTER

1. Plutarch, "Fabius," in *Lives,* trans. John Dryden (New York: Modern Library, 2001), I, 235.
2. Livy, *The History of Rome from Its Foundation, Books XXI–XXX*, trans. Aubrey de Sélincourt (London and New York: Penguin Books, 1965), XXII, 12.
3. Ibid., XXII, 17.
4. Ibid., XXI, 14.
5. Ibid., XXII, 23.
6. Ibid., XXII, 25.
7. Plutarch, "Fabius," I, 244.
8. Livy, *The History of Rome from Its Foundation,* trans. de Sélincourt, XXII, 29.
9. Ibid., XXII, 39.
10. Ibid., XXII, 49.
11. Elisabeth Kübler-Ross, *On Death and Dying* (New York: Scribner, 1969), p. 53.
12. Ibid., p. 63.
13. Lance Armstrong with Sally Jenkins, *It's Not About the Bike: My Journey Back to Life* (New York: Berkeley Books, 2001), p. 4.
14. Ibid., p. 119.
15. Kübler-Ross, *On Death and Dying*, p. 99.
16. Armstrong, *It's Not About the Bike*, p. 14.
17. Ibid., p. 70.
18. Kübler-Ross, *On Death and Dying*, p. 124.
19. Armstrong, *It's Not About the Bike*, p. 96.
20. Ibid., p. 95.
21. Ibid., p. 131.
22. Lance Armstrong in conversation with Bob Schieffer at the Aspen Ideas Festival on July 4, 2007, minutes 11 to 12, http://fora.tv/2007/07/04/A_Conversation_with_Lance_Armstrong.

23. Plutarch, "Fabius," I, 249.

24. Blanche Wiesen Cook, *Eleanor Roosevelt, Volume 1: 1884–1933* (New York: Penguin Books, 1993), p. 235.

25. Ibid.

26. Alfred Lansing, *Endurance: Shackleton's Incredible Voyage* (New York: Carroll & Graf, 1959), p. 14.

27. Ibid., p. 30.

28. Ibid., p. 38.

29. Ibid., p. 50.

30. Ibid., p. 9.

31. Ibid., p. 104.

32. Ibid., p. 137.

33. Roland Huntford, *Shackleton* (New York: Atheneum, 1986), p. 582.

34. Ibid., p. 597.

EIGHT. THE PRISON OF SUCCESS

1. Livy, *The History of Rome from Its Foundation, Books XXI–XXX*, trans. Aubrey de Sélincourt (London and New York: Penguin Books, 1965), XXIII, 45.

2. Ibid., XXII, 51.

3. Ibid., XXV, 7–10.

4. Plutarch, "Fabius," in *Lives*, trans. John Dryden (New York: Modern Library, 2001), I, 251–53.

5. Ibid., I, 253.

6. Adrian Goldsworthy, *The Punic Wars* (London: Cassell & Co., 2000), p. 226.

7. Livy, *The History of Rome from Its Foundation*, trans. de Sélincourt, XXVII, 16.

8. Serge Lancel, *Hannibal*, trans. Antonia Nevill (Oxford, UK, and Malden, MA: Blackwell, 1998), p. 124.

9. Livy, *The History of Rome from Its Foundation*, trans. de Sélincourt, XXIV, 44.

10. Ibid., XXVII, 49.

11. Ibid., XXVII, 51.

12. Ibid., XXX, 18–19.

13. Ibid., XXVI, 8.

14. Ibid., XXVI, 10.

15. Ibid., XXVI, 11.

16. Tennessee Williams, "The Catastrophe of Success," *The Glass Menagerie* (New York: New Directions Books [NDP874], 1999). All direct quotes from Williams come from this essay.

17. Interview with Amy Tan at the Academy of Achievement: http://www.achievement .org/autodoc/page/tan0int-1.

18. Ulrike Malmendier and Geoffrey Tate, "Superstar CEOs," March 15, 2007, available at http://ssrn.com/abstract=972725, p. 2.

19. Paul Samuelson, "Is There Life After Nobel Coronation?" http://nobelprize.org/ economics/articles/samuelson/index.html.

20. Cameron Anderson and Adam Galinsky, "Power, Optimism and Risk-taking," *European Journal of Social Psychology* 36 (2006): 511–36.

21. Michael Powell and Mike McIntire, "A Fall from White Knight to Client 9,"

New York Times, March 11, 2008. http://www.nytimes.com/2008/03/11/nyregion/11fall.html?fta=y.

22. "The Promise of Eliot Spitzer," *New York Times*, October 22, 2006. http://www.nytimes.com/2006/10/22/opinion/22sun2.html?scp=29&sq=eliot%20spitzer&st=cse.

23. Michael Powell and Nicholas Confessore, "4 Arrests, Then 6 Days to a Resignation," *New York Times*, March 13, 2008. http://www.nytimes.com/2008/03/13/nyregion/13recon.html?scp=1&sq=eliot%20spitzer%20%224%20arrests%22&st=cse.

24. John Cloud, "Was Spitzer Destined to Fall?" Time.com, March 13, 2008. http://www.time.com/time/nation/article/0,8599,1721968,00.html.

25. Serge Kovaleski and Ian Urbina, "For an Aspiring Singer, a Harsher Spotlight," *New York Times*, March 13, 2008. http://www.nytimes.com/2008/03/13/nyregion/12cnd-kristen.html?scp=16&sq=eliot%20spitzer&st=cse.

26. Cloud, "Was Spitzer Destined to Fall?"

27. Danny Hakim, "6 Months Later, Spitzer Is Contrite, Yes, but Sometimes Still Angry," *The New York Times*, September 28, 2008. http://www.nytimes.com/2008/09/28/nyregion/28spitzer.html?scp=44&sq=eliot%20spitzer&st=cse.

28. Malmendier and Tate, "Super CEOs," p. 5.

29. Walter Isaacson, *Einstein: His Life and Universe* (New York: Simon & Schuster, 2007), p. 22.

30. Ibid., p. 7.

31. Ibid., p. 27.

32. Ibid., p. 37.

33. Ibid., p. 56.

34. Ibid., p. 59.

35. Ibid., pp. 1–2.

36. Ibid., p. 295.

37. Ibid., p. 268.

38. Ibid., p. 272.

39. Ibid., p. 324.

40. Ibid., p. 325.

41. Ibid., p. 332.

42. Ibid., p. 463.

43. Ibid., p. 100.

44. Ibid., p. 514.

45. Ibid., p. 538.

46. Ibid., p. 317.

47. Ibid., pp. 511–12.

48. Ibid., p. 466.

49. Ibid., p. 7.

NINE. THE LIBERATION OF FAILURE

1. Polybius says he was seventeen, Livy says he was eighteen.

2. Polybius, *The Rise of the Roman Empire*, trans. Ian Scott-Kilvert (London: Penguin Books, 1979), X, 3.

3. Adrian Goldsworthy, *The Punic Wars* (London: Cassell & Co., 2000), p. 270.

4. Livy, *The History of Rome from Its Foundation, Books XXI–XXX*, trans. Aubrey de Sélincourt (London and New York: Penguin Books, 1965), XXII, 53.

5. Ibid., XXVI, 18–19.

6. Ibid., XXVI, 42.

7. Polybius, *The Rise of the Roman Empire*, X, 8.

8. Ibid., X, 13.

9. Ibid., X, 14.

10. Ibid., X, 15.

11. Ibid., X, 34.

12. Livy, *The History of Rome from Its Foundation,* trans. de Sélincourt, XXVI, 50.

13. Polybius, *The Rise of the Roman Empire*, X, 40.

14. Livy, *The History of Rome from Its Foundation,* trans. de Sélincourt, XXVII, 19.

15. B. H. Liddell Hart, *Scipio Africanus: Greater Than Napoleon* (Cambridge, MA: Da Capo Press, 1926), p. 58.

16. Ibid., p. 63, and Livy, *The History of Rome from Its Foundation,* trans. de Sélincourt, XXVII, 17–18.

17. Livy, *The History of Rome from Its Foundation,* trans. de Sélincourt, XXVIII, 40.

18. Ibid., XXVIII, 42.

19. Ibid., XXVIII, 43.

20. Ibid., XXVIII, 44.

21. Ibid.

22. Polybius, *The Rise of the Roman Empire*, XIV, 1–2.

23. After a book by the same title by Clayton Christensen at Harvard Business School.

24. Steve Jobs, Interview with Steve Jobs. *Smithsonian Institution Oral History Interview,* April 20, 1995, transcript available at http://www.cwheroes.org/archives/histories/jobs.pdf, p. 3.

25. Ibid., p. 4.

26. Ibid., p. 10.

27. Ibid., p. 11.

28. Andy Hertzfeld, "The End of an Era," May 1985, available at http://www.folklore.org/StoryView.py?project=Macintosh&story=The_End_Of_An_Era.txt.

29. Steve Jobs, Commencement Address, Stanford University, June 12, 2005, available at http://news-service.stanford.edu/news/2005/june15/jobs-061505.html.

30. Andy Hertzfeld, "The End of an Era."

31. Jobs, Interview with Steve Jobs, p. 12.

32. Jobs, Commencement Address.

33. Blanche Wiesen Cook, *Eleanor Roosevelt, Volume 1: 1884–1933* (New York: Penguin Books, 1993), p. 256.

34. Ibid., p. 313.

35. Ibid., p. 435.

36. Ibid., p. 492.

37. Ibid., p. 8.

TEN. THE THRESHOLD OF MIDDLE AGE

1. B. H. Liddell Hart, *Scipio Africanus: Greater than Napoleon* (Cambridge, MA: Da Capo Press, 1926), p. 164.

2. Polybius, *The Rise of the Roman Empire*, trans. Ian Scott-Kilvert (London: Penguin Books, 1979), XV, 6.

3. Livy, *The History of Rome from Its Foundation, Books XXI–XXX*, trans. Aubrey de Sélincourt (London and New York: Penguin Books, 1965), XXX, 30.

4. Polybius, *The Rise of the Roman Empire*, XV, 7.

5. Ibid., XV, 8.

6. Ibid., XV, 10.

7. Liddell Hart, *Scipio Africanus*, chapter 11.

8. Polybius, *The Rise of the Roman Empire*, XV, 19.

9. Livy, *The History of Rome from Its Foundation*, trans. de Sélincourt, XXX, 43–44.

10. Serge Lancel, *Hannibal*, trans. Antonia Nevill (Oxford, UK, and Malden, MA: Blackwell, 1998), p. 180.

11. Livy, *The History of Rome from Its Foundation, Books XXXI–XLV*, trans. Henry Betten-son (London and New York: Penguin Books, 1976), XXXIII, 46.

12. Ibid., XXXIII, 47.

13. Ibid., XXXIII, 45.

14. Ibid., XXXIII, 47.

15. *The Wisdom of Carl Jung*, ed. Edward Hoffman (New York: Citadel Press Books, 2003), p. 91.

16. Daniel Levinson, with Charlotte Darrow, Edward Klein, Maria Levinson, and Braxton McKee, *The Seasons of a Man's Life* (New York: Ballantine Books, 1978), p. 232.

17. Murray Stein, *In Midlife* (Putnam, CT: Spring Publications, 1983).

18. Ibid., p. 47.

19. Levinson, *The Seasons of a Man's Life*, p. 218.

20. David Blanchflower and Andrew Oswald, "Is Well-Being U-Shaped over the Life Cycle?" NBER Working Paper 12935, February 2007, available at www.nber.org/papers/w12935.

21. *The Wisdom of Carl Jung*, p. 5.

22. Ibid., p. 8.

23. Ibid., p. 13.

24. C. G. Jung, *Memories, Dreams, Reflections*, recorded and edited by Aniela Jaffe (New York: Vintage Books, 1989), p. 150.

25. Ibid., p. 152.

26. Ibid., p. 156.

27. *The Wisdom of Carl Jung*, p. 16.

28. Jung, *Memories, Dreams, Reflections*, p. 167.

29. *The Wisdom of Carl Jung*, p. 17.

30. Jung, *Memories, Dreams, Reflections*, p. 170.

31. *The Wisdom of Carl Jung*, p. 18.

32. Ibid., p. 17.

33. Ibid., pp. 25–28.

34. Ibid., p. 30.

35. Ibid., p. 40.

36. Roland Huntford, *Shackleton* (New York: Atheneum, 1986), p. 644.

37. Ibid., p. 630.

38. Ibid., p. 642.

39. Ibid., p. 652.

40. Ibid., p. 651.
41. Ibid., p. 657.
42. Ibid., p. 662.
43. Ibid., p. 666.
44. Ibid., p. 664.
45. Ibid., p. 667.
46. Ibid., p. 664.
47. Ibid., p. 669.
48. Ibid., p. 685.
49. Ibid.
50. Ibid., p. 690.
51. *The Wisdom of Carl Jung*, p. 102.
52. Ibid., p. 121.
53. Levinson, *The Seasons of a Man's Life*, p. 220.

ELEVEN. POLITICAL DEATH

1. Livy, *The History of Rome from Its Foundation, Books XXI–XXX*, trans. Aubrey de Sélincourt (London and New York: Penguin Books, 1965), XXX, 45.
2. Plutarch, "Marcus Cato," in *Lives*, trans. John Dryden (New York: Modern Library, 2001), I, 460–64.
3. Ibid., pp. 457–58.
4. Ibid., p. 459.
5. B. H. Liddell Hart, *Scipio Africanus: Greater than Napoleon* (Cambridge, MA: Da Capo Press, 1926), p. 239.
6. Livy, *The History of Rome from Its Foundation, Books XXXI–XLV*, trans. Henry Bettenson (London and New York: Penguin Books, 1976), XXXVIII, 51.
7. Serge Lancel, *Hannibal*, trans. Antonia Nevill (Oxford, UK, and Malden, MA: Blackwell, 1998), p. 210.
8. Alfred C. Mierzejewski, *Ludwig Erhard: A Biography* (Chapel Hill: University of North Carolina Press, 2004), p. 29.
9. Ibid., p. 31.
10. Ibid., p. 173.
11. Hans Ulrich Jörges and Walter Wüllenweber, "Ludwig Erhard war nie CDU-Mitglied," *Stern*, April 25, 2007. http://www.stern.de/politik/deutschland/cdu-altkanzler-ludwig-erhard-war-nie-cdu-mitglied-587764.html.
12. Mierzejewski, *Ludwig Erhard*, p. 184.
13. Ibid., p. 191.
14. Ibid.
15. Ibid., p. 200.
16. Harrison Salisbury, *The New Emperors: China in the Era of Mao and Deng* (New York: Avon Books, 1992), pp. 227–28.
17. Ibid., p. 226.
18. Nicholas Kristof, "Suicide of Jiang Qing, Mao's Widow, Is Reported," *The New York Times*, Wednesday, June 5, 1991.
19. Salisbury, *The New Emperors*, p. 234.
20. Ibid., pp. 235–36, 238.

21. Ibid., p. 268.
22. Ibid., p. 269.
23. Ibid., pp. 270–73.

TWELVE. AGING AND TRANSCENDING

1. Livy, *The History of Rome from Its Foundation, Books XXXI–XLV*, trans. Henry Betten-son (London and New York: Penguin Books, 1976), XXXV, 19.
2. Ibid., XXXV, 42.
3. Cornelius Nepos, trans. J. C. Rolfe (Cambridge, MA, and London: Harvard University Press, 1984), pp. 10–11.
4. *The Wisdom of Carl Jung*, ed. Edward Hoffman (New York: Citadel Press Books, 2003), p. 110.
5. A. H. Maslow, "A Theory of Human Motivation," *Psychological Review* 50 (1943): 383.
6. George Boeree, psychology professor at Shippensburg University, has a good explanation at http://webspace.ship.edu/cgboer/maslow.html.
7. Russell Freedman, *Eleanor Roosevelt: A Life of Discovery* (New York: Clarion Books, 1993), p. 154.
8. Ibid.
9. Ibid., p. 157.
10. Ibid., p. 154.
11. Ibid., p. 168.
12. Walter Isaacson, *Einstein: His Life and Universe* (New York: Simon & Schuster, 2007), pp. 76, 86–87.
13. Ibid., p. 516.
14. Ibid., p. 393.
15. Ibid., p. 371.
16. Ibid., p. 376.
17. Ibid., p. 386.
18. Ibid., pp. 357–58.
19. Ibid., pp. 427, 436.
20. Ibid., p. 435.
21. Ibid., p. 427.
22. Ibid., p. 439–40.
23. Ibid., p. 508.
24. Ibid., pp. 384–85.
25. Ibid., p. 387.
26. Ibid., p. 394.
27. Ibid., p. 520.
28. Ibid., p. 367.

THIRTEEN. THE LESSONS OF HANNIBAL

1. Plutarch, "Flamininus," in *Lives*, trans. John Dryden (New York: Modern Library, 2001), I, 515–16.
2. http://skyways.lib.ks.us/genweb/lincoln/success.htm.
3. *Bhagavad Gita*, trans. Stephen Mitchell (New York: Three Rivers Press, 2000), pp. 43, 211.

4. Paramahansa Yogananda, *God Talks with Arjuna: The Bhagavad Gita* (Los Angeles: Self-Realization Fellowship, 1999). See especially his genealogy chart of the characters on page xxxvi.

5. *Bhagavad Gita,* trans. Mitchell, p. 43.

6. *The Bhagavad Gita: A Walkthrough for Westerners,* trans. Jack Hawley (Novato, CA: New World Library, 2001), 2.37–38.

7. *Bhagavad Gita,* trans. Mitchell, 6.34.

8. Ibid., 2.50.

9. Ibid., 4.19–26.

BIBLIOGRAPHY

Ambrose, Stephen. *Undaunted Courage: Meriwether Lewis, Thomas Jefferson, and the Opening of the American West.* New York: Simon & Schuster, 1996.

Anderson, Cameron, and Adam Galinsky. "Power, Optimism and Risk-taking." *European Journal of Social Psychology* 36 (2006): 511–36.

Appian. *History of Rome: The Punic Wars.* Trans. Horace White. Online at Livius, http://www.livius.org/ap-ark/appian/appian_punic_00.html.

Armstrong, Lance, with Sally Jenkins. *It's Not About the Bike: My Journey Back to Life.* New York: Berkeley Books, 2001.

The Bhagavad Gita: A Walkthrough for Westerners. Trans. Jack Hawley. Novato, CA: New World Library, 2001.

Bhagavad Gita. Trans. Stephen Mitchell. New York: Three Rivers Press, 2000.

Blanchflower, David, and Andrew Oswald. "Is Well-Being U-Shaped over the Life Cycle?" NBER Working Paper 12935, February 2007. www.nber.org/papers/w12935.

Boeree, George. "Abraham Maslow." http://webspace.ship.edu/cgboer/maslow.html.

Brown, Chip. "It's Good to Be Immortal." *New York Times Magazine,* June 1, 2008.

Brown, Larry. "Mahabharata: The Great Epic of India." http://larryavisbrown.homestead.com/files/xeno.mahabsynop.htm.

Campbell, Joseph, with Bill Moyers. *The Power of Myth.* New York: Anchor Books, 1991.

Cook, Blanche Wiesen. *Eleanor Roosevelt. Volume 1: 1884–1933.* New York: Penguin Books, 1993.

Cornelius Nepos. Trans. J. C. Rolfe. Cambridge, MA, and London: Harvard University Press, 1984.

Diodorus Siculus. *The Library of History.* Vol. 11. Trans. F. R. Walton. Book XXV, section 10. http://penelope.uchicago.edu/Thayer/E/Roman/Texts/Diodorus_Siculus/25*.html. Accessed in 2008.

Fagan, Garrett G. *The History of Ancient Rome.* Chantilly, VA: The Teaching Company Limited, 1999.

Fears, J. Rufus. *Famous Romans.* Chantilly, VA: The Teaching Company Limited, 2001.

Fitzgerald, James L. "The Story of the Mahabharata." http://web.utk.edu/~jftzgrld/MBh1Story.html. Accessed in late 2009.

Freedman, Russell. *Eleanor Roosevelt: A Life of Discovery.* New York: Clarion Books, 1993.

Galenson, David W. *Old Masters and Young Geniuses: The Two Life Cycles of Artistic Creativity.* Princeton, NJ, and Oxford, UK: Princeton University Press, 2006.

Goldsworthy, Adrian. *Caesar: Life of a Colossus.* New Haven, CT, and London: Yale University Press, 2006.

———. *The Punic Wars.* London: Cassell & Co., 2003.

Grant, Michael. *Cleopatra.* Edison, NJ: Castle Books, 2004.

Greene, Robert. *The Art of Seduction.* New York: Penguin Books, 2003.

Haidt, Jonathan. *The Happiness Hypothesis: Finding Modern Truth in Ancient Wisdom.* New York: Basic Books, 2006.

Hertzfeld, Andy. "The End of an Era," May 1985. http://www.folklore.org/StoryView .py?project=Macintosh&story=The_End_Of_An_Era.txt.

Hodges, Bert H., and Anne L. Geyer. "A Nonconformist Account of the Asch Experiments: Values, Pragmatics, and Moral Dilemmas." *Personality and Social Psychology Review* 10 (2006): 2. http://psr.sagepub.com/cgi/content/abstract/10/1/2.

Hoffman, Joanna. Telephone interview. January 9, 2009.

Howard, Michael. *Clausewitz: A Very Short Introduction.* Oxford, UK, and New York: Oxford University Press, 2002.

Hunt, Patrick. *Hannibal.* Stanford University course ARC123 on iTunes University.

Huntford, Roland. *Shackleton.* New York: Atheneum, 1986.

Isaacson, Walter. *Einstein: His Life and Universe.* New York: Simon & Schuster, 2007.

Jobs, Steve. Commencement address. Stanford University, June 12, 2005. http://news -service.stanford.edu/news/2005/june15/jobs-061505.html.

———. Interview with Steve Jobs. *Smithsonian Institution Oral History.* April 20, 1995. www.cwheroes.org/archives/histories/jobs.pdf.

Jörges, Hans Ulrich, and Walter Wüllenweber. "Ludwig Erhard war nie CDU-Mitglied." *Stern,* April 25, 2007. http://www.stern.de/politik/deutschland/cdu-altkanzler-ludwig -erhard-war-nie-cdu-mitglied-587764.html.

Jung, C. G. *Memories, Dreams, Reflections.* Recorded and edited by Aniela Jaffe. New York: Vintage Books, 1989.

Kübler-Ross, Elisabeth. *On Death and Dying.* New York: Scribner, 1969.

Lancel, Serge. *Hannibal.* Trans. Antonia Nevill. Oxford, UK, and Malden, MA: Blackwell, 1998.

Lansing, Alfred. *Endurance: Shackleton's Incredible Voyage.* New York: Carroll & Graf, 1959.

Levinson, Daniel, with Charlotte Darrow, Edward Klein, Maria Levinson, and Braxton McKee. *The Seasons of a Man's Life.* New York: Ballantine Books, 1978.

Liddell Hart, B. H. *Scipio Africanus: Greater Than Napoleon.* Cambridge, MA: Da Capo Press, 1926.

Livy. *The History of Rome from Its Foundation, Books XXI–XXX.* Trans. Aubrey de Sélincourt. London and New York: Penguin Books, 1965.

———. *The History of Rome from Its Foundation, Books XXXI–XLV.* Trans. Henry Bettenson. London and New York: Penguin Books, 1976.

Lukomski, Jess. *Ludwig Erhard: Der Mensch und der Politiker.* Düsseldorf: Econ-Verlag, 1965.

Malmendier, Ulrike, and Geoffrey Tate. "Superstar CEOs," March 15, 2007. http://ssrn .com/abstract=972725.

Maslow, A. H. "A Theory of Human Motivation." *Psychological Review* 50 (1943): 370–96.

McAdams, Dan P. "The Psychology of Life Stories." *Review of General Psychology* 5, no. 2 (2001): 100–122.

McCullough, David. *Truman.* New York: Simon & Schuster, 1992.

Mierzejewski, Alfred C. *Ludwig Erhard: A Biography.* Chapel Hill: University of North Carolina Press, 2004.

Miles, Richard. *Carthage Must Be Destroyed.* London: Allen Lane, Penguin Group, 2010.

Miller, Steve. Telephone interview. January 22, 2008.

Obama, Barack. *Dreams from My Father.* New York: Three Rivers Press, 1995.

Plutarch. *Lives.* Trans. John Dryden. 2 vols. New York: Modern Library, 2001.

Polybius. *The Rise of the Roman Empire.* Trans. Ian Scott-Kilvert. London: Penguin Books, 1979.

Prevas, John. *Hannibal Crosses the Alps: The Invasion of Italy and the Punic Wars.* Cambridge, MA: Da Capo Press, 1998.

Rewald, John. *Cézanne: A Biography.* New York: Abrams, 1986.

Salisbury, Harrison. *The New Emperors: China in the Era of Mao and Deng.* New York: Avon Books, 1992.

Samuelson, Paul. "Is There Life After Nobel Coronation?" http://nobelprize.org/economics/articles/samuelson/index.html. Accessed 2008.

Skidmore, Joel. "Mythweb." http://www.mythweb.com. San Francisco, CA: Fleet Gazelle. Accessed in 2008.

Solomon, Deborah. "Questions for Amy Tan: The Good Daughter." *New York Times Magazine,* August 10, 2008.

Stein, Murray. *In Midlife.* Putnam, CT: Spring Publications, 1983.

Tan, Amy. Biography. Academy of Achievement. http://www.achievement.org/autodoc/page/tan0bio-1. Accessed in 2008.

———. Interview. Academy of Achievement. http://www.achievement.org/autodoc/page/tan0int-1. Accessed in 2008.

Ueshiba, Kisshomaru. *A Life in Aikido: The Biography of Founder Morihei Ueshiba.* Trans. Kei Izawa and Mary Fuller. Tokyo and New York: Kodansha International, 2008.

Williams, Tennesse. "The Catastrophe of Success." *The Glass Menagerie.* New York: New Directions Books (NDP874), 1999.

The Wisdom of Carl Jung. Ed. Edward Hoffman. New York: Citadel Press Books, 2003.

Yogananda, Paramahansa. *God Talks with Arjuna: The Bhagavad Gita.* Los Angeles: Self-Realization Fellowship, 1999.

INDEX

absent parent, 29–36, 52, 291
acceptance of circumstances
  by Armstrong, 157
  as characteristic of resilience, 153
  decision not to act, 291
  by Fabius, 146, 154, 157
  by Roosevelt, 159–60
  by Shackleton, 165, 168
  as stage in grief cycle, 157, 160
  state of flow, 153, 158–59, 168
  for survival and persistence, 206
  in Taoist philosophy, 158
Adenauer, Konrad, 253–55, 257
Africa
  Rome's Numidian alliances, 202, 205
  Scipio's plan to invade, 196, 202–5
  Zama battle, 217–21
aikido, 108–10, 158, 183
Alexander the Great, 23, 49, 123–24
Allucius, 198–99
Alps
  Carthaginian army crossing,
    2–3, 70–77
  in Hannibal's strategy to conquer Rome,
    68–70
  as impenetrable barrier, 3, 67–68
anger, 153–56, 179, 206, 290–91
anima/animus, 229
Antiochus, 227, 248, 267–69
Antony, Mark, 115–18, 135–37
anxiety, 11, 28, 177–79, 184
Apple computer. *See* Jobs, Steve

archetypes
  adolescent emulation of parent, 28, 52, 291
  adolescent rebellion against parent, 29,
    36–40, 52, 291
  hero on quest, 24, 52–53, 235
  human need for, 14–15
  in Jungian psychology, 14, 52
  quest for absent parent, 29–36, 52, 291
  triumph and disaster, 16
  See also dreamers; wanderers
Armstrong, Lance, 154–55, 156–57
Asia, Roman campaigns in, 248–49

balance
  inner calmness, 108–9, 183–84, 287
  opponent's center of gravity, 108, 124–26,
    127
  opponent's loss of, 104–5, 108–10, 112–13,
    158, 287
bargaining, 153, 155–56, 179
Bhagavad Gita, 284, 296–97
Bithynia, 270, 284–85
Bohr, Niels, 189
Born, Max, 190
Bradley, Omar, 139

Caesar, Gaius Julius, 111–15
calmness
  attitude of equanimity, 296–98
  inner balance, 108–9, 183–84, 287
Cannae
  Carthaginian army at, 47–48, 100

Cannae (*cont.*)
Fabius's acceptance of defeat, 154, 157
Hannibal's strategy, 100–102, 104–5
Hannibal's victory, 3–4, 152
report on victory to Carthaginian senate, 119–20
Rome at news of defeat, 102–3, 152
captivity by success
for Einstein, 184–85, 188–91, 289
for Hannibal, 170, 174, 177, 178, 183
imprisonment of imagination, 183–84, 289
for Tan, 178–79, 182, 183, 184, 289
for Williams, 177–78, 182–83, 184, 289
Capua, 119, 169–70, 176–77
Cartagena, 46, 197–99
Carthage
destruction by Rome, 5, 286
First Punic War, 21, 24–26
order of judges, 224
peace with Rome, 21–22, 25–26, 27
political structure, 22–23
power and sphere of influence, 22, 23, 27
sacrifice of firstborn sons, 45
Second Punic War, start of, 72
surrender to Rome, 221–23
Carthaginian army
Alpine crossing, 2–3, 70–76
composition, 2, 48, 70–71, 100
elephants, 71–72, 76, 96, 220
forces in Iberia, 46, 196, 199, 200
loyalty to Hannibal, 2, 47–49
rebel mercenary armies, 26–27
shrinkage, 71, 174
swamp crossing into central Italy, 97
See also Hannibal; *specific battles*
Casilinum, 148
Cato, Marcus Porcius, 245–47, 249, 293
Cézanne, Paul, 78, 80–83, 290
Charlemagne, 6
China
Jiang Qing, 259–60, 293
Liu Shaoqi, 258–59, 260, 261–64
Mao Zedong, 258, 260–64
Wang Guangmei, 258–60, 263–64
Cineas, 141–42
Clark, William, 84–87, 88, 89
Clausewitz, Carl von, 127–29
Cleopatra
family history, 110–11
goal, 111, 134–35
seduction of Antony, 115–18

seduction of Caesar, 111–15
strategic and tactical errors, 135–37
Corsica, 27, 69

Demoiselles d'Avignon, Les (Picasso), 79
denial, 154, 179, 206, 290–91
depression, 154, 156, 197, 206, 290–91
disaster, triumph from, 206–7, 210–16, 291
distraction by success, 182, 188
dreamers
early success and later discouragement, 77–78, 80, 83, 241–42, 288
Einstein, 184–91, 230–31, 278–83, 289–90, 294
goals, hero quest, 52–53
inexperience as asset, 77
Lewis, 54–56, 84–91, 228, 290
Picasso, 78–80, 82, 83, 90–91, 183, 288–89
as planners, 70, 77, 79, 84
Shackleton, 160–68, 236–41, 291–92, 295

Einstein, Albert, 184–91, 230–31, 278–83, 289–90, 294
emulation of parent, 28, 52, 291
ends. *See* goals
equanimity, 296–98
Erhard, Ludwig ("Uncle Lulu")
family background, 40
political decline and retreat from politics, 255–58
self-actualization, 274–76, 289, 294
success later in life, 65, 251–55, 290
as wanderer during youth, 59–65
Etruria, 98
exultation cycle following triumph, 179

Fabius Maximus, Quintus
acceptance of reality, 146, 152–54, 157, 171, 291
Carthage, declaration of war on, 50–51
death, 175
emotional self-control, 147, 152–53, 157
envy, 203, 204, 295
Hannibal, understanding of, 147–49, 174–75, 177
inaction, 145–46, 147–49, 151–52, 153, 158
leadership roles, 99, 145, 147, 152
physical appearance, 13, 144
resilience, 153–54
Roman distrust of, 149–51
on Scipio's African invasion plan, 203–5

slowness and methodical approach, 144–45
son's achievement, 145, 175
success, definition of, 146
tactical ruse at Tarentum, 173–74
Fabius Maximus, Quintus (Younger), 175
failure, triumph from, 206–7, 210–16, 291
First Punic War, 21, 24–26, 68
Flamininus, 271
Flaminius, 97–99, 104
flow
    acceptance of circumstances, 153, 158–59,
        168
    state of confidence and relaxation, 183–84
freedom. See liberation
Freud, Sigmund, 232–34

Galenson, David, 78
Gandhi, Mohandas, 296
Gauls
    at Cannae battle, 100, 101
    clashes with Carthaginian army, 71, 73–74
    in Hannibal's army, 70, 94, 98–99
    Roman conquest of, 93
    tribes, 69, 71
Gisco (Carthaginian senator), 222
Gisco (Carthaginian officer), 47–48
goals
    clarity of, 49, 52, 135
    Clausewitz on, 127–29
    of Cleopatra, 111, 134–37
    definition of success, 126–27, 291–92
    of fisherman, 140–41
    of Hamilcar, 8–9, 27–28
    of Hannibal, 1, 46, 49, 51–52, 68, 268
    hero on quest, 52–54
    of Pyrrhus, 141–42
    successes as means toward, 128, 142–43,
        287–88
    of Truman, 137–40
    of Woods, 130–34
Goerdeler, Carl Friedrich, 63–64
Greece
    attitude toward midlife, 230
    distrust of Romans, 23, 248
    as Mediterranean colonizer, 22
green-to-tee strategy, 132–33
grief cycle, 154–57, 160, 179, 209–10
Guernica (Picasso), 79

Hamilcar
    ambitions for sons, 19–20, 45–46
    confrontation with own soldiers, 26–27

in First Punic War, 25–26
goal, 8–9, 27–28
humiliation at submission to Rome, 21, 27
military and political shrewdness, 20–21
sacrifice of life for sons, 19–20, 46
Hannibal
    Alpine crossing, 1–3, 70–76
    Alpine strategy, 68–70
    blindness, 97
    brother Hasdrubal's death, 12, 176
    Cannae victory, 3–4
    catastrophe of success for, 177
    creativity, loss of, 288–89
    enemies in Carthage, 225–27, 267
    Fabius, understanding of, 148–49
    at Fabius's inaction, 147–49
    father's worldview and ambitions, 8–9, 20,
        27–28, 45–46, 228, 270
    goal, clarity of, 1, 46, 49, 51–52, 68, 268
    Hercules, comparison to, 3, 49, 68, 76,
        171
    as hero archetype, 8, 49, 77
    impasse, captivity by success, 4–5, 170, 171,
        174
    as leader, 2, 47–49, 92–93
    midlife transition, 224–27
    old age, return to Carthage in, 221–23
    Roman declaration of war, manipulation of,
        50–51
    Roman persecution of, 226, 267, 271,
        284–85
    Rome, march on, 171, 176–77
    Rome, peace offering to, 171
    Scipio, understanding of, 217–19, 265–67,
        292
    sea battles, 269, 270
    Seleucid Empire, as consultant to, 227, 248,
        268–69
    on strategy in war and life, 120–27, 286
    success, definition of, 52, 91, 127
    suicide, 285
    at surrender of Carthage to Rome, 223
    Tarentum siege, 172–74
    Ticinus River skirmish, 94, 192
    Trebia victory, 94–96
    winning, imperative of, 91, 93–94
    winning style, 103–5
    withdrawal from public life, 223–24
    youthful persona, 228
    Zama defeat, 219–21
Hannibal, lessons of
    acceptance of setbacks, 290–91

Hannibal, lessons of (*cont.*)
    alignment of tactics and strategies with goals,
        287–88
    attitude toward opponents, 292–94
    definition of success, 291–92
    duty and equanimity, 295–98
    self-actualization, 294
    self-balance, 104–5, 287
    self-discipline, 290
    style of winning, 103–5
    youthful ideas in later years, 288–89
Hanno, 120, 293
Hasdrubal Barca
    death, 12, 176
    father's military ambitions for, 19–20
    on Hannibal's plan to invade Italy, 68
    persona of youth, 228
    as troop commander, 69, 196, 199
Hasdrubal Gisco, 196, 200, 202, 205–6
Heisenberg, Werner, 189–90
hell, cultural metaphors for, 251
Hercules, 49, 67–68, 76, 171
hero on quest, 24, 52–53, 235. *See also*
        dreamers
hubris, 179–82, 290

Iberia
    Cartagena, 46, 197–99
    Carthaginian armies in, 46, 196, 199,
        200
    election of Hannibal to command army in,
        46–47
    Hamilcar's goal to conquer, 8–9, 28, 45–46
    Ilipa, 200–202
    Saguntum, 50
    Scipio's conquest for Rome, 202–3
    in Scipio's plan to invade Africa, 195–96
Ilipa, 200–202
inaction
    acceptance of setbacks, 291
    by Fabius, 145–46, 149–50, 153, 158
    by Shackleton, 160, 165–66, 168
    Taoist concept of nondoing, 158–59
individuation, 228–29
innovator's dilemma, 207
Italy
    Carthaginian alliances, 102
    Carthaginian army Alpine crossing, 2–3,
        70–77
    Hannibal's impasse in, 4–5, 170, 171, 174
    Hannibal's strategy in, 68–70
    See also specific cities and towns

Jefferson, Thomas, 54–56
Jiang Qing, 259–60, 293
Jobs, Steve
    career with Apple, 208–9, 211
    curiosity and creativity, 207–8, 210–11
    grief cycle, 209–10
    inaction, 291
    sense of liberation, 210–11, 291
Johnson, Lyndon, 256–57
Jung, Carl
    on archetypes, 14–15, 52
    creativity later in life, 289
    on individual's place in history, 286
    on individuation process, 228–29
    on midlife transition, 227–28, 241
    on spiritual unfulfillment in old age, 271
    successful midlife transition, 231–36

Kipling, Rudyard, 6, 16, 297
Kluth, Andreas
    adolescent identity, 40–43
    career, 6–7, 10–11, 17, 142
    emotional bargaining, 155–56
    interest in Hannibal, 5–6, 7–8
    on patterns of success and failure, 11–12
    personal myth, 8, 14
    strategic thinking about life, 142
    successes and failures in youth, 9–10
    as wanderer, 65–66
Kluth, Gerhard, 40–43, 64, 274–76
Kluth, Wilhelm, 62–63
Koch, Ed, 181
Krishna, 284, 296–98
Kübler-Ross, Elisabeth, 154, 155, 156, 157,
        160, 179

Lake Trasimene battle, 98–99, 104–5, 146
late bloomers. *See* wanderers
lateral thinking, 183–84
lessons of Hannibal. *See* Hannibal, lessons of
Lewis, Meriwether, 54–56, 84–91, 228, 290
liberation
    following disaster, 206–7, 210–16, 291
    intellectual freedom, 183–84, 185–87
Liu Shaoqi, 258–59, 261–64
Lucius Asiaticus, 248–49, 265, 269

MacArthur, Douglas, 138–40
Macedon, 248
Mago
    death, 176
    father's military ambitions for, 19–20

on Hannibal's plan to invade Italy, 68
persona of youth, 228
report to Carthage on Cannae victory,
119–20
as troop commander, 95–96, 196, 200
Maharbal, 170
Mamertines, 24
Mao Zedong, 258, 260–64
Masinissa, 200, 202
Maslow, Abraham, 271–73, 282
Mathos, 26–27
Messana, 24
Metapontum, 174–75
midlife transition
creativity during, 230–31
as crisis, 229–30
of Einstein, 230–31
in Greek and Roman mythology, 230
of Hannibal, 221–27
individuation process, 228–29
of Jung, 231–36
Jung on, 227
of Roosevelt, 228–29
of Shackleton, 236–41
successful transition, 227–31, 241–42
Miller, Steve, 130–33
Minucius, 147, 149, 150–51, 158

Napoleon, 6, 127
Nico, 172–73
Nobel Prize paradox, 179
Noland, Ethel, 56–57
nondoing. *See* inaction
North Korea, 137–40

Obama, Barack, 31
objectives. *See* goals
Octavian, 115, 118, 135–37
On War (Clausewitz), 128
Oppenheimer, Franz, 62

paranoia following success, 182–83
parents
absent, 29–36, 52, 291
emulation of, 28, 52, 291
rebellion against, 29, 36–40, 52, 291
Paullus, Lucius Aemilius, 99, 102, 151–52
Pendergast, Tom, 57–58
Pergamum, 248
persona of youth, 227–29, 291–92
Philemenus, 172–73
Phoenicia and Phoenicians, 22, 45, 226

Picasso, Pablo, 78–80, 82, 83, 90–91, 183,
288–89
planners, dreamers as, 70, 77, 79, 84, 161
Plutarch, 141
prison of success. *See* captivity by success
Prusias, 270, 271, 285
Pyrrhus, 23, 123–24, 141–42, 172

reality. *See* acceptance of circumstances
rebellion against parent, 29, 36–40, 52, 291
resilience, 153, 157
Rhodes, 248
Rome
aggressive warfare style, 23–24, 68
Cannae defeat, 3–4, 102–3, 152
Carthage, declaration of war on, 50–51
Carthage, destruction of, 5, 286
Carthage, peace with, 21–22, 25–26, 27
First Punic War, 21, 24–26
governmental structure, 22–23, 68–69
grief cycle, 153–54, 156–57
Hannibal, persecution of, 226, 267, 271,
284–85
at Hannibal's advances, 13, 76, 153–54
Mediterranean dominance, 23, 247–48, 270
midlife, attitude toward, 230
military command structure, 94, 99–100
naval fleet, 25
protection by Alps, 3, 67–68
Trebia defeat, 94–96
See also Fabius Maximus, Quintus; Scipio,
Publius Cornelius
Roosevelt, Eleanor
acceptance of reality, 291
creativity and self-actualization, 212–16,
231, 276–78, 289, 294
grief cycle, 159–60
inaction, 291
individuation, 228–29
persona of youth, 228
respectful relationship with Franklin, 292–93
search for absent parent, low self-esteem,
32–36
Roosevelt, Sara Delano, 34

Saguntum, 50
Samuelson, Paul, 179
Sardinia, 27, 69
Sartre, Jean-Paul, 251
Scipio, Publius Cornelius
Africa strategy, 195–96, 202, 203–6
Africanus as name, 244

Scipio, Publius Cornelius (*cont.*)
    enemies in Rome, 203–5, 244–47, 249–50
    father, battlefront rescue of, 94, 192–93
    father's and uncle's deaths, 13, 195
    Hannibal, respect for, 13, 193–94, 199,
        201–2, 217–19, 265–67, 292
    Iberia conquest, 195–202
    inaction, 291
    innocence and vulnerability, 251
    Locri scandal, 245
    old age, bitterness during, 295
    reputation and popularity, 193, 203,
        243–44, 247–48
    Seleucid victory, 248–49, 269–70
    strategic generosity, 198–99, 200
    withdrawal from public life, death, 250
    Zama victory and Carthaginian surrender,
        219–23
Scipio, Publius Cornelius (elder), 72, 76–77,
    94, 192–93
Sculley, John, 209, 211
search for parent, 29–36, 52, 291
searchers. *See* wanderers
Second Punic War, start of, 72
seduction
    as Cleopatra's strategy, 110–18, 134–35, 287
    by trappings of success, 178, 182
    use of suggestion, 103
Seleucid Empire and Antiochus, 226–27, 248,
    267–69
self-actualization
    characteristics of self-actualizers, 272–73
    by Einstein, 278–83
    by Erhard, 274–76
    inner peace and fulfillment, 271–72
    by Roosevelt, 276–78
    transcendence of success or failure, 273, 283,
        294, 298
Sempronius, 94–96, 104, 145
Shackleton, Ernest, 160–68, 236–41, 291–92,
    295
shadow, in Jungian philosophy, 229
Sicily, 24–26, 69, 76, 94, 205, 244–47
Silenus, 22
Sosylus, 22, 120–27, 286
South Korea, 137–40
Souvestre, Marie, 33–34
Spain. *See* Iberia
Spendius, 26–27
Spitzer, Eliot, 180–82
Stanley, Bessie, 294–95
strategy. *See* tactics and strategy

success
    anxiety following, 11, 177–79, 184
    anxiety to succeed, 28
    defining, 126–27, 291–92
    from disaster, 206–7, 210–16, 291
    as distraction, 182, 188
    early in life, 77–78, 80, 83, 241–42, 288
    exultation cycle, 179
    hubris following, 179–82, 290
    later in life, 53–54, 66, 78
    as means toward goal, 128, 142–43,
        287–88
    paranoia following, 182–83
    paths to, 52–54, 66
    self-actualization, 271–72, 294
    trappings of, 178, 182
    versus winning, 103
    See also captivity by success
Sun Tzu, 158
Syphax, 202, 205–6

tactics and strategy
    alignment with desired end, 128, 142–43,
        287–88
    Clausewitz on, 127–29
    of Cleopatra, 134–37
    of fisherman, 140–41
    of Hannibal, 120–26
    of Pyrrhus, 141–42
    of Truman, 137–40
    of Woods, 130–34
    See also inaction
Tan, Amy
    entrapment by success, 178–79, 182, 183,
        184, 289
    persona of youth, 228
    rebelliousness, 36–38
    success, 38–40
Taoist *wu wei* principle, 158–59
Tarentum, 172–74
Theseus myth, 29–31, 52–53
Ticinus River battle, 94, 192
transcendence of success or failure, 273, 283,
    294, 298
Trasimene battle, 98–99, 104–5, 146
Trebia River battle, 94–96, 104–5, 145
triumph. *See* success
Truman, Harry, 6, 7, 56–59, 138–40, 290
Tyre, 22, 226–27

Ueshiba, Morihei ("O Sensei"), 105–10, 158,
    183

Varro, 99–102, 104, 150, 151–52
Vom Kriege (Clausewitz), 128

wanderers
 Cézanne, 78, 80–83, 290
 creativity later in life, 288–89
 gradual achievement of success, 66, 78
 self-knowledge and experience, 53–54, 78
 Truman, 56–59, 138–40, 290
 Ueshiba, 105–10, 158, 183
 See also Erhard, Ludwig ("Uncle Lulu")
Wang Guangmei, 258–60, 263–64
Williams, Tennessee, 177–78, 182–83, 289

Woods, Tiger, 130–34, 180, 290
wu wei, 158–59

youth
 emulation of parent, 28, 52, 291
 persona of, 227–29, 291–92
 quest for absent parent, 29–36, 52, 291
 rebellion against parent, 29, 36–40, 52, 291
youthful ideas in later years, 288–89

Zama, battle at, 217–21
Zola, Émile, 80–82